The Penguin Book of

# Baby
# Names
## for
## Canadians

PENGUIN
CANADA

PENGUIN CANADA

Published by the Penguin Group

Penguin Group (Canada), 90 Eglinton Avenue East, Suite 700,
Toronto, Ontario, Canada M4P 2Y3 (a division of Pearson Canada Inc.)

Penguin Group (USA) Inc., 375 Hudson Street, New York, New York 10014, U.S.A.
Penguin Books Ltd, 80 Strand, London WC2R 0RL, England
Penguin Ireland, 25 St Stephen's Green, Dublin 2, Ireland
(a division of Penguin Books Ltd)
Penguin Group (Australia), 250 Camberwell Road, Camberwell, Victoria 3124, Australia
(a division of Pearson Australia Group Pty Ltd)
Penguin Books India Pvt Ltd, 11 Community Centre, Panchsheel Park,
New Delhi – 110 017, India
Penguin Group (NZ), 67 Apollo Drive, Rosedale, North Shore 0632,
New Zealand (a division of Pearson New Zealand Ltd)
Penguin Books (South Africa) (Pty) Ltd, 24 Sturdee Avenue, Rosebank,
Johannesburg 2196, South Africa

Penguin Books Ltd, Registered Offices: 80 Strand, London WC2R 0RL, England

First published 2009

1 2 3 4 5 6 7 8 9 10 (WEB)

Copyright © Penguin Group (Canada), 2009

Manufactured in Canada.

Library and Archives Canada Cataloguing in Publication

The Penguin book of baby names for Canadians.

ISBN 978-0-14-317255-0

1. Names, Personal--Canada--Dictionaries. 2. Names, Personal--Dictionaries.
I. Title: Baby names for Canadians.

CS2377.P45 2009          929.4'40971          C2009-903954-0

Visit the Penguin Group (Canada) website at **www.penguin.ca**

Special and corporate bulk purchase rates available; please see
**www.penguin.ca/corporatesales** or call 1-800-810-3104, ext. 477 or 474

# Contents

# Introduction

Believe it or not, choosing a name for your baby is actually one of the easiest parts of becoming a parent (just ask anyone who has ever given birth). However, picking the perfect name isn't always plain sailing. Your friends will doubtless have an opinion on what's hot and what's not. Your partner's favourite name may remind you of someone you hated at school. And your family may bring serious pressure to bear on immortalizing Great-Aunt Eunice with the naming of the latest addition to the clan.

This book contains over 3,500 names for boys and girls, plus a selection that works equally well for both sexes (see page 87). Each name is listed alphabetically and includes a country or language of origin, together with well-known spelling variations and shortened forms.

But before you plunge straight into the baby-name game, take a moment to read the following introductory sections. Here you'll find some invaluable tips on choosing a name that both you and your child will be happy to live with for the rest of your lives.

## Naming Trends in Canada

A quick glance at Canada's most popular baby names (see page 21) shows that many baby names turn up on the list year after year, even century after century. There is an equal amount of movement away from and toward classic names such as William and Elizabeth. Some parents enjoy the more traditional approach, while others are abandoning it in favour of names that will make their child stand out. Sometimes this is done by simply modifying the traditional spelling or pronunciation—for example, from John to Jhon, or Simon to Symon. It can also be done by rearranging the order of existing words, such as Nevaeh or Neleh (which are heaven and Helen spelled backwards, and which are becoming increasingly popular in Western Canada).

Many new parents are moving toward giving baby girls traditionally male names, such as Sydney, Chris, Cameron, or Jay. (Boys are still rarely given female names.) Other parents enjoy the process of creating a name that is unique to their child. However, this option has many pitfalls for the unwary, which are covered in detail on pages 5–8.

# The Basics of Choosing a Name

In essence, choosing your child's name all comes down to finding a name that you like, that sounds good, and that will help and not hinder your child in his or her path through life. While this is very much a matter of personal preference, some common issues are worth taking into consideration:

## Name length

In these days of computerized forms, it's a good idea to choose a name that will fit easily into the boxes provided. Find a commonly used one, and input your chosen first name with the middle name and surname to make sure it all fits. Odd punctuation, such as an apostrophe in the middle of a name, can also create difficulties when dealing with officialdom. Try to choose a name or combination of names that won't be too much hassle for your child in later life. A name that can be easily spelled and pronounced is a gift indeed.

## Rhythm

Some names sound better than others because they have a natural flow and rhythm. This rhythm can be created in a number of ways, either through the number of syllables in each part of the name or through the actual sounds of the vowels and consonants. Examples of good syllable patterns include:

| | |
|---|---|
| 1-1 | Brad Pitt |
| 1-2-1 | Jane Marie Hall |
| 2-1-2 | Gary S. Oldman |
| 1-2-3 | John Kevin O'Reilly |

As a general rule, if you have a complicated surname with many syllables, it's best to keep the other names short and simple. But if your surname is short and strong, like Smith, then a more ornate first name can help balance the rhythm.

Alliteration can also create an attractive rhythm within a name. For example, the repetition of a consonant at the start of the first and last name may be pleasing to the ear, as in Harrison Holmes or Benjamin Blair.

The inclusion of similar vowel sounds can also help—for example, the name of the actor Leonardo DiCaprio. However, watch out for first and last names that run into each other, such as Allen Owen or Nancy Symons. Said quickly, it can be difficult to tell where the first name stops and the next starts.

## Versatility

Think about how your child might use his or her name in the future. If you choose a strong traditional first name, consider coupling it with a more imaginative middle name so your child has the option of using that name later in life if it better suits his or her personality. Or choose a first name that can be adapted to suit different circumstances. For example, Samora Berry (named after the late president of Mozambique, Samora Machel) may grow up to become an accountant and choose to be known as Sam. In a parallel universe, he could run away to join the circus as a sword swallower and revel in the exotic name Samora.

## Nicknames

Consider, too, which nicknames or shortened forms are commonly associated with your child's chosen name. While you may declare that your son Jerome will never be known as Jerry, the kids at school may have another opinion—one over which you will have no control. Likewise, Cornelius may be a family name that appeals to your sense of tradition, but how would you feel about him being known as Neil or Corny?

One way around the problem is to choose a name with a variety of shortened forms or nicknames. For example, Elizabeth has over twenty pet and diminutive variations.

Finally, if you'd really like to know what nicknames may be derived from your prospective name, ask a group of eight- to ten-year-olds. They will quickly come up with more nicknames than you would have dreamed possible.

## Initials

Write down the initials of your child's proposed name and check for any cutesy or unfortunate combinations. Try to stay away from names that form silly or negative combinations, such as PIG, ASS, or MAD.

You should also check that the initials and last name don't create a silly expression; for example, Macklin Thomas Place (MT Place) could become known among his friends as The Void.

## Associations

Names usually come with associations to historical figures, celebrities, characters from literature or film, and people we know personally. These associations can be either positive or negative. Say the name Madonna, for instance, and people will generally think of the often controversial blond rock star. Elvis is inextricably linked with Elvis Presley, Adolf with Adolf Hitler, and Atticus with the lawyer from Harper Lee's classic book *To Kill a Mockingbird*.

Even names that are not linked to someone famous can have immediate associations. For example, Bertha easily becomes Big Bertha, while Bambi brings to mind a timid fawn. Think of any good or bad links to names you are considering before you make a final choice.

Name associations not only matter in the playground—where children can be notoriously cruel—but also later in life. Given a choice of employing Grace, Fifibelle, or Rebecca for a senior accountant's job, there's a chance that Fifibelle will be looked on less favourably merely because her name sounds rather ditzy.

## Silliness

While it may be tempting to go for laughs with a name, remember that your child will have to live with your choice for life—or at least until he or she is old enough to register a legal change of name. Justin Case, Hugh Jass, Richard Head, and Krystall Ball are unlikely to appreciate the humour in their names—but if you need more convincing, listen to the famous Johnny Cash song "A Boy Named Sue." It makes sense to give your child a name that will be an asset rather than a liability.

# Unique and Unusual Baby Names

Although coming up with an unusual name can be very satisfying, you also need to make sure that you are not setting your child up for years of schoolyard taunts and snickers from bureaucrats every time there's a form to fill in. You should also consider how well the name will work at different stages of his or her life. For example, a made-up name like Honeybeigh may be cute for a baby but is less impressive for a lawyer.

Unusual names can also be very frustrating. Before opting for something like Ayeeshaquahh, think how many times your child will have to explain how to say or spell that name over the course of his or her life.

Remember that while an unusual name can be charming, an eccentric one may label your child in an unpleasant way. If you are set on something uncommon, perhaps look for a classic name that has fallen out of favour. Go through your family tree, reread classic literature, or look at names from times gone by that appeal to you (see page 81).

The last few years have seen a resurgence in popularity of names from the early twentieth century, such as Ruby. Check out names from other decades to find something that is currently neglected but attractive.

But be aware that in our multicultural society, one person's perfect name may unintentionally cause grief to another. Caffar, which means "helmet" in Gaelic, can sound a lot like "kaffir," an extremely derogatory term used to refer to black South Africans during the Apartheid era. Do some research and be very careful what you may end up yelling across the playground!

## DIY monikers

Creating a completely new name for your child can be a very satisfying experience. You could achieve this by combining two names you really love or perhaps by altering an existing name. You could also try naming him or her after something that holds particular meaning for you and your partner, as Victoria and David Beckham did with their son, Brooklyn. Just be careful that the meaning doesn't pose potential problems for your little one. (Dragonfruit is unlikely to hold much appeal, likewise Banana, if you were to follow Gwyneth Paltrow's fruity example.)

Also, be cautious when attempting to invent a completely new name; your idea of what sounds good may not go down so well with others. Ask family and friends for their honest opinion before committing to an invented name, such as Gorblan or Sunberry. They may not wish to hurt your feelings, but you can usually get an accurate impression from their faces and the time it takes them to reply.

Remember too that exotic spellings of common names can lead to great confusion. Just because you decide to spell Jake as Jaiykhe does not alter the fact that it is essentially the same name. Your son may still end up being one of six Jakes in his class, while also being condemned to a lifetime of having to always spell out his name. Insisting on unnecessary punctuation (such as Jaiyk'he) will create further problems when he needs to fill out a form.

Changing the spelling can also change the meaning of a name. Unless you're absolutely certain, you could end up saddling your child with a name that's rather different from what you intended. For example, let's say you want to name your son Mael, which is Gaelic for "prince." If you change the spelling to Male or Mail, you will give him a lot of grief as he grows up. (This name could also cause some confusion when yelled across the playground.)

## Names from places far and near

Listen to the roll call in any Canadian classroom these days, and you'll hear names from all around the world. This reflects not only the growing number of Canadians with diverse ethnic heritages but also an increased interest in giving our children unusual names.

For instance, few people in our parents' generation would have thought of calling a child an Arabic name such as Jamila, a Native Australian name like Kylie, or a German name such as Alaric, unless there was a family link. Nowadays, however, people are more than happy to move beyond their own cultural boundaries in search of that perfect name.

Some final words of caution if you are picking an unusual name: First, make sure you know how to pronounce it correctly ("Ale-handra" for Alejandra, for example). Second, if it is complicated to spell, consider using an anglicized version (such as Riona for the Gaelic name Ríoghnach, meaning "queenly").

## A note on Native Canadian names and naming

Canada's First Peoples have a rich and vibrant history; they are an extremely valuable part of Canada's past and future. You may be inspired by this contribution to give your baby a traditional Native Canadian name from Six Nations, Inuit, Innu, or Métis sources.

Be very careful! While certain indigenous-derived names may be popular (think Dakota, Lakota, etc.), they may not mean what you think they do. For example, Dakota is a plural noun used to refer to the Dakota people. Using it as a child's name is comparable to naming your child Scotsmen or Italians. Always be sensitive to the origin of a name; even if you love what you think is a Native name, it may not quite be what you intended.

You should also know that each Native Canadian naming tradition is different. Often a baby is named after the most recently deceased elder. Sometimes the parents will name the baby, while in other cases the oldest woman or man in the community will give the name. Names can be both intensely personal and passed down from generation to generation; they are usually descriptive in nature and very long to write out in English (for example, Tekakwitha ["she moves things"] and Tekahionwake ["double wampum/double life"]).

If you are not of Native Canadian heritage but are still set on giving your child an indigenous-derived name, probably the best way to do so is to go through lexicon lists of Native languages and choose something with a meaning and spelling that appeals to you. This book contains over two hundred indigenous-derived names from across Canada, ranging from Anwatin ("calm weather" in Algonquin) to Makwa ("bear" in Algonquin), from Kunik ("kiss" in InupiaQ) to Seskiku ("she is beautiful" in Maliseet).

# Naming Multiples

If naming one baby is a challenge, how about naming two or three or even five? Adding to the natural incidence of multiple births, the rising number of fertility treatments in Canada, such as IVF, often result in more than one child being born at a time. This makes choosing names an even more complicated task, as you not only have to consider how well one name works, but also how the different names will work together when you're in the supermarket trying to keep a gaggle of kids under control.

Choosing similar-sounding names may result in constant confusion, with all three children coming at the same time. Conversely, choosing names that all start with the same letter can cut down on labelling school clothes and lunch boxes.

Some parents opt for names that emphasize their children's connection with each other. Others believe in giving their multiples distinct names that will help them establish separate identities. Ultimately, it's up to you!

Some options include:

## Names that begin with the same letter

- Samantha, Sarah, and Serena
- Bronwyn and Brian
- Priya and Patrick
- Winona and William

## Names that relate to each other through form or meaning

- Chaya and Eve (both mean "life")
- Shona, Siân, Sinead, Siobhan, Joanna, Jack, and Ian (all mean "God is gracious")
- Saffron, Jasmine, and Rosie (all are flowers)
- Sadie, Sarah, and Zara (all mean "princess")
- Melanie, Ciaran, and Darcy (all mean "dark-haired")
- Kevin and Alan (both mean "handsome")

- Eloise and Quinn (both mean "wise")
- Archie and Patrick (both mean "noble")

## Anagrams
- Myra and Mary
- Amy and May
- Jonah and Johan

## Favourite characters from literature or film
- Jonathan and David (from the Bible story about an everlasting friendship)
- Elizabeth and Jane (the two older Bennet sisters from Jane Austen's *Pride and Prejudice*)
- Anne and Diana (from *Anne of Green Gables*)
- Peter and Wendy (from *Peter Pan*)

## Alphabetically linked
(this can also be used for naming successive children in a family)

- Alexander, Brian, Charles, Dara, and Elaine
- Zachary, Xavier, Yannick, and Wendy
- Minette, Nathan, and Owen

## Culturally linked
- Heather and Hamish (Scottish)
- Priya, Parvati, and Padma (Hindu)
- Jonathan and Matthew (Hebrew)

## Letter swapping
(be careful with this option, as many combinations sound similar and may lead to a great deal of confusion)

- Dara and Cara
- Xan and Dan

- Merry and Jerry
- Seth and Beth
- Britt and Brett
- Ross and Rose

## Boy/girl variations
(again you need to be careful with this type of naming as not only are the sounds similar, but the children may end up with similar shortened forms or nicknames)

- Daniel and Daniella
- Alan and Alannah
- Paul and Pauline
- Charles and Charlotte
- Alexander and Alexis
- Nicholas and Nicole

## Derivatives of the same name
- Elizabeth, Bess, and Lisa
- Alex and Xander
- Anne and Nina
- Mollie and Maria

Whichever option you decide to go for—even if you give the children completely unrelated names—beware the temptation to overload on the cute factor when naming more than one child. So while Millie and Billy may be sweet names for babies, they may not be quite so appealing for surly teenagers or serious adults. Likewise, combinations such as Cara and Mia (which put together mean "my darling") may elicit more groans than sighs of admiration at your cleverness. As time goes by, your children may wish to assert their own individuality and could, in fact, resent names that are too similar.

# Middle Names

Middle names are much more than just the filling in the name sandwich. As already mentioned, they can provide your child with flexibility in what he or she wishes to be called. Middle names can also add more individuality to a name, giving you the chance to honour an important member of your family or to reflect something important about the family's cultural history. Most parents include one middle name, although there is no rule saying there has to be any. It's worth bearing in mind that most legal forms provide a place to write your first and last name as well as your middle name, or at least an initial. Having more than one middle name can complicate things for your child, so it's lucky that William Arthur Philip Louis (Prince William) and Henry Charles Albert David (Prince Harry) aren't likely to fill out many forms in their lives.

Think about how the middle name works with any proposed first name, as well as with the surname. Belinda Linda Lindenmayer is unlikely to be a happy bunny. But Belinda Jane Lindenmayer may feel a little less aggrieved.

Inspiration for a middle name can come from anywhere, just like a first name, but some common starting points include:

## Mother's maiden name

If the mother of the baby has taken her partner's surname or the baby will be called by the father's surname, then you can honour the mother by including her birth surname as a middle name. For example, Elaine Marvell and her husband Samuel Blake call their daughter Rebecca Marvell Blake.

## Important family members

If you'd like to carry on your father's first name, Stewart, but can't bear the idea of your child being known as Stewie in the playground, then consider tucking it away as a middle name instead. You can also use a middle name to create something that reflects both sides of the family—for example, by combining the names of two grandmothers into one. Thus Emma Brown, the granddaughter of Rosalie and Carina, becomes Emma Rosina Brown, and both grandmothers feel suitably flattered. (This does, of course, depend on the grandmothers having appropriate names. Your child is unlikely to appreciate being called Emma Brittabeth Brown.)

## Friends or inspirational figures

A middle name is a great way to recognize someone who has been important to you, especially if you can't do it with the first name for some reason. This could be anyone from the person who introduced you to your partner to an inspirational celebrity, such as Nelson Mandela or your favourite sports hero.

## Your social, cultural, or ethnic background

Even if you are not actively religious or have little interest in your ancestors, you may want to reflect your family's background with a middle name from your country of origin or religion. This will doubtless please at least one set of grandparents and create a link between your child and previous generations.

## Symbolism or messages of hope

Giving your baby a middle name that relates to your hopes for his or her future is a lovely way of letting that child know how you feel. Choosing a name such as Joy is one way. Or you could choose a more subtle name, such as Simcha, which means "joy in life" in Hebrew.

# A Family Affair

Your choice of name for your baby will probably generate a great deal of interest and excitement within your extended family. Sometimes even the sanest of families gets hysterical over name choices. Others will accept your chosen name without question. The important thing is to remember that deciding on a child's name is basically down to the parents or parent involved. The fallout can be dealt with later, and chances are that any apprehensions will pass once the concerned family members realize how delightful your new little one is and how apt your name choice is.

## A joint decision

Some couples spend their first date plotting potential names for their possible offspring. Others only face the challenge once the pregnancy becomes viable. Whichever camp you fall into, there's no doubt that some compromise will need to be made.

Your partner may love the name Jordana, while for you it conjures up memories of a girl who bullied you in Grade 4. Your partner's mother may also be campaigning—subtly, of course—for her role in the family to be recognized somehow. Balancing all these competing opinions and desires is no easy task!

When dealing with your family, there are two options open to you. Either keep your chosen name(s) secret and bear the consequences later, or be open about your choice before the birth—and bear the consequences immediately. The important thing to remember is that whatever name you finally select, it should be a name that you and your partner like and feel will suit your baby. No name will ever please everybody equally.

## Compromising in the name of peace

Perhaps the best way to look at choosing a name for your child is to treat it as a relationship-building exercise and to make sure that the final choice is made from a list of names that both parents like. If one of you insists on a name that the other detests then the second parent may always feel awkward about calling that child by his or her name. Decide on something you both agree will be suitable and only then open up the discussion for others' opinions.

If you are a single parent, you will avoid this potential source of friction. Rest secure in the knowledge that you have chosen the best name for your new little one, and be prepared to celebrate it for the rest of your life!

## Coping with family traditions

Some families and cultural groups have strict ideas about the naming of babies. Perhaps your family assumes that your child will be named after a grandparent. Or maybe you are expected to use a religious or culturally significant name. Catholics, for instance, often give a baby a name from the calendar of saints, and Muslims frequently name a child after names derived from the prophet Mohammed or his relations. Jewish families may follow the custom of naming a newborn child after a relative who has died. Each Native Canadian indigenous group has a different tradition for naming the newest arrival. Whatever your individual circumstances, there are ways of getting your own way without putting family noses too severely out of joint:

- Use a must-have family name as a middle name. This way, your preferred name comes first (and is the name your child will be known by), and the traditional or family name is included tactfully as a middle name. Now everyone is happy.
- Hide an unpleasant family name behind an initial. Choose a name that starts with the same letter as the family name you are expected to include, and tell your family the reason why you have chosen a name that you prefer. (If your parents or relatives have always resented a tradition, such as having to include the name Edwina, they are likely to be sympathetic to your ideas.) Sometimes concerned families only want to know that you have considered family customs when naming your child and will be happy enough to be able

to tell their friends that baby Bree was named in honour of Uncle Bruce.

- Another way of pleasing demanding family members is to choose a name with the same meaning. For example, if your mother, Molly, is expecting that her first grandchild will be named after her, you can honour her by calling your daughter Marina (which has the same Mary root meaning).

- Mine your family tree. You may be familiar with names in the immediate preceding generations, but what about going even farther back to your great-great-great-great-grandparents or even beyond? The internet offers some excellent genealogy research tools, and your family tree may reveal some truly wonderful names that will link past and future generations. Make sure to run your choice past members of your family first, though, just in case there are any negative associations with that name. You don't want to name your child after the family renegade.

- Create your own tradition. Some families have long-standing naming traditions, but remember that all traditions have to start somewhere. There is no rule saying that traditions can't be updated or modified, and you may be surprised at how little resistance you encounter when you decide to start afresh. The important thing is that you and your partner are happy with the name for your baby, even if it means ruffling a few familial feathers.

## Make an event out of it

Choosing a name for your child is not something that should be sandwiched between washing-up and rushing out the door to a movie. Instead, take a night off—or several—to discuss possible options over dinner, away from all other pressures. Turn off your cellphones and iPods, unplug the landline, and keep the world at bay for at least an hour or so. This way, you can both give each other—and the challenge—your undivided attention. If you are a single parent, you can have a similar celebratory planning dinner with a trusted family member and/or close friend who will help with the naming process. Who knows? Having an official naming dinner could become a new family tradition.

## Name Choice Checklist

Once you have a list of names that resonate with you and your partner, it's time to get down to details. First, write down all the spellings or variations of the names you like best. This will give you an even longer list, but don't worry. You will now apply some practical considerations to each name so you can narrow it back down to something manageable:

- Is the name so popular that half the kids in your child's class will have the same one? Are you prepared for him to be known as Jack H in a sea of Jack Ms, Jack Ks, and Jack Ts?
- Is the name so unusual that it will come across as weird or make your child a laughing stock?
- Does the name sound good on its own?
- Does the name work well with your last name?
- Do you like the nicknames or variations your child is likely to be called?
- Do you like the image this name conveys? Will it be positive or negative?
- Do you have a positive or negative impression of the most famous namesakes?
- Is the name difficult to spell?
- Is the name likely to be mispronounced?
- Does this name clearly show whether your child is a girl or a boy? Does this matter to you? Is it likely to result in teasing?
- Do you like the combination of initials that the name forms with the middle and last name? Do they spell anything silly or inappropriate?

- Is the meaning of his or her name positive? Does it have any rude or unpleasant connotations in other languages or cultures?
- Does this name suit your own family, religious, and/or cultural traditions?

## Kickstart Questionnaire

If you are stuck for inspiration for your baby's name, then the following questionnaire may help you identify some possibilities. It's all about choosing a name that you feel comfortable with and one that means something personal to you. Get your partner to go through the same process—chances are you'll find several names that you have in common, or at least you'll have a starting point for debate. (If you don't have a partner, simply enlist a good friend or family member to do the same thing—make sure it's someone whose taste you trust.)

Make a list of possible names by writing down your answers to the following questions:

1   What country did your parents, grandparents, or great-grandparents come from?
2   Do you have strong religious, cultural, or social beliefs?
3   What do you think or hope your baby's personality will be?
4   What do you think your baby will be like physically?
5   What will be your baby's star sign?
6   Where was your baby conceived?
7   In what season will your baby be born?
8   Who do you most admire?
9   Who are your favourite artists?
10  Who are your favourite authors?
11  Who are your sports heroes?
12  Who are your favourite characters from literature, film, theatre, and mythology?

13 Who are your favourite celebrities? If they have children, what are their names?

14 What are your favourite unisex names (see page 87)?

15 What is your favourite holiday destination? Where in the world would you most like to live? Do you speak any other languages?

16 What are your favourite boys and girls names from the list of most popular Canadian names (see page 21)?

17 What are your favourite boys and girls names from the most recent list of popular names (see page 21)?

18 Who are your favourite relatives? (Make sure to keep this list top secret!)

19 What are your favourite colours, animals, flowers, plants, gemstones, and minerals?

20 What kind of music inspires you? Who are your favourite singers, composers, and musicians?

## Final Naming Guidelines
### Verbal Tests

1 Yell the name out the back door twenty times. If you're embarrassed to do it after the first five times—or if it sounds as if you're calling your dog—you may want to reconsider.

2 Ask a group of ten-year-olds how many nicknames they can come up with using the name. Kids can be both inventive and cruel. It's worth finding out right from the start what potential nicknames lie in wait for your little one, because teasing can have a big impact on childhood development.

3 List your final top ten names. Ask friends and family what they really think of them. Pay close attention to their facial expressions as they answer. Do they hesitate before replying? They may not want to hurt your feelings. If more than two or three people react in the same way, you may want to rethink your decision.

## Paper Tests

1 Write down your top choices of first and middle name(s) with your surname. Check for any unfortunate combinations of initials like ASS, MAD, NAD, NERD, or DORK.

2 Write down the following and leave the space for the given names blank:

a) Prime Minister _____ [your surname]
b) Supreme Court Justice _____ [your surname]
c) Professor _____ [your surname]

Then write the following, leaving the space for the given names blank:

a) Live onstage at the Frisky Beaver Gentlemen's Club: _____ [your surname]
b) Appearing nightly at Remington's Men of Steel Club: _____ [your surname]
c) _____ [your surname] vs. The Queen

How do the various names look in print? Which names sound better in which context?

These simple exercises should be enough to bring you to the final step: deleting any names that you are unsure about or have definitely decided against. Now you will probably have a very short list of likely options for your baby's name. All you have to do is make the final decision. Good luck!

# Most Popular Canadian Baby Names

Want to know what other Canadians are naming their new little ones? Whether you wish to be inspired by your neighbours or avoid the possibility of having your child be one of many with the same name, you should check out these lists. Organized from west to east, they will give you an idea of what's hot and what's not in Canadian naming.

## Top Ten Canadian Baby Names (2008)**

|  | Boys | Girls |
| --- | --- | --- |
| 1 | Ethan | Ava |
| 2 | Nathan | Emma |
| 3 | William | Olivia |
| 4 | Jacob | Chloë |
| 5 | Noah | Sarah |
| 6 | Samuel | Emily |
| 7 | Matthew | Hannah |
| 8 | Joshua | Madison |
| 9 | Logan | Abigail |
| 10 | Alexander | Sophia |

**Results based on data from those provinces and territories that provided data. Prince Edward Island, Nunavut, and the Northwest Territories did not provide data. In certain cases, data from 2008 were not available; 2007 data have been substituted.

## British Columbia

(http://www.vs.gov.bc.ca/babynames/baby2008.html)

|    | Boys     | Girls    |
|----|----------|----------|
| 1  | Ethan    | Ava      |
| 2  | Jacob    | Chloe    |
| 3  | James    | Emma     |
| 4  | Logan    | Emily    |
| 5  | Nathan   | Hannah   |
| 6  | Noah     | Olivia   |
| 7  | Joshua   | Ella     |
| 8  | Matthew  | Sophie   |
| 9  | Benjamin | Abigail  |
| 10 | Liam     | Isabella |

## Alberta

(http://www.servicealberta.gov.ab.ca/807.cfm)

|    | Boys      | Girls    |
|----|-----------|----------|
| 1  | Ethan     | Ava      |
| 2  | Jacob     | Olivia   |
| 3  | Alexander | Emma     |
| 4  | Joshua    | Emily    |
| 5  | Liam      | Sarah    |
| 6  | Logan     | Isabella |
| 7  | Nathan    | Sophia   |
| 8  | Matthew   | Hannah   |
| 9  | Noah      | Madison  |
| 10 | Owen      | Chloe    |

## Saskatchewan

|   | Boys   | Girls  |
|---|--------|--------|
| 1 | Ethan  | Ava    |
| 2 | Noah   | Emma   |
| 3 | Joshua | Hannah |

| 4 | Liam | Emily |
|---|---|---|
| 5 | Logan | Taylor |
| 6 | Alexander | Olivia |
| 7 | Carter | Hailey |
| 8 | Jacob | Madison |
| 9 | Benjamin | Abigail |
| 10 | Matthew | Brooklyn |

## Manitoba

| | Boys | Girls |
|---|---|---|
| 1 | Ethan | Emily |
| 2 | Noah | Hannah |
| 3 | Alexander | Emma |
| 4 | Aiden | Ava |
| 5 | Liam | Madison |
| 6 | Joshua | Olivia |
| 7 | Jayden | Abigail |
| 8 | Benjamin | Hailey |
| 9 | Logan | Taylor |
| 10 | Evan | Brooke |

## Ontario

| | Boys | Girls |
|---|---|---|
| 1 | Ethan | Emma |
| 2 | Matthew | Olivia |
| 3 | Joshua | Emily |
| 4 | Jacob | Ava |
| 5 | Ryan | Sarah |
| 6 | Noah | Isabella |
| 7 | Nathan | Hannah |
| 8 | Daniel | Abigail |
| 9 | Alexander | Madison |
| 10 | Owen | Ella |

## Quebec

|    | Boys    | Girls     |
|----|---------|-----------|
| 1  | William | Léa       |
| 2  | Samuel  | Jade      |
| 3  | Gabriel | Rosalie   |
| 4  | Nathan  | Florence  |
| 5  | Alexis  | Juliette  |
| 6  | Thomas  | Gabrielle |
| 7  | Olivier | Sarah     |
| 8  | Félix   | Coralie   |
| 9  | Antoine | Maika     |
| 10 | Justin  | Noëmie    |

## New Brunswick

|    | Boys      | Girls     |
|----|-----------|-----------|
| 1  | Jacob     | Emma      |
| 2  | Samuel    | Madison   |
| 3  | Nathan    | Olivia    |
| 4  | Zachary   | Abigail   |
| 5  | Alexander | Chloë     |
| 6  | Ethan     | Sarah     |
| 7  | Lucas     | Ava       |
| 8  | Noah      | Emily     |
| 9  | Logan     | Brooklyn  |
| 10 | Aiden     | Gabrielle |

## Nova Scotia

|   | Boys  | Girls |
|---|-------|-------|
| 1 | Noah  | Emma  |
| 2 | Ethan | Emily |
| 3 | Jack  | Ava   |

| 4 | Liam | Olivia |
| 5 | Logan | Madison |
| 6 | Owen | Chloë |
| 7 | Jacob | Hannah |
| 8 | Alexander | Abigail |
| 9 | William | Ella |
| 10 | Nicholas | Sophia |

## Newfoundland and Labrador

| | Boys | Girls |
| --- | --- | --- |
| 1 | Logan | Ava |
| 2 | Nathan | Cloë |
| 3 | Jacob | Sarah |
| 4 | Ethan | Claire |
| 5 | Noah | Abigail |
| 6 | Liam | Madison |
| 7 | Jack | Emma |
| 8 | Riley | Peyton |
| 9 | Jayden | Olivia |
| 10 | William | Leah |

## Yukon

| | Boys | Girls |
| --- | --- | --- |
| 1 | Logan | Emily |
| 2 | Ethan | Hannah |
| 3 | Andrew | Emma |
| 4 | Daniel | Madison |
| 5 | James | Olivia |
| 6 | Joshua | Alyssa |
| 7 | Tristan | Sarah |
| 8 | Cameron | Brooke |
| 9 | Jacob | Jessica |
| 10 | Adam | Morgan |

# Registering Your Baby

Now that you're baby has been born, and you are doing more loads of laundry than before, eating casseroles that friends and family have brought over, and adapting to the schedule of your new housemate, you may think that the hardest part is finished. But don't let your sleeplessness distract you from the fact that you have to register Baby with the government! By Canadian law, you're required to register your child within a certain time frame (this differs from province to province). Sometimes you are personally responsible for this, and sometimes the hospital processes the form. If you aren't sure who's responsible, or if your baby wasn't born in a hospital, make sure you visit your provincial website to find out.

Here are some basic guidelines. Be aware that naming requirements differ across the country; Quebec in particular has quite strict rules about what you can and cannot name your child. Make sure that you visit your home province's website to get all the latest naming information.

## British Columbia
(http://www.vs.gov.bc.ca)

Form:              http://www.vs.gov.bc.ca/forms/vsa404c_fill.pdf
Mailing Address:   Vital Statistics Agency
                   P.O. Box 9657, Stn. Prov. Govt
                   Victoria, BC  V8W 9P3
Phone:             250-952-2681
Time Limit:        30 days after birth

To register your child's birth in British Columbia, complete and return the Registration of Live Birth form to the B.C. Vital Statistics Agency within thirty days of your child's birth. If you or your partner gave birth in a hospital, you will receive this form in the birth package given to parents during the hospital stay. You can also pick one up at any Vital Statistics office.

You can also apply for your child's Social Insurance Number (SIN) at the same time; no fee is required. Just check the SIN Number box at the bottom of the Registration of Live Birth form and sign in the space provided for Release of Information. Your child's SIN card will arrive within five days of the birth being registered.

If only one parent is being named on the registration, different rules apply. A mother applying on her own must complete the form and check the statement section indicating the father is not being registered. If the father is incapable, the mother must provide proof of the father's incapacity in the form of a statutory declaration. Fathers or third parties applying to register a birth should contact a service representative at 250-952-2681 for further information.

When registering the child's name, be sure to follow the guidelines given here. Remember, if only one parent completes the registration, the surname must be the one chosen by the parent. If both parents register, the child's surname may be any surname chosen by the parents. If the parents do not agree on the name, the agency will register the child's birth using both parents' surnames.

## Alberta
(http://www.servicealberta.gov.ab.ca)

Email:              vs@gov.ab.ca
Mailing Address:  Service Alberta
                  Alberta Registries, Vital Statistics
                  P.O. Box 2023
                  Edmonton, AB   T5J 4W7

| Phone: | Dial 310-0000 toll free, followed by |
| | 780-427-7013 (within AB only) |
| Time Limit: | 10 days after birth |

It is the responsibility of the baby's parents (if they are married) or the baby's mother (if unmarried) to complete a Registration of Birth form. The birth registration should be left with the hospital where your baby was born so that the document can be forwarded from there to Vital Statistics. The birth registration must be sent to the Vital Statistics Office within ten days of the child's birth.

Only under special circumstances may the parent(s) mail the registration directly to Vital Statistics. When you do mail it in, you will need one of the following Class A documents to reinforce the form. It must

- be dated before the baby's fourth birthday
- contain all the following information:
  a) full name of the child
  b) date of birth
  c) place of birth
  d) parents' or parent's names (father may not be listed)
  e) date of record

The following are examples of Class A Evidence documents:

1  A baptismal, christening, blessing, or similar church or religious record. If a baptismal certificate is obtained, you will also be required to supply
   - a letter with the name, location, and phone number of the church or diocese that issued the certificate
   - a photocopy of the page from the baptismal register where the birth information was recorded

2   A document from the medical records department in the hospital where the baby was born

3   A letter or report from the doctor or midwife present at the baby's birth.

Alberta's laws allow the parent(s) various options when choosing a child's last name. The baby's surname is based on the relationship and marital status of the parents. Some restrictions may apply, so please refer to the website for guidelines.

When you register your newborn's birth, you have the option to apply for your child's Social Insurance Number (SIN) at the same time. To apply for a child's SIN, simply add your signature in the "Request for a Social Insurance Number for My Child" section found at the bottom of the Registration of Birth form. When completed, this is considered the SIN application for your child. The information will be sent to Service Canada over a secure network after the birth has been registered. There is no fee to apply.

## Saskatchewan
(http://www.isc.ca/Default.aspx?DN=2015,2010,10,1,Documents)

Email:        ask@isc.ca
Address:      1942 Hamilton Street
              Regina, SK  S4P 3V7
Phone:        1-800-667-7551 or 1-866-275-4721
Fax:          306-787-2288
Time Limit:   15 days after birth

In Saskatchewan, you must register your baby within fifteen days of his or her birth. Registering the birth is the responsibility of

- the mother of the child, the father of the child, or both;
- where the father is unacknowledged or either parent is incapable, the other parent; or
- where both parents are incapable, the person standing in the place of the parents.

To register a birth, complete and sign the Registration of Live Birth form. Your baby's surname must contain no more than two names hyphenated or combined. It can be any name chosen by the parent(s) and does not have to be the same name as that of either parent. (Check the website for more rules about choosing a surname.)

If your baby was born in a hospital, the hospital will require that you complete the Registration of Live Birth form before it discharges the baby; the hospital will then forward the form to the appropriate office. If your baby was not born in a hospital, the mother and/or father must contact the Vital Statistics office to obtain a Registration of Live Birth form for completion.

Once Vital Statistics receives the Registration of Live Birth, they will check and verify the information on the form and follow up with you if there is any missing or incorrect information. There is no fee to register within one year of the date of birth.

## Manitoba
(gov.mb.ca)

| | |
|---|---|
| Email: | vitalstats@gov.mb.ca |
| Address: | 254 Portage Avenue |
| | Winnipeg, MB  R3C 0B6 |
| Phone: | 204-945-3701 or 1-800-282-8069 (toll free) |
| Fax: | 204-948-3128 |
| Time Limit: | 5 days after birth |

You must make sure your baby is registered within five days after birth. The child's mother or father can do this by filling out a Registration of Live Birth form, which is available online or will be provided by hospital staff. Make sure that you establish who will be submitting the form to avoid unpleasant surprises.

# Ontario

(https://www.orgforms.gov.on.ca/eForms/start.do)

Online Registry: http://www.ontario.ca/en/services_for_
residents/STEL01_105212
Email: cbsinfo@cbs.gov.on.ca
Address: P.O. Box 4600
189 Red River Road
Thunder Bay, ON P7B 6L8
Telephone: 416-325-8305 or 1-800-461-2156 (toll free)
Fax: 807-343-7459
Time Limit: 30 days after birth

There are two ways you can register your baby's birth in Ontario, but it must be done within thirty days of his or her birth. You can use the Online Registry Service (see link above) if you live in a municipality that permits it; otherwise, the hospital or midwife will give you a Statement of Live Birth form. This is your child's permanent identity record. Fill out the form, ensuring the information is clear and accurate, sign it, and mail it to the municipality where the child was born. You can apply for your child's birth certificate and Social Insurance Number (SIN) at the same time—just complete and sign the relevant portions of the form. Don't forget that the birth registration must be signed by each parent whose information is included on the birth registration form, unless a parent is incapable due to illness or death.

# Quebec

(http://www.etatcivil.gouv.qc.ca/en/default.html)

Email: etatcivil@dec.gouv.qc.ca
Address: 2535 boulevard Laurier
Sainte-Foy, QC G1V 5C5

| Phone: | 418-643-3900 or 1-800-567-3900 (toll free) |
| Fax: | 418-646-3255 |
| Time Limit: | 30 days after birth |

You must complete a Declaration of Birth form, either at the hospital or at home, which must also be signed by a witness of legal age. Whoever assists with the delivery of your baby (the *accoucheur*) will draw up an Attestation of Birth. These two forms should be sent to the directeur de l'état civil within thirty days of the birth. If your baby was born in a hospital, give the forms to the hospital staff, who will do this for you. If your baby was born at home, send the *green* copy of the Attestation of Birth and the *original* of the Declaration of Birth to the directeur de l'état civil and keep the *green* copy of the Declaration of Birth.

Make sure that you check the website for naming guidelines. Quebec is quite strict when it comes to naming regulations.

## New Brunswick
(http://www.snb.ca/e/1000/1000-01/e/index-e.asp)

| Email: | vitalstatistics@snb.ca |
| Address: | P.O. Box 6000 |
| | 435 King Street, Room 203 |
| | Fredericton, NB  E3B 5H1 |
| Phone: | 506-453-2385 |
| Fax: | 506-444-4139 |
| Time Limit: | 30 days after birth |

You must complete the Registration of Birth form within thirty days of your baby's birth and send it to the Vital Statistics office. If your baby was born in a hospital, you can ask the hospital staff to assist you with any questions you may have.

## Nova Scotia
(http://www.gov.ns.ca/snsmr/vstat/)

Email:      vstat@gov.ns.ca
Office:      Vital Statistics Office
              Joseph Howe Building, Ground Floor
              1690 Hollis Street
              Halifax, NS  B3J 3J9
Address:    Vital Statistics Office
              P.O. Box 157
              Halifax, NS  B3J 2M9
Phone:      902-424-4381 or 1-877-848-2578 (toll free)
Fax:         902-424-0678
Time Limit: 30 days after birth

In Nova Scotia, you must register your baby within thirty days of birth, using a Registration of Birth form that you'll receive in the hospital. Once you've completed the form, give it to the hospital staff, and the medical director will forward it to Vital Statistics. If your baby was not born in hospital, you can obtain the form from any registrar of births and stillbirths—check the website for details. If you need to find a registrar, you can always reach one through the medical records director at your local hospital.

## Prince Edward Island
(http://www.gov.pe.ca/health/index.php3?number=1020358&lang=E)

Office:      126 Douses Road
              Montague, PE  C0A 1R0
Address:    P.O. Box 3000
              Montague, PE  C0A 1R0
Phone:      902-838-0880 or 1-877-320-1253 (toll free)
Fax:         902-838-0883
Time Limit: 30 days after birth

In Prince Edward Island, you must register your baby within thirty days of birth. If your baby was born in a hospital, you may fill out a Registration of Birth form there, and the hospital will submit it to the office of Vital Statistics for you. After the birth is registered, you will receive an official Confirmation of Birth follow-up letter. If it is returned within thirty days of the birth, you may make changes to the information on this form. The letter also provides the opportunity to request a birth certificate.

If your baby was not born in hospital, contact an Access PEI site or the office of Vital Statistics for information on obtaining a Registration of Birth form.

## Newfoundland and Labrador
(http://www.gs.gov.nl.ca/gs/vs/birth-cert.stm)

| | |
|---|---|
| Form: | http://www.health.gov.nl.ca/mcp/forms/ newborn.pdf |
| Email: | gsinfo@gov.nl.ca |
| Address: | P.O. Box 8700 |
| | St. John's, NL  A1B 4J6 |
| Phone: | 709-729-3308 |
| Fax: | 709-729-0946 |
| Time Limit: | 30 days after birth |

You must register your new baby within thirty days of his or her birth. If your child was born in a hospital, you'll receive a Medical Care Plan (MCP) Newborn Registration form as part of your hospital package. Complete the form and return it to your nearest MCP office. If you have questions, ask hospital staff for assistance or visit the MCP website.

If your baby was not born in a hospital, you can obtain the MCP form from most doctors' offices and hospitals. Forms are available at all MCP offices. You can also print the form from the website (please see the link above).

## Yukon

(http://www.hss.gov.yk.ca/programs/vitalstats/birth/)

Email:         Vital.Statistics@gov.yk.ca
Address:       4th Floor – 204 Lambert Street
               Whitehorse, YT  Y1A 3T2
Phone:         1-800-661-0408 ext. 5207 (yoll free in YT only)
Fax:           867-393-6486
Time Limit:    30 days after birth

You can register your child's birth in several ways:

1   in person at any Vital Statistics office or Territorial agent;
2   by mailing a completed Application for Service form
    (available on the website); or
3   by phone, paying by VISA, Mastercard, or American
    Express.

The birth of every child in the territory must be registered within thirty days after the birth. The mother and father must register the birth—or where one parent is unacknowledged or incapable, by the other parent. If both parents are incapable, the guardian/person standing in place of the parents must register the birth.

No birth may be registered that contains more than two surnames hyphenated or combined. If either the mother or father, or both, have a hyphenated or combined surname, only one of the names in the surname or surnames may be used. The one name used must be the name that alphabetically precedes the other.

## Northwest Territories

(http://www.hlthss.gov.nt.ca/english/services/vital_statistics/
birth_registration/default.htm)

| Form: | http://www.hlthss.gov.nt.ca/content/ |
| | Publications/Forms/Certificates/ |
| | ApplicationCertificateEng.pdf |
| Address: | Bag 9 |
| | Inuvik, NT  X0E 0T0 |
| Phone: | 867-777-7420 or (toll free) 1-800-661-0830 |
| Fax: | 867-777-3197 |
| Time Limit: | 30 days after birth |

Your baby must be registered within thirty days of his or her birth in the Northwest Territories; you can find the Registration of Birth form online (see the link above). If your child was born in hospital, the hospital staff will give you a Registration of Birth form with all medical information completed; you just need to sign it. Registering the birth is the responsibility of:

1  the baby's mother;
2  if the mother is incapable, the child's father;
3  where either parent is incapable, the other parent; and
4  where both parents are incapable, the person standing in the place of the parents.

Check the website for valuable information about choosing your baby's surname.

## Nunavut
(http://www.gov.nu.ca/)

| Form: | http://www.gov.nu.ca/documents/ |
| | Vital%20Statistics-Birth-Marriage-Death- |
| | Applications.pdf |
| Address: | Vital Statistics Office |
| | Bag 3 |
| | Rankin Inlet, NU  X0C 0G0 |

Phone:        1-800-661-0833
Fax:          867-645-8092
Time Limit:   30 days after birth

You must register your child within thirty days of his or her birth. While there is no website for the Office of Vital Statistics in Nunavut, you can find a Registration of Birth form online (please see the link above). If you have any questions, please contact the registrar-general of Vital Statistics at the phone number above.

# Famous Canadian Names

Canada has a long and proud history of outstanding citizens who have contributed to its positive international reputation. What better way to honour your Canadian roots or your new Canadian home than by giving your little one a name that reflects an honourable part of Canada's past? Whether you're looking for a name shared by a cherished hockey hero, a beloved author, or an inspirational musician, there are plenty to choose from!

## Males

| | |
|---|---|
| **Alan Doyle** | musician (guitarist, singer: Great Big Sea) |
| **Alan Maitland** | journalist |
| **Alan Thicke** | actor, host |
| **Alex Baumann** | athlete (swimming) |
| **Alex Colville** | artist |
| **Alex Lifeson** | musician (guitarist, Rush) |
| **Alex Trebek** | broadcaster, entertainer |
| **Alexander Graham Bell** | inventor (telephone) |
| **Alexander Milton Ross** | abolitionist, philanthropist |
| **Alexander Young "A.Y." Jackson** | artist, member of the Group of Seven |
| **Alexandre Despatie** | athlete (diving) |
| **Alfred Joseph "A.J." Casson** | artist, member of The Group of Seven |

| | |
|---|---|
| **Alfred Sung** | fashion designer |
| **Alistair MacLeod** | author |
| **André Alexis** | missionary, priest |
| **André Besette / "Miracle Man of Montreal"** | priest, religious figure |
| **Anton Kuerti** | musician (pianist) |
| **Arthur Erickson** | architect |
| **Arthur Lismer** | artist, member of The Group of Seven |
| **Ashley MacIsaac** | musician (violinist) |
| **Atom Egoyan** | director / producer |
| **Austin Clarke** | author |
| **Ben Barry** | fashion designer |
| **Ben Heppner** | musician (singer) |
| **Ben Wicks** | cartoonist / auther |
| **Big Bear** | band chief, politician |
| **"Billy" William Avery Bishop** | WWI flying ace |
| **Bjarni Tryggvason** | astronaut |
| **Blair Thornton** | musician (guitarist, Bachman Turner Overdrive) |
| **Bob Hallett** | musician (singer, bagpiper, fiddler: Great Big Sea) |
| **Bob Rae** | politician |
| **Brendan Fraser** | actor |
| **Brent Butt** | comedian |
| **Bret "The Hitman" Hart** | athlete (wrestling) |
| **Brett Polegato** | musician (singer) |

| | |
|---|---|
| **Brian Orser** | athlete (figure skating) |
| **Bronko Nagurski** | athlete (football) |
| **Bruce Cockburn** | musician (singer) |
| **Bruce McCulloch** | actor, comedian |
| **Bruno Gerussi** | actor |
| **Bruny Surin** | athlete (track) |
| **Bryan Adams** | musician (singer) |
| **"Buck 65" Richard Turfry** | DJ, musician |
| **Buddy MacMaster** | musician (violinist) |
| **Burton Cummings** | musician (singer, Bachman Turner Overdrive and The Guess Who) |
| **"Cadence Weapon" Rollie Pemberton** | musician (singer) |
| **Chad Allan** | musician (singer, Bachman Turner Overdrive and The Guess Who) |
| **Chad Kroeger** | musician (singer, Nickelback) |
| **Charles Best** | scientist, co-discoverer of insulin |
| **Charles Thomas "Stompin' Tom" Connors** | musician (singer) |
| **"Choclair" Kareem Blake** | musician (singer) |
| **Chris Hadfield** | astronaut |
| **Christopher Plummer** | actor |
| **Chuck Comeau** | musician (drummer, Simple Plan) |
| **Clyde Gilmour** | broadcaster |
| **Colin Mochrie** | actor, comedian |
| **Colm Feore** | actor |
| **"Cone" Jason McCaslin** | musician (guitarist, Sum 41) |

| | |
|---|---|
| Corey Haim | actor |
| Corey Hart | musician (singer) |
| Craig Kielburger | humanitarian |
| Curtis Joseph | athlete (hockey) |
| Dallas Green | musician (singer), songwriter |
| Dan Aykroyd | actor |
| Dan George | band chief, politician |
| Daniel Lanois | musician, producer |
| Daniel Nestor | athlete (doubles tennis) |
| Darrell Power | musician (singer, guitarist, fiddler: Great Big Sea) |
| Dave Broadfoot | comedian; member of Royal Canadian Air Farce |
| Dave Foley | actor, comedian |
| Dave Irwin | athlete (downhill skiing), one of the "Crazy Canucks" |
| Dave Murray | athlete (downhill skiing), one of the "Crazy Canucks" |
| Dave Thomas | comedian |
| David Bauer | athlete, priest |
| David Cronenberg | filmmaker, producer |
| David Desrosiers | musician (bassist, Simple Plan) |
| David Pelletier | athlete (pairs figure skating) |
| David Suzuki | scientist |
| David Usher | musician (singer, Moist) |
| Dean McDermot | actor |
| Denys Arcand | director |
| Deryck Whibley | musician (singer, guitarist: Sum 41) |

| | |
|---|---|
| **Don Cherry** | athlete (hockey), sports personality |
| **Don Ferguson** | comedian; member of Royal Canadian Air Farce |
| **Don McKellar** | actor, filmmaker |
| **Donald Sutherland** | actor |
| **Donovan Bailey** | athlete (track and field) |
| **Doug Henning** | magician |
| **Ed Mirvish** | entrepreneur, philanthropist; founder of Honest Ed's store and Mirvish Productions |
| **Ed Robertson** | musician (singer, guitarist: Barenaked Ladies) |
| **Egerton Ryerson** | educator |
| **Elijah Harper** | band chief, politician |
| **Elvis Stojko** | athlete (figure skating) |
| **Éric Bédard** | athlete (speed skating) |
| **Éric Gagné** | athlete (baseball) |
| **Eugene Levy** | actor |
| **Evan Solomon** | journalist |
| **Foster Hewitt** | journalist |
| **Francis Pegahmagabow** | WWI sharpshooter |
| **Frank Gehry** | architect |
| **Frank Johnston** | artist, member of The Group of Seven |
| **Frank Shuster** | comedian |
| **Franklin Carmichael** | artist, member of The Group of Seven |
| **Fred Turner** | musician (bassist, Bachman Turner Overdrive) |

| | |
|---|---|
| **Frederick Banting** | scientist, co-discoverer of insulin |
| **Frederick Varley** | artist, member of The Group of Seven |
| **Gabriel Arcand** | actor |
| **Gaétan Boucher** | athlete (speed skating) |
| **Geddy Lee** | musician (singer, Rush) |
| **George Elliott Clarke** | author |
| **George Stroumboulopoulos** | journalist |
| **Georges St.-Pierre** | athlete (mixed martial arts) |
| **Geraint Wyn Davies** | actor |
| **Gilles Villeneuve** | automobile racing |
| **Gino Vannelli** | musician (singer) |
| **Glenn Gould** | musician (pianist) |
| **Gord Downie** | musician (singer, The Tragically Hip) |
| **Gordon Korman** | author |
| **Gordon Lightfoot** | musician (singer) |
| **Gordon Pinsent** | actor |
| **Gordon Tootoosis** | actor |
| **Graham Greene** | actor |
| **Greg Curnoe** | artist |
| **Greg Thomey** | comedian |
| **"Grey Owl" Archie Belaney** | author, environmentalist |
| **Guy Laliberté** | entrepreneur; founder / owner of Cirque du Soleil |
| **Guy Lombardo** | musician (bandleader) |
| **Guy Vanderhaeghe** | author |
| **Hagood Hardy** | musician (pianist) |

| | |
|---|---|
| **Hal Foster** | cartoonist, artist |
| **Harold Ramis** | actor |
| **Harry Somers** | composer |
| **"Hawksley Workman"** **Ryan Corrigan** | musician (singer, guitarist) |
| **Hayden Christensen** | actor |
| **Howard Shore** | composer |
| **Howie Mandel** | comedian |
| **Hume Cronyn** | actor |
| **Ian Millar** | athlete (equestrian) |
| **Ian Tyson** | musician (singer) |
| **Irving Layton** | poet |
| **Isaac Brock** | soldier |
| **Isadore Sharp** | entrepreneur, founder of Four Seasons hotel chain |
| **Ivan Reitman** | filmmaker |
| **"Izzy" Israel Asper** | entrepreneur, founder of CanWest Global Communications |
| **Jack Warner** | entrepreneur, founder of Warner Bros. Studios |
| **Jacques Villeneuve** | automobile racer |
| **James Collip** | scientist, co-discoverer of insulin |
| **James Doohan** | actor |
| **James Ehnes** | musician (violinist) |
| **James Naismith** | inventor (basketball) |
| **James Edward Hervey** **"J.E.H." Macdonald** | artist, member of The Group of Seven |
| **"Jarvis Church"** **Gerald Eaton** | musician (singer, The Philosopher Kings), producer |

| | |
|---|---|
| **Jay Silverheels** | actor |
| **Jason Priestley** | actor |
| **Jean Marchand** | politician |
| **Jean Vanier** | priest, humanitarian |
| **Jean-Luc Brassard** | athlete (freestyle skiing) |
| **Jeff Healey** | musician (guitarist, singer) |
| **Jeff Stinco** | musician (guitarist, Simple Plan) |
| **Jeffrey Buttle** | athlete (figure skating) |
| **Jeremy Gara** | musician (drummer, Arcade Fire) |
| **Jeremy Wotherspoon** | athlete (speed skating) |
| **Jian Ghomeshi** | broadcaster, musician (singer, Moxy Früvous) |
| **Jim Carrey** | actor |
| **Jim Creeggan** | musician (bassist, Barenaked Ladies) |
| **Jim Cuddy** | musician (guitarist, Blue Rodeo) |
| **Jim Day** | athlete (equestrian) |
| **Joe Flaherty** | comedian |
| **Joe Mendelson / Mendelson Joe** | artist, musician |
| **Joe Shuster** | artist / cartoonist, co-creator of Superman |
| **John Candy** | actor |
| **John Kricfalusi** | animator, cartoonist |
| **John McCrae** | doctor, poet, author of "In Flanders Fields" |
| **John Molson** | entrepreneur, founder of Molson Breweries |
| **John Morgan** | comedian, member of Royal Canadian Air Farce |

| | |
|---|---|
| John Polanyi | scientist, winner of the Nobel Prize |
| John Ralston Saul | author, philosopher |
| Johnny Wayne | comedian |
| Jon Kimura Parker | musician (pianist) |
| Joseph Boyden | author |
| Joseph Brant | politician, band chief |
| Joseph-Armand Bombardier | inventor (snowmobile) |
| Joshua Jackson | actor |
| Josiah Henson | author, community founder |
| "Kardinal Offishall" Jason Harrow | musician |
| Ken Read | athlete (downhill skiing), one of the "Crazy Canucks" |
| Kenneth G. Mills | fashion designer |
| Kevin Hearn | musician (keyboardist, Barenaked Ladies) |
| "Kid Koala" Eric San | DJ, musician |
| "K'naan" Kanaan Warsame | musician (singer) |
| Kurt Browning | athlete (figure skating) |
| Kyle Shewfelt | athlete (gymnastics) |
| Lawren Harris | artist, member of The Group of Seven |
| Leon Mandrake | magician |
| Leonard Cohen | poet, singer |
| Leslie Nielsen | actor |
| Lincoln Alexander | first black MP, lieutenant governor of Ontario |
| Lloyd Eisler | athlete (figure skating) |

| | |
|---|---|
| **Lloyd Robertson** | journalist |
| **Lorne Greene** | actor |
| **Lorne Michaels** | comedian, comedy promoter |
| **Louis B. Mayer** | entrepreneur, co-founder of Metro-Goldwyn-Mayer studios |
| **Louis Quilico** | musician (singer) |
| **Louis Riel** | Métis leader, politician |
| **Louis-Joseph Papineau** | politician |
| **Lucien Bouchard** | politician |
| **M. G. Vassanji** | author |
| **Marc Garneau** | astronaut |
| **Mario Bernardi** | musician (conductor, pianist) |
| **Mark McKinney** | actor, comedian |
| **Mark Tewksbury** | athlete (swimming) |
| **Marshall McLuhan** | intellectual, media savant |
| **Martin Short** | actor, comedian |
| **Matthew Perry** | actor |
| **Maurice Duplessis** | politician |
| **Maury Chaykin** | actor |
| **Max Aitken** | entrepreneur |
| **Michael Bublé** | musician (singer) |
| **Michael Cera** | actor |
| **Michael Ignatieff** | author, politician |
| **Michael J. Fox** | actor |
| **Michael Lee-Chin** | architect |
| **Michael Ondaatje** | author |
| **Mike Bullard** | comedian |
| **Mike Myers** | actor |

| | |
|---|---|
| Mike Weir | athlete (golf) |
| Moe Koffman | musician (flautist, saxophonist) |
| Mordecai Richler | author |
| Morley Callaghan | author |
| Moses Znaimer | entrepreneur, co-founder of Citytv |
| Mychael Danna | musician (composer) |
| Neil Peart | musician (drummer, Rush) |
| Neil Young | musician (singer) |
| Nicholas Campbell | actor |
| Norman Bethune | doctor, humanitarian |
| Norman Jewison | filmmaker, producer |
| Norman McLaren | animator, director |
| Northrop Frye | author, literary theorist, philosopher |
| Norval Morrisseau | artist |
| Oscar Peterson | musician (pianist) |
| Ovide Mercredi | chief of Assembly of First Nations, politician |
| Owen Hart | athlete (wrestling) |
| Patrick Huard | actor |
| Paul Anka | musician (singer) |
| Paul Gross | actor |
| Paul Shaffer | musician (keyboardist) |
| Paul Tracy | auto racer |
| Peter Gzowski | journalist |
| Peter Jennings | journalist |
| Peter C. Newman | journalist |
| Peter Mansbridge | journalist |

| | |
|---|---|
| **Phil Hartman** | actor |
| **Pierre Berton** | journalist |
| **Pierre Bouvier** | musician (singer, Simple Plan) |
| **Preston Manning** | politician |
| **Randy Bachman** | musician (guitarist, Bachman Turner Overdrive and The Guess Who) |
| **Ray Hnatyshyn** | governor general, politician |
| **Raymond Burr** | actor |
| **Raymond Massey** | actor |
| **Red Pollard** | athlete (equestrian) |
| **Reginald Fessenden** | inventor (sonar); patented first TV system |
| **René Levesque** | politician; founder of the Parti Québécois |
| **Rex Murphy** | journalist |
| **Richard Margison** | musician (singer) |
| **Richard Reed Parry** | musician (bassist, keyboardist: Arcade Fire) |
| **Rick Green** | comedian |
| **Rick Hansen** | athlete, humanitarian |
| **Rick Mercer** | comedian |
| **Rick Moranis** | actor |
| **Robbie Bachman** | musician (drummer, Bachman Turner Overdrive) |
| **Robbie Robertson** | musician (singer) |
| **Robert Bateman** | artist |
| **Robert Goulet** | actor, musician |
| **Robert McNeil** | journalist |
| **Robert Munsch** | author |

| | |
|---|---|
| **Robert Service** | poet |
| **Robert Thirsk** | astronaut |
| **Robert Davies** | author |
| **Roch Carrier** | author |
| **Roch Voisine** | musician (singer) |
| **Roger Abbott** | comedian; member of Royal Canadian Air Farce |
| **Rohinton Mistry** | author |
| **Roméo Dallaire** | diplomat, humanitarian, soldier |
| **Ron Joyce** | entrepreneur; co-founder of Tim Hortons coffee shop chain |
| **Ron MacLean** | broadcaster |
| **Ron Sexsmith** | musician (singer) |
| **Ross Rebagliati** | athlete (snowboarding) |
| **"Rowdy Roddy Piper" Roderick Toombs** | athlete (wrestling) |
| **Roy Brown** | WWI flying ace; shot down the Red Baron |
| **Roy Thomson** | entrepreneur; media baron |
| **Rudy Wiebe** | author |
| **Rufus Wainwright** | musician (singer) |
| **Russell Baze** | athlete (equestrian) |
| **Russell Braun** | musician (singer) |
| **Ryan Gosling** | actor |
| **Ryan Peake** | musician (guitarist, Nickelback) |
| **Ryan Reynolds** | actor |
| **Sam Roberts** | musician (singer / songwriter) |
| **Samuel Bronfman** | entrepreneur, acquired Seagram Co. Ltd. |

| | |
|---|---|
| **Samuel Cunard** | entrepreneur, shipping magnate |
| **Sandford Fleming** | scientist, proposed worldwide standard time zones |
| **"Saukrates" Amani Wailoo** | musician (singer) |
| **Scott Thompson** | actor, comedian |
| **Séan McCann** | musician (singer, percussionist: Great Big Sea) |
| **Sébastien Lefebvre** | musician (guitarist, Simple Plan) |
| **Selwyn G. Blaylock** | entrepreneur, scientist |
| **"Seth" Gregory Gallant** | artist, cartoonist |
| **Seth Rogen** | actor |
| **Simon Whitfield** | athlete (triathlon) |
| **St. Jean de Brébeuf** | missionary, priest |
| **Stephen Page** | musician (singer, Barenaked Ladies) |
| **Steve Nash** | athlete (basketball) |
| **Steve Podborski** | athlete (downhill skiing), one of the "Crazy Canucks" |
| **Steve "Red Green" Smith** | comedian |
| **Steven MacLean** | astronaut |
| **Stockwell Day** | politician |
| **Stu Hart** | athlete (wrestling) |
| **Tecumseh** | band chief, politician |
| **Terry Fox** | athlete, humanitarian |
| **Thomas D'Arcy McGee** | politician |
| **Tim Horton** | athlete (hockey), entrepreneur, founder of Tim Hortons coffee shop chain |
| **Tim Kingsbury** | musician (guitarist, Arcade Fire) |

| | |
|---|---|
| **Timothy Eaton** | entrepreneur, founder of Eaton's department store chain |
| **Timothy Findley** | writer |
| **Todd Brooker** | athlete (downhill skiing), one of the "Crazy Canucks" |
| **Todd Macfarlane** | artist, cartoonist |
| **Toller Cranston** | athlete (figure skating) |
| **Tom Cochrane** | musician (singer) |
| **Tom Green** | actor, comedian |
| **Tom Jackson** | actor |
| **Tom Longboat** | athlete (track) |
| **Tom Thomson** | artist |
| **Tommy Chong** | actor, comedian |
| **Tommy Douglas** | activist, politician |
| **Tomson Highway** | author |
| **Tyler Stewart** | musician (drummer, Barenaked Ladies) |
| **Victor Davis** | athlete (swimming) |
| **Walter Ostanek** | bandleader, musician (accordion) |
| **Wilf Carter** | musician (singer) |
| **William B. Davis** | actor |
| **William Butler** | musician (guitarist, keyboardist: Arcade Fire) |
| **William Kurelek** | artist, author |
| **William Shatner** | actor |
| **Win Butler** | musician (singer, Arcade Fire) |

## Females

| | |
|---|---|
| **Adelaide Hoodless** | activist, educator |
| **Adrienne Clarkson** | broadcaster, governor general |
| **Agnes Macphail** | activist, educator, first female member of House of Commons |
| **Aimee Semple McPherson** | founder of the Foursquare Church |
| **Alanis Morissette** | musician (singer) |
| **Alannah Myles** | musician (singer) |
| **Alice Munro** | author |
| **Alison Sydor** | athlete (mountain biking) |
| **Amanda Marshall** | musician (singer) |
| **Amy Sky** | musician (singer) |
| **Andrea Joy "A.J." Cook** | actor |
| **Anna McGarrigle** | musician (singer) |
| **Anna Paquin** | actor |
| **Anne Hébert** | activist, poet |
| **Anne Murray** | musician (singer) |
| **Annette Dionne** | activist; one of the Dionne Quintuplets |
| **Avril Lavigne** | musician (singer) |
| **Barbara Frum** | journalist |
| **Barbara McDougall** | politician |
| **Barbara Smucker** | author |
| **Beckie Scott** | athlete (cross-country skiing) |
| **Betty Oliphant** | dancer, co-founder of the National Ballet School |
| **"Bif Naked" Beth Torbert** | musician (singer) |
| **Buffy Sainte-Marie** | musician (singer) |
| **Carol Huynh** | athlete (freestyle wrestling) |
| **Carol Shields** | author |

| | |
|---|---|
| **Carolyn Waldo** | athlete (synchronized swimming) |
| **Carrie-Anne Moss** | actor |
| **Catherine Callbeck** | politician |
| **Catherine O'Hara** | actor |
| **Catherine Parr Traill** | author |
| **Catherine Robbin** | musician (singer) |
| **Cathy Jones** | comedian |
| **Catriona Le May Doan** | athlete (speed skating) |
| **Cécile Dionne** | activist; one of the Dionne Quintuplets |
| **Celia Franca** | dancer; co-founder of the National Ballet School |
| **Céline Dion** | musician (singer) |
| **Chan Hon Goh** | dancer |
| **Chantal Kreviazuk** | musician (singer) |
| **Chantal Petitclerc** | athlete (wheelchair racing) |
| **Charmion King** | actor |
| **Cindy Klassen** | athlete (skiing) |
| **Cindy Nicholas** | athlete (long-distance swimming) |
| **Colleen Dewhurst** | actor |
| **Cookie Rankin** | musician (singer) |
| **Cree Summer** | voice actor |
| **Crystal Shawanda** | musician (singer) |
| **Cynthia Dale** | actor |
| **Daphne Odjig** | artist |
| **Deanna Durbin** | actor, singer |
| **Deborah Cox** | musician (singer) |
| **Deborah Grey** | politician |
| **Deepa Mehta** | filmmaker |

| | |
|---|---|
| **Denise Bombardier** | journalist |
| **Diana Krall** | musician (singer, pianist) |
| **Divine Brown** | musician (singer) |
| **Dorothy Livesay** | journalist |
| **E. Pauline Johnson / Tekahionwake** | poet |
| **Elisha Cuthbert** | actor |
| **Elizabeth Arden** | entrepreneur; founder of Elizabeth Arden cosmetics |
| **Elizabeth Manley** | athlete (figure skating) |
| **Elizabeth Smart** | author, journalist |
| **Ellen Page** | actor |
| **Ember Swift** | musician (singer, guitarist) |
| **Emilie Dionne** | activist; one of the Dionne Quintuplets |
| **Emily Carr** | artist |
| **Emily Murphy** | first female judge in British Empire, member of "Famous Five" |
| **Estella Warren** | actor, model |
| **Eva Avila** | musician (singer) |
| **Evangeline Lilly** | actor |
| **Evelyn Lau** | author |
| **Fanny "Bobbie" Rosenfeld** | athlete (track) |
| **Fay Wray** | actor |
| **Fefe Dobson** | musician (singer) |
| **Fifi D'Orsay** | actor |
| **Gabrielle Roy** | author |
| **Geneviève Bujold** | actor |

| | |
|---|---|
| **Ginette Reno** | musician (singer) |
| **Grace Park** | actor |
| **Greta Krause** | musician (harpsichordist) |
| **Gwendolyn MacEwan** | author |
| **Heather Rankin** | musician (singer) |
| **Henrietta Edwards** | activist, founding member of Victorian Order of Nurses, member of "Famous Five" |
| **Hilary Weston** | politician |
| **Holly Cole** | musician (singer) |
| **Irene Parlby** | first female cabinet minister in Alberta, member of "Famous Five" |
| **Irshad Manji** | activist, author |
| **Isabel Bayrakdarian** | musician (singer) |
| **Issa / Jane Siberry** | musician (guitarist, singer) |
| **Jackie Burroughs** | actor |
| **Jamie Salé** | athlete (pairs figure skating) |
| **Jan Wong** | author, journalist |
| **Jane Bunnett** | musician (saxophonist, flautist) |
| **Jane Jacobs** | activist, author |
| **Jane Urquhart** | author |
| **Jann Arden** | musician (singer) |
| **Jean Stilwell** | musician (singer) |
| **Jeanne Mance** | doctor |
| **Jeanne Sauvé** | former governor general |
| **Jennie Trout** | one of Canada's first female doctors |
| **Jennifer Tilly** | actor |
| **Jill Hennessy** | actor |

| | |
|---|---|
| Joannie Rochette | athlete (figure skating) |
| Joni Mitchell | musician (singer) |
| Josée Chouinard | athlete (figure skating) |
| Joyce Wieland | artist |
| Judy LaMarsh | politician |
| Julie Doiron | musician (bassist, singer: Eric's Trip) |
| Julie Payette | astronaut |
| June Callwood | journalist, activist |
| k.d. Kathryn Dawn Lang | musician (singer) |
| Karen Kain | dancer |
| Kate Nelligan | actor |
| Kateri Tekakwitha | religious figure |
| Kathleen Edwards | musician (singer) |
| Kerrin Lee-Gartner | athlete (alpine skiing) |
| Kim Cattrall | actor |
| Kinnie Starr | musician (singer) |
| Kristin Kreuk | actor |
| Laura Secord | folk hero, patriot |
| Léa Pool | director |
| Lee Aaron | musician (singer) |
| Leslie Feist | musician (singer) |
| Liane Balaban | actor |
| Linda Evangelista | model |
| Linda Griffiths | actor, playwright |
| Liona Boyd | musician (guitarist) |
| Lorraine Segato | musician (singer) |
| Louise McKinney | first woman in the British Empire elected to a legislative assembly, member of "Famous Five" |

| | |
|---|---|
| **Luba Goy** | comedian, member of Royal Canadian Air Farce |
| **Lucy Maud Montgomery** | author |
| **Lynn Johnston** | artist, cartoonist |
| **Margaret Atwood** | author |
| **Margaret Laurence** | author |
| **Margaret Marshall Saunders** | author |
| **Margaret Trudeau** | author, public figure |
| **Margo Timmins** | musician (singer, Cowboy Junkies) |
| **Margot Kidder** | actor |
| **Marie Dionne** | activist; one of the Dionne Quintuplets |
| **Marilyn Bell** | athlete (long-distance swimming) |
| **Marjorie Harris** | author, gardener |
| **Marnie McBean** | athlete (rowing) |
| **Martha Wainwright** | musician (singer) |
| **Mary Brant** | politician; leader of Six Nations' Womens' Federation |
| **Mary Jane Lamond** | musician (singer) |
| **Mary Pickford** | actor |
| **Mary Walsh** | actor, comedian |
| **Maud Menten** | medical scientist |
| **Maureen Forrester** | musician (singer) |
| **Maureen McTeer** | author, lawyer |
| **Mavis Gallant** | author |
| **Meg Tilly** | actor |
| **Megan Follows** | actor |

| | |
|---|---|
| Melanie Turgeon | athlete (alpine skiing) |
| Melissa Auf der Maur | musician (guitarist) |
| Mia Kirshner | actor |
| Michaëlle Jean | governor general, journalist |
| Mitsou Gélinas | broadcaster, musician (singer) |
| Molly Parker | actor |
| Monika Schnarre | model |
| Myriam Bédard | athlete (biathlon) |
| Myriam Boileau | athlete (swimming) |
| Nancy Greene | athlete (skier) |
| Natalie MacMaster | musician (violinist) |
| Natasha Henstridge | actor, model |
| Nellie McClung | activist, educator, member of "Famous Five" |
| Nelly Furtado | musician (singer) |
| Neve Campbell | actor |
| Nia Vardalos | actor |
| Norma Shearer | actor |
| Pamela Anderson | actor |
| Pamela Wallin | journalist |
| Pauline Jewett | academic, politician |
| "Peaches" Merrill Nisker | musician (singer) |
| Perdita Felicien | athlete (track) |
| Phan Thị Kim Phúc | activist, UNESCO ambassador |
| Rachel McAdams | actor |
| Rae Dawn Chong | actor |
| Raylene Rankin | musician (singer) |
| Régine Chassagne | musician (singer, pianist, accordionist: Arcade Fire) |

| | |
|---|---|
| **Rita MacNeil** | musician (singer) |
| **Roberta Bondar** | astronaut |
| **Rosalie Silberman Abella** | Supreme Court justice |
| **Samantha Bee** | comedian |
| **Sandra Oh** | actor |
| **Sandra Schmirler** | athlete (curling) |
| **Sara Quin** | musician (singer) |
| **Sara Renner** | athlete (cross-country skiing) |
| **Sarah Harmer** | musician (singer) |
| **Sarah McLachlan** | musician (singer) |
| **Sarah Neufeld** | musician (violinist, Arcade Fire) |
| **Sarah Polley** | actor, filmmaker |
| **Sarah Slean** | musician (singer) |
| **Serena Ryder** | musician (singer) |
| **Shalom Harlow** | model |
| **Shania Twain** | musician (singer) |
| **Shannon Tweed** | actor, model |
| **Sheila Copps** | politician |
| **Shirley Douglas** | actor |
| **Silken Laumann** | athlete (rowing) |
| **Sonja Smits** | actor |
| **Ste. Marguerite Bourgeoys** | first Canadian saint |
| **Ste. Marie-Marguerite d'Youville** | founder of the Grey Nuns |
| **Suhana Meharchand** | journalist |
| **Susan Aglukark** | musician |
| **Susan Auch** | athlete (speed skating) |
| **Susan Musgrave** | poet |

| | |
|---|---|
| Susanna Moodie | writer |
| Sylvia Tyson | musician (singer) |
| Sylvie Bernier | athlete (diving) |
| Sylvie Daigle | athlete (speed skating) |
| Tantoo Cardinal | actor |
| Tanya Tagaq Gillis | musician (singer) |
| Tegan Quin | musician (singer) |
| Teresa Stratas | musician (singer) |
| Tricia Helfer | actor |
| "Trish Stratus" Patricia Stratigias | athlete (wrestling) |
| Valerie "Lights" Poxleitner | musician (singer, keyboardist) |
| Valerie Pringle | journalist |
| Vicki Keith | athlete (long-distance swimming) |
| Violet Archer | composer |
| Wendy Mesley | journalist |
| Yasmeen Ghauri | model |
| Yvonne Dionne | activist; one of the Dionne Quintuplets |

# Prime Ministers of Canada
## 1867-2009

John A. Macdonald (1867–1873, 1878–1891)

Alexander Mackenzie (1873–1878)

John Abbott (1891–1892)

John Thompson (1892–1894)

Mackenzie Bowell (1894–1896)

Charles Tupper (1896)

Wilfrid Laurier (1896–1911)

Robert Borden (1911–1920)

Arthur Meighen (1920–1921, 1926)

William Lyon Mackenzie King (1921–1926, 1926–1930, 1935–1948)

Richard Bedford Bennett (1930–1935)

Louis St. Laurent (1948–1957)

John Diefenbaker (1957–1963)

Lester B. Pearson (1963–1968)

Pierre Elliott Trudeau (1968–1979, 1980–1984)

Joe Clark (1979–1980)

John Turner (1984)

Brian Mulroney (1984–1993)

Kim Campbell (1993)

Jean Chrétien (1993–2003)

Paul Martin (2003–2006)

Stephen Harper (2006–present)

# Famous Canadian Hockey Names

Do you have ice dreams for your baby? Check out these popular names in the long and honourable Canadian hockey tradition that are associated with men and women who have proudly represented Canada on ice all over the world.

## Males

**A**

Adam Foote
Adam Graves
Albert "Babe" Siebert
Alex Delvecchio
Allan "Al" Jensen
Andrew Brunette
Andrew Ference
Andy Bathgate
Andy Hebenton
Andy Moog
Aurel Joliat

**B**

Barret Jackman
Bernie Geoffrion
Bernie Parent
Bill Cowley
Bill Durnan
Bill Masterton

Bill Mosienko
Billy Burch
Billy Smith
Blake Dunlop
Bob Bourne
Bob Froese
Bob Gainey
Bob MacMillan
Bob Sauvé
Bobby Bauer
Bobby Clarke
Bobby Hull
Bobby Orr
Brad Park
Brad Richards
Brendan Shanahan
Brenden Morrow
Brett Hull
Bronco Horvath
Brian Hayward

Bryan Allen
Bryan McCabe
Bryan Trottier

## C
Cam Neely
Camille Henry
Charles Apps
Charlie Hodge
Charlie Simmer
Chris Osgood
Chris Phillips
Chris Pronger
Clark Gillies
Claude Provost
Claude "Chuck" Rayner
Clint Smith
Colby Armstrong
Cory Stillman
Craig Ramsay
Craig Rivet
Curtis Joseph

## D
Dan Ellis
Dan Snyder
Dany Heatley
Darren Jensen
Darren McCarty
Dave Andreychuk
Dave Keon
Dave Poulin
Dave Taylor

Denis DeJordy
Denis Harron
Denis Potvin
Denis Savard
Derek Sanderson
Dion Phaneuf
Dirk Graham
Don Cherry
Don Luce
Don McKenney
Doug Bentley
Doug Gilmour
Doug Harvey
Doug Jarvis
Duncan Keith
Dwayne Roloson

## E
Earl "Dutch" Reidel
Ebenezer "Ebbie"
Goodfellow
Ed Belfour
Ed Jovanovski
Ed Westfall
Eddie Shore
Edgar Laprade
Elmer Lach
Elwin "Al" Rollins
Elwyn Romnes
Emmanuel "Manny"
Fernandez
Eric Brewer
Eric Lindros

Eric Staal
Ethan Moreau

**F**

Félix Potvin
Frank Boucher
Frank Mahovlich
Frank Nighbor
Frederick Taylor

**G**

Gary Roberts
George Armstrong
George Hainsworth
Georges Laraque
Georges Vézina
Gerry Cheevers
Gilbert Perreault
Glenn Hall
Glenn "Chico" Resch
Gord Kluzak
Gordie Drillon
Gordie Howe
Grant Fuhr
Guy Carbonneau
Guy Lafleur

**H**

Hector "Toe" Blake
Henri Richard
Herb Gardiner
Herbert "Buddy" O'Connor

Howie Morenz
Hubert "Pit" Morton
Hubert "Bill" Quackenbush

**I**

Ian Laperrière

**J**

Jacques Plante
Jamal Mayers
Jarome Iginla
Jason Arnott
Jason Pominville
Jason Spezza
Jay Bouwmeester
Jay McClement
Jay McKee
Jean Béliveau
Jean-Pierre Dumont
John Cullen
John Madden
Johnny Bower
Johnny Bucyk
Jonathan Cheechoo
Jonathan Toews
Jordan Staal
José Théodore
Joe Nieuwendyk
Joe Primeau
Joe Sakic
Joe Thornton
Joseph "Jean" Ratelle

**K**

Kelly Chase
Kelly Hrudey
Ken Brown
Ken Daneyko
Ken Dryden
Kenny Wharram
Kevin Lowe
Kris King
Kristopher Draper

**L**

Lanny McDonald
Larry Robinson
Leonard "Red" Kelly
Lorne "Gump" Worsley
Lowell MacDonald
Luc Robitaille

**M**

Marc-André Fleury
Marcel Dionne
Mario Lemieux
Mark Fitzpatrick
Mark Messier
Martin Brodeur
Martin St. Louis
Marty Barry
Marty Turco
Maurice Richard
Max Bentley
Michael Peca

Mike Bossy
Mike Liut
Mike Richards
Mike Sillinger
Mike Vernon
Milton Schmidt

**N**

Nels Stewart

**P**

Patrice Bergeron
Pat Riggin
Patrick Marleau
Patrick Roy
Patrick Sharp
Paul Henderson
Paul Kariya
Pavel Buré
Phil Esposito
Phil Goyette
Pierre Dagenais
Pierre Turgeon

**R**

Ray Bourque
Ray Whitney
Réjean Lemelin
Rick Kehoe
Rick Meagher

Rick Middleton
Rick Nash
Rick Wamsley
Riley Armstrong
Rob Blake
Rob Niedermayer
Rob Ray
Robert "Butch" Goring
Roberto Luongo
Robyn Regehr
Rod Brind'Amour
Rod Gilbert
Rogatien Vachon
Roger Crozier
Roland Melanson
Ron Francis
Ron MacLean
Ron Sutter
Roy Worters
Ryan Getzlaf

**S**

Scott Hannan
Scott Niedermayer
Serge Savard
Shane Doan
Shawn Horcoff
Shea Weber
Sheldon Souray
Sid Abel
Sid Smith
Sidney Crosby
Simon Gagné

Stan Mikita
Stéphane Robidas
Stephen Weiss
Steve Ott
Steve Staios
Steve Sullivan
Steve Yzerman
Steven Reinprecht
Syl Apps

**T**

Tahir "Tie" Domi
Ted Hampson
Ted Kennedy
Terry Sawchuk
Tim Horton
Tim Kerr
Tommy Anderson
Tony Esposito
Trevor Linden
Troy Murray

**V**

Vincent Damphousse
Vincent Lecavalier

**W**

Walter "Babe" Pratt
Wendel Clark
Willie Mitchell

## Females

### A
Abby Hoffman
Andria Hunter
Angela James

### B
Becky Kellar

### C
Carla MacLeod
Carol Scheibel
Caroline Ouellette
Cassie Campbell
Cathy Phillips
Charline Labonté
Cherie Piper
Cheryl Pounder
Colleen Sostorics

### D
Dana Antal
Danièle Sauvageau
Danielle Dubé
Danielle Goyette
Dawn McGuire

### E
Erin Whitten

### F
Fanny "Bobbie" Rosenfeld
Fiona Smith
Fran Rider
France St-Louis

### G
Geraldine Heaney
Gillian Apps
Gillian Ferrari
Gina Kingsbury
Glynis Peters

### H
Hayley Wickenheiser

### I
Isabelle Minier
Isobel Stanley

### J
Jane Robinson
Jayna Hefford
Jennifer Botterill
Judy Diduck

### K
Kathy McCormack
Karen Hughes

Karen Nystrom
Karen Wallace
Katie Weatherston
Kim Ratushny
Kim St-Pierre

**L**
Laura Leslie
Laura Schuler
Leslie Reddon
Lori Dupuis
Luce Letendre

**M**
Manon Rhéaume
Margot Page
Marianne Grnak
Meghan Acosta
Melody Davidson

**N**
Nancy Deschamps
Nancy Drolet
Nathalie Picard

**R**
Rebecca Fahey

**S**
Sami Jo Small
Sarah Vaillancourt
Shannon Miller
Shirley Cameron
Stacy Wilson
Susan Dalziel

**T**
Tammy Shewchuk
Thérèse Brisson

**V**
Vicky Sunohara

# Celebrities' Babies' Names

Weird, wacky, and sometimes wonderful, celebrities not only influence our taste in fashion and music, they also provide a whole new take on what babies may be called. In some cases, their creative ideas either inspire or misfire. If you're considering a similarly creative name for your baby, make sure you review the final naming guidelines on page 19. Check out the ✤ for Canadian parental creativity.

| Baby Name(s) | Parent(s) |
| --- | --- |
| Aanisah, Cassius, and Tahmel | Macy Gray and Tracy Hinds |
| Aaron Elvis, Ava, and Ezra Ann | Acheson and Larry Mullen Jr. |
| Adelaide Rose and Banjo Patrick | Rachel Griffiths and Andrew Taylor |
| Adrian Edward, Lulu, and Gabriel Elijah | Edie Brickell and Paul Simon |
| Alaafia Jehu-T, Akhenaten Kihwa-T, Alimayu Moa-T, Iset Jua-T, and Jelani Asar | Wesley Snipes |
| Alaia | Stephen Baldwin |
| Alexa Ray, Jack Paris, and Sailor Lee | Christie Brinkley |
| Alexa, Austin, Laura, and Stephanie | Nathalie Asselin and ✤ Mario Lemieux |

| Baby Name(s) | Parent(s) |
|---|---|
| Alexandra, Avis Ann, Atticus, and Kahlea | Daniel Baldwin |
| Alexandria Zahra and Duncan Zowie Haywood | David Bowie |
| Alfie, Charlie John, and Gulliver Flynn | Gary Oldman |
| Amandine and Loewy | John Malkovich |
| Amba Isis and Assisi Lola | Jade Jagger |
| André, Huguette, Jean, Maurice Jr., Normand, Paul, and Suzanne | ❦ Lucille and Maurice Richard |
| Angel Iris, Bella Zahra, Bria, Christian, Eric, Miles, Shayne Audra, and Zola Ivy | Eddie Murphy |
| Angel Iris and Phoenix-Chi | Melanie "Scary Spice" Brown |
| Angus Moore | Amanda Pays and Corbin Bernsen |
| Annaliza, Arissa, Ayako, Dominic, Kentaro, and Savannah | Steven Seagal |
| Apple Blythe Alison and Moses Bruce Anthony | Gwyneth Paltrow and Chris Martin |
| Aquinnah Kathleen and Schuyler Frances (twins), Esmé Annabelle, and Sam Michael | Tracy Pollan and ❦ Michael J. Fox |
| Arpad Flynn Alexander and Aurelius Cy Andrea | Elle Macpherson and Arpad Busson |
| Arran, Blue Angel, Hollie, Levi, and Sian | Dave "The Edge" Evans |

| Baby Name(s) | Parent(s) |
|---|---|
| Arshile | ♣ Arsinée Khanjian and Atom Egoyan |
| Audio Science | Shannyn Sossamon and Dallas Clayton |
| Augustin James | ♣ Linda Evangelista |
| Autumn, Jaffar, Jaimy, Jermaine Jr., Jermajesty, Jeremy Maldonado, and Jourdynn Micheal | Jermaine Jackson |
| Autumn, Ocean, Sonnet, and True | Keisha Nash and Forest Whitaker |
| Ava and Deacon | Reese Witherspoon and Ryan Philippe |
| Barron William, Donald Jr., Eric, Ivanka, and Tiffany | Donald Trump |
| Belle Kingston, Danielle Alexandra, and Stella Irene August | Donna Dixon and ♣ Dan Aykroyd |
| Billy Ray and Nell | Helena Bonham Carter and Tim Burton |
| Birgen and Sean | Brynn Omdahl and ♣ Phil Hartman |
| Braison Chance, Brandi, Christopher Cody, Miley, Noah Lindsey, and Trace | Billy Ray Cyrus |
| Brandon Thomas and Dylan Jagger | ♣ Pamela Anderson and Tommy Lee |
| Brawley and Sophie Lane | Nick Nolte |
| Bridget Michael, Eliot Pauline, Fuchsia Catherine, Giacomo Luke, Jake, and Joseph | Gordon "Sting" Sumner |

| Baby Name(s) | Parent(s) |
| --- | --- |
| Brooklyn, Cruz, and Romeo | Victoria and David Beckham |
| Bruno Paul and Cosima Thomasina | Nigella Lawson and John Diamond |
| Buck | Roseanne Barr |
| Calico, Dashiel, and Sonora | Sheryl Goddard and Alice Cooper |
| Chelsea, Liv, Mia, and Taj Monroe | Steven Tyler |
| Chester, Colin, Elizabeth Ann, and Truman | Tom Hanks |
| Coco Riley | Courtney Cox and David Arquette |
| Corde, Cordell, and Cori | Shante and Calvin "Snoop Dogg" Broadus Jr. |
| Daisy Boo, Petal Blossom, Rainbow, and Poppy Honey | Juliette "Jools" and Jamie Oliver |
| David Banda Mwale, Lourdes Maria, and Rocco | Madonna Ciccone |
| Dawn and William | ❦ Anne Murray |
| Declyn Wallace | Cyndi Lauper and David Thornton |
| Destry Allyn, Jessica Capshaw, Max Samuel, Mikaela George, Sasha Rebecca, Sawyer Avery, and Theo | Kate Capshaw and Steven Spielberg |
| Dex and Thomas | Paula Zwagerman and Dana Carvey |

| Baby Name(s) | Parent(s) |
|---|---|
| Dexter and Duke | Diane Keaton |
| Dexter Henry Lorcan and Frank Harlan James (twins) | ❦ Diana Krall and Elvis Costello |
| Dree and Langley | Mariel Hemingway and Stephen Crisman |
| Dylan Frances and Hopper Jack | Robin Wright and Sean Penn |
| Eja D'Angelo | ❦ Shania Twain and Mutt Lange |
| Elijah Bob Patricius Guggi Q, John Abraham, Jordan, and Memphis Eve | Alison and Paul "Bono" Hewson |
| Elizabeth Scarlett, Gabriel Luke Beauregard, Georgia May Ayeesha, Jade Sheena Jezebel, James Leroy Augustin, Karis Hunt, and Lucas Maurice Morad | Mick Jagger |
| Emma Marie, Paulina Mary Jean, Trevor Douglas, Tristan Wayne, and Ty Robert | Janet Jones and ❦ Wayne Gretzky |
| Felix, Oscar, and Piper Maru | Gillian Anderson |
| Fifi Trixibelle, Peaches Honeyblossom Michelle Charlotte Angel Vanessa, and Little Pixie | Paula Yates and Bob Geldof |
| Finlay Munro, Iris, Rafferty, and Rudy | Sadie Frost and Jude Law |
| Frances Bean | Courtney Love and Kurt Cobain |

| Baby Name(s) | Parent(s) |
| --- | --- |
| Freda George, George Jr., George III, George IV, George V, George VI, Georgette, Leola, Michi, and Natalie | George Foreman |
| Gilbran, Paris, Precious, Rae Dawn, and Robbi | Maxine Sneed and ♣ Tommy Chong |
| Grier Hammond and Rowan Frances | Brooke Shields and Chris Henchy |
| Griffin Archer, Holden Fletcher, and Leland Francis | Afton Smith and ♣ Brendan Fraser |
| Harley Quinn | Jennifer and Kevin Smith |
| Hazel Patricia and Phinnaeus Walter | Julia Roberts and Daniel Moder |
| Heaven Love'on, God'Iss Love, and Justin McKenzie Phillip | Cynthia "Lil' Mo" Loving |
| Heavenly Hiraani Tiger Lily | Paula Yates and Michael Hutchence |
| Hud, Justice, Michelle, Speck, and Teddi Jo | John Cougar Mellencamp |
| India Ann and Taja Summer | ♣ Sarah McLachlan and Ashwin Sood |
| Ireland Eliesse | Kim Basinger and Alec Baldwin |
| Jack, Lewis, and Maesa | Tamara Hurwitz and Bill Pullman |
| Jaden Christopher Syre and Willow Camille Reign | Jada Pinkett and Will Smith |

| Baby Name(s) | Parent(s) |
|---|---|
| Jane Erin | ♣ Jim Carrey |
| John "Jack" Christopher and Lily-Rose Melody | Vanessa Paradis and Johnny Depp |
| Junior and Princess Tiaamii | Katy "Jordan" Perry and Peter André |
| Kal-El Coppola and Weston Coppola | Nicolas Cage |
| Kyd Miller and Madelaine West | Téa Leoni and David Duchovny |
| Laura, Sarika, Severn, Tamiko, and Troy | ♣ David Suzuki |
| Leaf Joaquin, Liberty Mariposa, River Jude, Rainbow Joan of Arc, and Summer Joy | Arlyn "Heart" and John Phoenix |
| Leslie Carol, Lisabeth Mary, and Melanie | ♣ William Shatner |
| Levon Roan and Maya Ray | Uma Thurman and Ethan Hawke |
| Lola and Tali | Annie Lennox and Uri Fruchtmann |
| Lolita and Piper | Brian De Palma |
| Maddox Chivan, Knox Léon, Pax Thian, Shiloh Nouvel, Vivienne Marcheline, and Zahara Marley | Angelina Jolie and Brad Pitt |
| Makena'lei Gordon | Helen Hunt and Matthew Carnahan |
| Mars Merkaba, Puma Rose Sabti, and Seven Sirius | Erykah Badu |

| Baby Name(s) | Parent(s) |
| --- | --- |
| Moon Unit, Dweezil, Ahmet Emuukha Rodan, and Diva Muffin | Gail and Frank Zappa |
| Moxie CrimeFighter and Zolten Penn | Emily Zolten and Penn Jillette |
| Nahla Ariela | Halle Berry and ♣ Gabriel Aubry |
| Nevis | ♣ Nelly Furtado |
| Nico and Ripley | Thandie Newton and Ol Parker |
| Paris Michael Katherine, "Prince" Michael Joseph Jackson Jr., and Prince Michael Jackson II | Michael Jackson |
| Pilot Inspektor | Jason Lee |
| Racer Maximilliano, Rebel Antonio, Rhiannon Elizabeth, Rocket Valentino, and Rogue Joaquin | Elizabeth Avellán and Robert Rodriguez |
| Ramona | Maggie Gyllenhaal and Peter Sarsgaard |
| Rebop | Michelle and Todd Rundgren |
| Rumer Glenn, Scout LaRue, and Tallulah Belle | Demi Moore and Bruce Willis |
| Sage Moonblood, Scarlett Rose, Seargeoh, Sistine Rose, and Sophia Rose | Sylvester Stallone |
| Scarlet Starr | Melanie "Sporty Spice" Chisholm and Thomas Starr |

| Baby Name(s) | Parent(s) |
| --- | --- |
| Sean Preston and Jayden James | Britney Spears and Kevin Federline |
| Seraphina Rose Elizabeth and Violet Anne | Jennifer Garner and Ben Affleck |
| Sosie Ruth and Travis Sedgwick | Kyra Sedgwick and Kevin Bacon |
| Suri | Katie Holmes and Tom Cruise |

# Biblical Names

| Boys | Girls |
|------|-------|
| Abel | Abigail |
| Abraham | Adah |
| Adam | Agatha |
| Amos | Anne |
| Angus | Azubah |
| Asa | Bathsheba |
| Cain | Bernice |
| Caleb | Catherine |
| Christian | Chloë |
| Daniel | Claudia |
| Darth | Deborah |
| David | Delilah |
| Eli | Dinah |
| Elijah | Dorcas |
| Enoch | Edna |
| Ephraim | Elisheba |
| Ethan | Emma |
| Ezekiel | Esther |
| Felix | Evangeline |
| Gabriel | Eve |
| Gideon | Faith |
| Hosea | Felicity |
| Isaac | Grace |
| Isaiah | Hagar |
| Israel | Hannah |

| Boys | Girls |
|------|-------|
| Jacob | Hope |
| James | Jezebel |
| Jared | Joy |
| Jason | Judith |
| Joel | Keziah |
| John | Leah |
| Jonathan | Lucia |
| Joseph | Madonna |
| Joshua | Magdalene |
| Judah | Mara |
| Luke | Margaret |
| Malcolm | Martha |
| Mark | Mary |
| Matthew | Moriah |
| Michael | Priscilla |
| Moses | Rachel |
| Nathan | Regina |
| Noah | Salome |
| Paul | Sapphira |
| Peter | Sarah/Sarai |
| Samson | Susannah |
| Samuel | Sylvia |
| Saul | Tabitha |
| Seth | Thamar |
| Stephen | Tirzah |
| Thomas | Vashti |
| Tobias | Vera |
| Victor | Zillah |
| Vincent | Zipporah |
| Zacharias | Zoë |

# Timeless Names

Names can go in and out of fashion very quickly, but the classic names below have all stood the test of time:

| Boys | Girls |
| --- | --- |
| Alexander | Alexandra |
| Daniel | Alice |
| David | Anne |
| Edward | Catherine |
| Henry | Claire |
| James | Elizabeth |
| John | Emma |
| Joseph | Grace |
| Joshua | Helen |
| Mark | Jane |
| Matthew | Julia |
| Michael | Laura |
| Nicholas | Lucy |
| Patrick | Maria |
| Richard | Olivia |
| Robert | Rachel |
| Samuel | Rebecca |
| Simon | Sarah |
| Thomas | Sophie |
| William | Victoria |

# Shakespearean Names

Have you always loved classic names that stand the test of time? Did you sigh over *Romeo and Juliet* as a teenager? If so, consider using a name from one of William Shakespeare's plays for your new baby. These names are elegant, classy, and good for both little ones and adults; most of them can be easily shortened to a nickname.

Shakespeare liked some names so much that he used them several times—Antonio, for example, is used in at least five plays! Some names that were originally used for males, like Ariel, Cymbeline, and Paris, are now used primarily for females. They've been included on both lists in case you want to keep with tradition or try something new.

## Males

Aaron (*Titus Andronicus*)

Achilles (*Troilus and Cressida*)

Adrian (*Coriolanus*)

Adriano (*Love's Labour's Lost*)

Aemilius (*Titus Andronicus*)

Alonso (*The Tempest*)

Andrew (*Twelfth Night*)

Angelo (*The Comedy of Errors*) (*Measure for Measure*)

Antonio (*The Merchant of Venice*) (*Much Ado About Nothing*) (*The Tempest*) (*Twelfth Night*) (*Two Gentlemen of Verona*)

Antony (*Antony and Cleopatra*)

Ariel (*The Tempest*)

Autolycus (*The Winter's Tale*)

Balthazar (*The Comedy of Errors*) (*Much Ado About Nothing*)

Banquo (*Macbeth*)

Bassanio (*The Merchant of Venice*)

Belarius (*Cymbeline*)

Benedick (*Much Ado About Nothing*)

Benvolio (*Romeo and Juliet*)

Bertram (*All's Well That Ends Well*)

Brutus (*Julius Caesar*)

Caesar (*Julius Caesar*)

Caius (*Coriolanus*)

Camillo (*The Winter's Tale*)

Cassio (*Othello*)

Cassius (*Julius Caesar*)

Charles (*As You Like It*)

Chiron (*Titus Andronicus*)

Christopher (*The Taming of the Shrew*)

Claudio (*Measure for Measure*) (*Much Ado About Nothing*)

Claudius (*Hamlet*)

Clifford (*Henry VI*)

Cloten (*Cymbeline*)

Corin (*As You Like It*)

Cornelius (*Cymbeline*)

Cymbeline (*Cymbeline*)

Demetrius (*Titus Andronicus*) (*A Midsummer Night's Dream*)

Dion (*The Winter's Tale*)

Donalbain (*Macbeth*)

Duncan (*Macbeth*)

Edgar (*King Lear*)

Edmund (*King Lear*)

Edward (*Henry VI*)

Egeus (*A Midsummer Night's Dream*)

Escalus (*Romeo and Juliet*)

Fabian (*Twelfth Night*)

Falstaff (*The Merry Wives of Windsor*)

Fenton (*The Merry Wives of Windsor*)

Ferdinand (*The Tempest*) (*Love's Labour's Lost*)

Ford (*The Merry Wives of Windsor*)

Fortinbras (*Hamlet*)

Frederick (*As You Like It*)

Gonzalo (*The Tempest*)

Gratiano (*The Merchant of Venice*)

Hamlet (*Hamlet*)

Hector (*Troilus and Cressida*)

Henry (*Henry IV, Henry V, Henry VI*)

Horatio (*Hamlet*)

Hugh (*The Merry Wives of Windsor*)

Iago (*Othello*)

Jaques (*As You Like It*)

John (*Much Ado About Nothing*)

Julius (*Julius Caesar*)

Laertes (*Hamlet*)

Laurence (*Romeo and Juliet*)

Lear (*King Lear*)

Leonardo (*The Merchant of Venice*)

Leonato (*Much Ado About Nothing*)

Leontes (*The Winter's Tale*)

Lodovico (*Othello*)

Lorenzo (*The Merchant of Venice*)

Louis (*Henry V*)

Lucentio (*The Taming of the Shrew*)

Lucio (*Measure for Measure*)

Lucius (*Titus Andronicus*)

Lysander (*A Midsummer Night's Dream*)

Macbeth (*Macbeth*)

Malcolm (*Macbeth*)

Marcius (*Coriolanus*)

Marcus (*Titus Andronicus*)

Mercutio (*Romeo and Juliet*)

Nathaniel (*Love's Labour's Lost*)

Oberon (*A Midsummer Night's Dream*)

Oliver (*As You Like It*)

Orlando (*As You Like It*)

Orsino (*Twelfth Night*)

Oswald (*King Lear*)

Othello (*Othello*)

Owen (*Henry IV*) (*Henry V*)

Paris (*Romeo and Juliet*)

Pedro (*Much Ado About Nothing*)

Petruchio (*The Taming of the Shrew*)

Polonius (*Hamlet*)

Prospero (*The Tempest*)

Proteus (*Two Gentlemen of Verona*)

Richard (*Richard II*)
(*Richard III*)

Robin (*The Merry Wives of
Windsor*)

Roderigo (*Othello*)

Romeo (*Romeo and Juliet*)

Sebastian (*The Tempest*)
(*Twelfth Night*)

Shylock (*The Merchant of
Venice*)

Silvius (*As You Like It*)

Stephano (*The Tempest*)

Theseus (*A Midsummer Night's
Dream*)

Titus (*Titus Andronicus*)

Toby (*Twelfth Night*)

Troilus (*Troilus and Cressida*)

Tybalt (*Romeo and Juliet*)

Valentine (*Twelfth Night*) (*Two
Gentlemen of Verona*)

Vincentio (*Measure for
Measure*) (*The Taming of the
Shrew*)

William (*As You Like It*)

## Females

Adriana (*The Comedy of Errors*)

Aemilia (*The Comedy
of Errors*)

Alice (*Henry V*)

Anne (*The Merry Wives of
Windsor*)

Ariel (*The Tempest*)

Audrey (*As You Like It*)

Beatrice (*Much Ado About
Nothing*)

Bianca (*Othello*) (*The Taming of
the Shrew*)

Calpurnia (*Julius Caesar*)

Cassandra (*Troilus and
Cressida*)

Celia (*As You Like It*)

Cleopatra (*Antony and
Cleopatra*)

Cordelia (*King Lear*)

Cressida (*Troilus and Cressida*)

Cymbeline (*Cymbeline*)

Desdemona (*Othello*)

Diana (*All's Well That Ends
Well*)

Eleanor (*Henry VI*)

Emilia (*Othello*)
(*The Winter's Tale*)

Francisca (*Measure
for Measure*)

Gertrude (*Hamlet*)

Goneril (*King Lear*)

Helen (*Troilus and Cressida*)

Helena (*A Midsummer Night's Dream*) (*All's Well That Ends Well*)

Hermia (*A Midsummer Night's Dream*)

Hermione (*The Winter's Tale*)

Hero (*Much Ado About Nothing*)

Hippolyta (*A Midsummer Night's Dream*)

Imogen (*Cymbeline*)

Isabel (*Henry V*)

Isabella (*Measure for Measure*)

Jessica (*The Merchant of Venice*)

Julia (*Two Gentlemen of Verona*)

Juliet (*Romeo and Juliet*) (*Measure for Measure*)

Katharine (*Henry V*) (*The Taming of the Shrew*)

Lavinia (*Titus Andronicus*)

Lucetta (*Two Gentlemen of Verona*)

Luciana (*The Comedy of Errors*)

Margaret (*Henry VI*) (*Much Ado About Nothing*)

Margery (*Henry VI*)

Maria (*Twelfth Night*)

Mariana (*Measure for Measure*)

Miranda (*The Tempest*)

Nerissa (*The Merchant of Venice*)

Octavia (*Antony and Cleopatra*)

Olivia (*Twelfth Night*)

Ophelia (*Hamlet*)

Paris (*Romeo and Juliet*)

Paulina (*The Winter's Tale*)

Perdita (*The Winter's Tale*)

Portia (*The Merchant of Venice*) (*Julius Caesar*)

Regan (*King Lear*)

Rosalind (*As You Like It*)

Rosaline (*Love's Labour's Lost*) (*Romeo and Juliet*)

Silvia (*Two Gentlemen of Verona*)

Tamora (*Titus Andronicus*)

Titania (*A Midsummer Night's Dream*)

Ursula (*Much Ado About Nothing*)

Valeria (*Coriolanus*)

Viola (*Twelfth Night*)

Virgilia (*Coriolanus*)

# Unisex Names

If you don't know whether you're having a boy or a girl, or you'd like a name that stands on its own without any preexisting gender associations, consider a name that can do equally well for a girl or a boy. Some work well as nicknames or shortened versions of longer names. A word of caution: some of the spellings have traditionally been used to indicate gender (for example, Lesley for a girl, Leslie for a boy), although this is quickly changing. They're flagged here as (M) and (F) for your reference.

Adair

Addison

Ainslie (M), Ainsley (F)

Alex

Ashley

Aubrey

Bailey

Brett

Cameron

Casey

Chris

Dale

Daryl

Drew

Gene (M), Jean (F)

Gerry (M), Jerry (F)

Glenn

Harley

Harper

Jamie

Jay

Jesse (M), Jessie (F)

Joe (M), Jo (F)

Jordan

Kai

Kelly

Lane

Lee (M), Leigh (F)

Leslie (M), Lesley (F)

Mackenzie

Madison

Mickey (M), Mickie (F)

Nat

Nick (M), Nicky (F)

Paris

Pat

Quinn

Ray (M), Rae (F)

Reagan (M), Regan (F)

Reece

Reilly (M), Riley (F)

Robin

Rory

Sam

Sandy

Sasha

Sean (M), Shawn (F)

Taylor

Terry

# Names from Nature

Plant and flower names are generally best suited to girls, but some, such as Basil or Heath, are more traditionally used for boys. You can also use names that are inspired by colours, gemstones, wildlife, weather, and other natural phenomena—but be aware that this naming trend has been sharply declining since the hippie-inspired naming fads of the sixties and seventies. Little Sunshine and Scarlett may be the only ones in their school with such names! Don't forget to apply the naming guidelines on page 19 when choosing a name from nature.

## Trees and Flowers

### Boys

| | |
|---|---|
| Alder | Heath |
| Ashley | Leaf, Leif |
| Basil | Linden |
| Bay | Lockwood |
| Burnet, Burnett | Oakley |
| Eldridge | Oliver |
| Filbert | Perry |
| Florian | Sage |
| Forrest | Silvanus |
| Fraser, Frasier | Speedwell |
| Grover | Stockton |
| Harwood | Thorne |
| Hawthorn | Valerian |

## Girls

Acacia
Alyssa, Alyssum
Amaranth
Amaryllis
Angelica
Aster
Azalea
Belladonna
Blossom
Briar
Bryony
Calla
Camellia
Cassia
Cherry
Cicely
Columbine
Daffodil
Dahlia
Daisy
Fern
Fleur, Fleurette
Forsythia
Ginger
Gladiola
Goldberry
Hazel
Heather
Holly
Hyacinth
Iris
Ivy
Jasmine

Juniper
Laurel
Lavender
Liatris
Lilac
Lily
Lotus
Lupine
Magnolia
Marguerite
Marigold
Mimosa
Myrtle
Olive
Orchid
Pansy
Peony
Petunia
Poppy
Posy
Protea
Rhoda
Rose
Rosemary
Rue
Safflower
Saffron
Scilla
Tansy
Violet
Willow
Zinnia

# Names from the Night Sky

Here are some heavenly names for heavenly babies: a mixture of Arabic star names and the names of constellations based on Greek mythology.

| Boys | Girls |
|------|-------|
| Algebar – the giant | Adhara – the maidens |
| Alioth – the black horse | Alioth – the black horse |
| Almeisan – the shining one | Almeisan, Meissa – the shining one |
| Alnair – the bright one | |
| Altair – the flying eagle | Alnair – the bright one |
| Apus – bird of paradise | Alnilam – the string of pearls |
| Auriga – charioteer | Altair – the flying eagle |
| Caelum – sky | Andromeda – mythological princess |
| Canis – dog | |
| Castor – mythological twin in the Gemini constellation | Aquila – eagle |
| | Ara – altar |
| Cepheus – mythological king of Ethiopia | Aurora – Northern Lights |
| | Carina – ship's keel |
| Cetus – whale | Cassiopeia – mythological queen |
| Corvus – crow | |
| Cygnus – swan | Columba – dove |

| Boys | Girls |
|------|-------|
| Delphinus – dolphin | Corona – crown |
| Dorado – dolphin fish | Cygna – swan |
| Draco – dragon | Delphina – dolphin |
| Dubhe – the bear | Dorada – dolphin fish |
| Eridanus – river | Hydra – water snake |
| Errai – the shepherd | Lacerta – lizard |
| Herakles/Hercules – mythological hero | Lyra – lyre |
| Hydrus – water snake | Phoenix – mythological firebird |
| Lupus – wolf | Sadalbari – lucky star of the excellent one |
| Orion – mythological hunter | Sagitta – arrow |
| Pavo – peacock | Saiph – the sword |
| Pegasus – winged horse | Ursa – bear |
| Perseus – mythological hero | Vega – the stooping eagle |
| Phoenix – mythological firebird | Vela – sails |
| Pollux – mythological twin in the Gemini constellation | |
| Sadalbari – lucky star of the excellent one | |
| Saiph – the sword | |
| Sirius – the Dog Star | |
| Ursa – bear | |
| Vega – the stooping eagle | |

# Names to Reconsider

It's a shame when it happens—but sometimes you discover something about a favourite name that radically changes your perception of it. Much of this is culturally determined, but you might want to keep these nuances in mind when trying out potential names for your new little one.

## Boys and Girls

1   **The name of any fruit or vegetable**. Gwyneth Paltrow's daughter, Apple, notwithstanding, naming your child after produce will cause problems for any child who is not born to a major movie star. The child will get snickered at wherever she goes, and simple trips to the grocery store will become ordeals: "Hand me that apple, Papaya."

2   **The name of any musical instrument**. Rachel Griffiths did name her son Banjo, but he can legally change it when he turns sixteen. Unless your son becomes a blues musician and wants a memorable stage name, please do not saddle him with an instrumental name: "Ukelele Jones says he's having a sleepover for his birthday."

3   **The name of any controversial or strongly divisive figure**. While it may be tempting to name your child to prove a point, please remember that your child is an individual. He or she may grow up to cherish a completely different set of experiences and viewpoints than you, and having to cope with a strongly polarized name may only hurt. Keeping your parents' beliefs in

mind is hard to do when you're getting beaten up every day on the playground. So commit the first selfless act of your selfless parenting career: choose a name with your *child's* future in mind, not yours.

## Boys

| | |
|---|---|
| **Adolf** | Means "noble wolf," but has strong Fascist overtones |
| **Butch** | Slang for masculine—sometimes used to describe lesbians in a derogatory way |
| **Calvin** | Means "little bald one" |
| **Cameron** | Means "crooked nose" |
| **Campbell** | Means "crooked mouth" |
| **Claud(e)** | Means "crippled" or "lame" |
| **Dick** | Slang for penis |
| **Esau** | Means "hairy" |
| **Gaylord** | Can be used to refer to homosexuals in a derogatory way |
| **Job** | Means "the persecuted one" |
| **John Thomas** | Old-fashioned slang for penis |
| **Johnny** | Slang for condom (primarily in England) |
| **Johnson** | Old-fashioned slang for penis |
| **Kennedy** | Means "ugly head" |
| **Melville** | Means "bad town" |
| **Oedipus** | Mythological Greek figure who unknowingly killed his father and married his mother |
| **Peter** | Slang for penis |
| **Ralph** | Slang for vomiting |
| **Randi / Randy** | Slang for sexually excited |

| Tristan / Tristram | Means "sad" |
|---|---|
| Tullio | Depending on pronunciation, sounds like toolio; tool is slang for penis |
| Willie / Willy | Slang for penis |
| Woody | Slang for an erection |

## Girls

| Ademia | Means "without husband" |
|---|---|
| Agrippa | Means "sick" or "painful" |
| Alexia | An inability to read; associated with brain damage |
| Andromache | Means "she who fights against men" |
| Audun | Means "deserted" |
| Balbina | Means "stammers" |
| Bertha | Associated with "Big Bertha," a piece of heavy artillery |
| Candida | Means "glowing" but is also the name of an unpleasant yeast infection |
| Cassandra | Means "entangler of men" or "prophet of doom" |
| Cherry | Associated with losing one's virginity ("popping the cherry") |
| Desdemona | Means "ill-fated one" |
| Electra | Associated with the psychoanalytic Electra complex; named after a mythical Greek figure who killed her mother and slept with her father |
| Fanny | Means "vagina" in Europe and "bottom" in North America |
| Gay | Slang for homosexual |

| | |
|---|---|
| **Jezebel** | Wicked Biblical figure |
| **Jocasta** | Means "scorned"; Oedipus' mother, whom he unwittingly slept with |
| **Mara** | Means "bitter" or "sorrowful" |
| **Mary Jane** | Slang for marijuana |
| **Pansy** | Derogatory slang for a feminine man |
| **Patsy** | Slang for someone who has been set up to take responsibility for a crime |
| **Randi / Randy** | Slang for sexually excited |
| **Salome** | Wicked Biblical figure |
| **Sarai** | Means "quarrelsome" |
| **Zanita** | Means "long teeth" |

# Names
## *for*
# GIRLS

# A

**Aaliyah** *(Arabic, Hebrew)* High, exalted.

**Aasivak** *(InupiaQ)* Spider.

**Aba** *(African)* Born on Thursday.

**Abbey** *See* Abigail.

**Abby** *(Latin)* Head of a monastery.
  *See also* Abigail.

**Abella** *(Latin)* Beautiful.

**Abeni** *(African)* Girl prayed for.

**Abha** *(Hindu)* Lustrous beauty.

**Abia** *(Arabic)* Great.

**Abigail** *(Hebrew)* A father's joy.
  *Variants:* Abbey, Abby, Gail.

**Abina** *(Ghanaian)* Born on a Tuesday.

**Abira** *(Hebrew)* Strong.

**Abnauraq** *(InupiaQ)* Girl; little woman.

**Abra** *(Hebrew)* Mother of multitudes.

**Acacia** *(Greek)* The name of a flower.

**Acelin** *(Germanic)* Noble.

**Achal** *(Hindu)* Steady; mountainous.

**Achazia** *(Hebrew)* The Lord holds.

**Achen** *(Ugandan)* A twin.

# A

**Ada** *(Germanic)* Prosperous and happy.
*Variants:* Etta; Aida, Eda *(English)*.

**Adah** *(Hebrew)* Ornament.

**Adalia** *See* Adelaide.

**Adamina** *(Hebrew)* Of the red earth. Feminine form of Adam.

**Adara** *(Arabic)* Virgin; *(Greek)* Beauty.

**Adela** *See* Adèle.

**Adelaide** *(Germanic)* Of noble rank.
*Variants:* Adalia, Adelaida, Aline, Alyna, Delia; Adeline *(English)*; Adelia *(French)*; Adelina *(Italian)*; Alina *(Latin)*.

**Adèle** *(French)* Of noble cheer.
*Variants:* Adela, Adelie, Adelia, Adelle, Adila, Edila, Edla.
*See also* Della.

**Ademia** *(Greek)* Without husband.

**Adena** *See* Adina.

**Aderes** *(Hebrew)* Protector.

**Adhira** *(Hindu)* Lightning.

**Adila** *See* Adèle.

**Adina** *(Indigenous Australian)* Good; *(Hebrew)* Gentle, delicate, adorned, noble. *Variants:* Adena, Adinah.

**Aditi** *(Hindu)* Free and unbounded.

**Adiva** *(Arabic)* Pleasant; gentle.

**Adonia** *(Greek)* Beautiful goddess. Feminine form of Adonis.

**Adora** *(French)* Beloved.

**Adriana** *(Greek)* Woman of the Adriatic; *(Latin)* Wealthy dark one. Feminine form of Adrian.
*Variants:* Adriane, Adrianna, Adrianne *(English)*; Adrienne *(French)*; Hadriane *(Greek)*; Adria *(Italian)*.

**Affrica** *(Gaelic)* Pleasant.

**Afra** *See* Aphra.

# A

**Agatha** *(Greek)* Good, kind woman.
*Variants:* Agat *(Abenaki)*; Agace, Agacia, Ageuda; Agathe *(French)*; Agata *(Germanic)*; Agafia *(Russian)*.

**Aglaia** *(Greek)* Splendid beauty; one of the three Graces of Greek mythology (the goddess of harmony).
*Variant:* Aglaea.

**Agnes** *(Greek)* Pure; chaste.
*Variants:* Agna, Agnelia, Agnies, Aigneis, Aneda, Anese, Annais, Anneyce, Annis, Annys, Inesita, Neysa, Neza, Ynez; Agneta *(Scandinavian)*; Ines, Inez, Ynes *(Spanish)*; Nesta *(Welsh)*.

**Agnola** *See* Angela.

**Agostina** *See* Augusta.

**Ahava** *(Hebrew)* Love; the name of a river.

**Ah Cy** *(Chinese)* Lovely.

**Ahimsa** *(Hindu)* Non-violent virtue.

**Ah Lam** *(Chinese)* Like an orchid.

**Ai** *(Japanese)* Love.

**Aida** *(English)* Joyful; helper; reward.
*See also* Ada.

**Aiesha** *(Arabic)* Woman.

**Aigneis** *See* Agnes.

**Aiko** *(Japanese)* Beloved one; little love.

**Aila** *(Finnish)* Light-bearer.

**Aileen** *(Celtic) See* Eileen, Helen.

**Ailis** *See* Alice.

**Ailsa** *(Scottish)* Of good cheer.
*Variants:* Aillsa, Ailssa, Elsa, Ilsa.

**Aimée** *See* Amy.

**Ain** *(Arabic)* Precious; eye.

**Aindrea** *See* Andrea.

**Aine** *(Celtic)* Joy.

**Aingeal** *See* Angela.

**Ainsley** *(English)* Meadow; clearing.
*Variants:* Ainslea, Ainslee, Ainsleigh, Anslea.

**Airlia** *(Greek)* Ethereal.

**Aisha** *See* Asha.

**Aislinn** *(Celtic)* A dream, vision, inspiration.

**Aissa** *(African)* Grateful.

**Aithne** *(Celtic)* Little fire.
*Variants:* Eithne, Ethene, Ethne.

**Akane** *(Japanese)* Deep red.

**Akina** *(Japanese)* Bright spring flower.

**Alana** *(Celtic)* Beautiful, harmonious one. Feminine form of Alan.
*Variants:* Alaine, Alanah, Alanna, Alanne, Alayna, Alayne, Aleine, Alina, Aline, Allene, Allyn, Lana, Lane, Lanna.

**Alarice** *(Germanic)* Ruler of all.

**Alatea** *(Spanish)* Truth.

**Alavda** *(French)* Lark.

**Alayna, Alayne** *See* Alana.

**Alazne** *(Basque)* Miracle.

**Alba** *(Latin)* White; fair. Medieval name for Scotland.

**Alberta** *(Germanic)* Noble and bright. Feminine form of Albert.
*Variants:* Albertina, Albertine, Albertyna, Albrette, Elberta.

**Albreda** *See* Alfreda.

**Alcina** *(Greek)* Strong-minded.

**Alda** *(Germanic)* Old.

# A

**Aldea** *(Germanic)* Rich.

**Aldora** *(Greek)* Winged gift.

**Aleece** *See* Alice.

**Aleine** *See* Alana.

**Alejandra, Aleksandrina** *See* Alexandra.

**Alena** *(Greek)* Pretty; *(Slavic)* Light.

**Alenka** *See* Helen.

**Alesia** *See* Alice.

**Alethea** *(Greek)* Truth.
> *Variants:* Aleethea, Aletea, Aletha, Aletheia, Alithea, Thea; Alatea *(Spanish)*.

**Aletta** *(Latin)* Winged; bird-like.
> *Variants:* Alida, Alita, Alouetta; Alette *(French)*; Aleta *(Spanish)*.

**Alexandra** *(Greek)* Helper and protector of mankind. Feminine form of Alexander. *Variants:* Aleksandrina, Alexa, Alexandraine, Alexina, Alexine, Elexis, Sandra, Sandrine, Sondra, Xandy, Zandra; Alexandrine, Alix *(French)*; Alex, Alexandria, Alexandrina, Alexia, Alexis *(Greek)*; Alessandra *(Italian)*; Sacha, Sashenka *(Russian)*; Alejandra, Xandra *(Spanish)*.

**Alfreda** *(Germanic)* Elf counsel; wise. Feminine form of Alfred.
> *Variants:* Albreda, Alfreta.
> *See also* Elfrida.

**Alice** *(French)* Noble; kind.
> *Variants:* Ailis, Aleece, Alesia, Ali, Alicen, Alis, Alise, Alisone, Alisoun, Alize, Allis, Allisa, Allissa, Allysa, Allyson, Alson, Alyce, Alus, Lycia; Alicia *(English)*; Alison, Eilish *(Gaelic)*; Elisha, Elissa *(Greek)*; Eilis *(Hebrew)*; Alisa *(Italian)*.

**Alida, Alita** *See* Aletta.

**Alienor** *See* Helen.

**Alima** *(Arabic)* Wise; learned.

**Alina** *(Polish)* Bright; beautiful.
*See also* Adelaide, Alana.

**Aline** *See* Adelaide, Alana.

**Alis** *See* Alice.

**Alisa** *See* Alice, Alysia.

**Alise** *See* Alice.

**Alisia** *See* Alysia.

**Alisone, Alisoun, Alisson** *See* Alice.

**Alita** *(Spanish)* Noble.

**Alithea** *See* Alethea.

**Alivia** *(English)* Alive.

**Alix** *See* Alexandra.

**Aliz** *(Hungarian)* Kind.

**Aliza** *(Hebrew)* Joyous.

**Alize** *See* Alice.

**Alizée** *(French)* Noble.

**Alla** *(English)* The only one.

**Allegra** *(Italian)* Joyful and cheerful.

**Allene** *See* Alana.

**Allis, Allisa, Allissa** *See* Alice.

**Allyn** *See* Alana.

**Allysa, Allyson** *See* Alice.

**Alma** *(Latin)* Fair and kind; soulful.

**Almeta** *(Latin)* Ambitious.

**Almira** *(Arabic)* Princess.
*Variants:* Almeria, Ameerah, Elmira, Mira.

**Aloha** *(Hawaiian)* Greetings; farewell; love and kindness.

# A

**Aloisa, Aloise** *See* Louisa.

**Alouetta** *See* Aletta.

**Aloysia** *See* Louisa.

**Alpha** *(Greek)* First.

**Alson** *See* Alice.

**Althea** *(Greek)* A healer; wholesome.
*Variants:* Althaea, Althee, Altheta, Thea.

**Alula** *(Latin)* Winged one.

**Alus** *See* Alice.

**Alvina** *(Germanic)* Beloved by all.

**Alvira** *See* Elvira.

**Alvita** *(Latin)* Anointed.

**Alwyn** *(Germanic)* Elf friend.

**Alyna** *See* Adelaide.

**Alyce** *See* Alice.

**Alysia** *(Greek)* Captivating.
*Variants:* Alisa, Alisia, Alysa.

**Alyssa** *(Greek)* Logical; the name of a flower.

**Alzena** *(Arabic)* Woman.
*Variant:* Amabelle.

**Amaia** *(Basque)* End.

**Amalur** *(Basque)* Homeland.

**Amanda** *(Latin)* Worthy of love; loveable.
*Variant:* Amandine, Manda, Mandi, Mandy.
*See also* Mandy.

**Amara** *(Greek)* Unfolding.

**Amara** *(Sanskrit)* Immortal.

**Amarante** *(French)* The name of a flower.
*Variants:* Amarantha, Amaranthe.

# A

**Amaris** *(English)* Child of the moon.

**Amaryllis** *(Greek)* Country girl; sparkling stream.
*Variants:* Amarilla, Amarillis, Amaryl, Marilla.

**Amata** *(Spanish)* Beloved.
*See also* Amy.

**Amaya** *See* Amy.

**Ambar** *(Hindu)* Sky.

**Amber** *(Egyptian)* Light; precious jewel.

**Ame** *See* Amy.

**Ameerah** *See* Almira.

**Amélie, Amelita** *See* Emily.

**Amena** *(French)* Yielding.

**Amethyst** *(Greek)* Wine-coloured.

**Amia, Amice, Amie, Amieia, Amina** *See* Amy.

**Amik** *(Algonquin)* Beaver.

**Aminar** *(Arabic)* Honest; faithful.

**Aminta** *(Greek)* Protected.

**Amity** *(French)* Friendly.
*Variants:* Amissa *(Hebrew)*; Ami *(Japanese)*.
*See also* Amy.

**Amo** *(Algonquin)* Bee.

**Amoretta, Amorita** *See* Amy.

**Amrita** *(Hindu)* Immortality.

**Amuwes** *(Maliseet)* Honeybee.

**Amy** *(French)* Well loved.
*Variants:* Aimée, Amaya, Ame, Amia, Amice, Amie, Amieia,
Amina, Amity, Amoretta, Amorita, Amye, Esmé, Esmée;
Amata *(Latin)*.

**An** *(Chinese)* Peace.

# A

**Ana** *See* Anne.

**Anaëlle** *(French)* Grace.
See also Anaïs.

**Anahid** *(Armenian)* Goddess of the moon.

**Anaïs** *(French)* Grace.
See also Anaëlle.

**Anan** *(Arabic)* Clouds.

**Anastasia** *(Greek)* Resurrection. Feminine form of
Anastasius.
*Variants:* Anastasie, Anastassia, Anastatia, Anestasia, Anstace,
Anstey, Anstice, Anstyce, Natassia, Stacia, Stacie, Stacy,
Tasia; Anastazia, Nastenka *(Czech)*; Nastasia, Nastassja,
Nastasya, Nastya *(Russian)*.

**Anca** *See* Anne.

**Ancelin** *(Latin)* Handmaiden.

**Andrea** *(Greek)* Womanly. Feminine form of Andrew or
Andreas.
*Variants:* Aindrea, Andreana, Andrée, Andriana, Andrina.

**Andria** *(Italian)* Love; joy.

**Andromache** *(Greek)* She who fights against men; battle of a
man; the name of the wife of Hector in Greek mythology.

**Aneda** *See* Agnes.

**Anemone** *(Greek)* Breath; windflower.

**Anese** *See* Agnes.

**Anestasia** *See* Anastasia.

**Aneta** *See* Anne.

**Angela** *(Greek)* Heavenly messenger. Feminine form of
Angel.
*Variants:* Aingeal, Angeletta, Angiola; Anjela *(Czech)*; Angel,
Angele, Angeline *(French)*; Engel, Engelchen *(Germanic)*;
Agnola, Angelina, Aniela *(Italian)*; Angelita *(Spanish)*.

**Angelica** *(Latin)* Angelic.
  *Variants:* Angelika, Angelique, Angyelika.

**Angevin** *(French)* Angel of wine.

**Angharad** *(Welsh)* Greatly beloved.

**Angiola** *See* Angela.

**Angyelika** *See* Angelica.

**Anh** *(Vietnamese)* Flower.

**Aniela** *See* Angela.

**Anika** *(Hindu)* Very beautiful; graceful.

**Anisa** *(Arabic)* Friendly.

**Anita** *See* Anne.

**Anjela** *See* Angela.

**Anke** *(Hebrew)* Grace.

**Anna** *See* Hannah.

**Annabel** *See* Belle.

**Annais** *See* Agnes.

**Anne** *(Hebrew)* Full of grace.
  *Variants:* Anca, Aneta, Annan, Annetta, Annina, Annuschka, Anona, Chana, Chanah, Channa, Hana, Hanicka, Hannah, Nan, Nancy, Nanny, Ninette, Nita, Ona, Vanka; Anais, Ann, Anna, Anne, Annie *(English)*; Annette, Nanette *(French)*; Anka *(Polish)*; Nina *(Russian)*; Annika *(Scandinavian)*; Ana, Anica, Anita *(Spanish)*.

**Anneyce, Annis** *See* Agnes.

**Annick** *(French)* Favour; grace.
  *Variants:* Annouk, Anouk; Anoushka *(Russian)*.

**Annora** *(Latin)* Honour.

**Annouk, Anouk** *See* Annick.

**Annys** *See* Agnes.

# A

**Anona** *See* Anne.

**Anoush** *(Armenian)* Sweet.

**Anslea** *See* Ainsley.

**Anstace**, **Anstey**, **Anstice**, **Anstyce** *See* Anastasia.

**Anthea** *(Greek)* Lady of the flowers.
*Variants:* Anthia, Bluma, Thea, Thia.

**Antigone** *(Greek)* Contrary; born against.

**Antje** *(Germanic)* Grace.

**Antonia** *(Italian)* Beyond price; inestimable. Feminine form of Anthony.
*Variants:* Anthonia, Antonette, Antoni, Antonya, Netta, Netti, Netty, Toinette, Toni; Antoinette, Toinette *(French)*; Tonya *(Russian)*.

**Anuradha** *(Hindu)* Bright star.

**Anwatin** *(Algonquin)* Calm, peaceful weather.

**Aolani** *(Hindu)* Cloud from heaven.

**Aphra** *(Hebrew)* Dust.
*Variant:* Afra.

**Apolline** *(Greek)* Of Apollo; sunshine and strength.
*Variants:* Apollonia; Appollonie *(French)*.

**April** *(Latin)* The open; month of the year.
*Variant:* Avril *(French)*.

**Aquene** *(Native American)* Peace.

**Ara** *(Germanic)* Eagle maid.

**Arabelle** *(Germanic)* Beautiful eagle.

**Aralie** *See* Aurelia.

**Araminta** *(Hebrew)* Lofty.

**Arashel** *(Hebrew)* Strong and protected hill.

**Araxie** *(Armenian)* The name of a river said to inspire poetic expression.

**Arcadia** *(Greek)* Happy and peaceful; *(Spanish)* Adventurous.

**Ardelia** *(Latin)* Zealous; industrious.
  *Variants:* Ardelle, Ardella.

**Ardere** *(Latin)* Fire.

**Arella** *(Hebrew)* Angel messenger.

**Areta** *(Greek)* Divine; holy; virtuous.
  *Variants:* Arete, Aretha, Aretta, Arette.

**Aria** *(Latin)* Beautiful melody.

**Ariadne** *(Greek)* Very holy one.
  *Variants:* Ariadna, Ariane, Arianna.

**Ariana** *(Welsh)* Silvery.
  *Variant:* Ariene.

**Arica** *See* Erica.

**Aricia** *See* Avis.
  *Variant:* Arielle.

**Arilda** *(Germanic)* Hearth; home.

**Arina** *See* Irene.

**Arista** *(Latin)* Harvest.

**Arizona** *(Native American)* Little creeks.

**Arleen** *(Germanic, Celtic)* A promise.
  *Variant:* Arlene.

**Armida** *(Persian)* Beautiful sorceress.

**Armina** *(Latin)* Of a high degree.

**Armilda** *(Latin)* Braceleted.
  *Variant:* Armilla.

**Aroha** *(Maori)* Love.

**Arrabel** *See* Belle.

**Artemisia** *(Greek)* Belonging to Artemis.

# A

**Aruna** *(Hindu)* Radiance.

**Arziki** *(African)* Prosperity.

**Asa** *(Hebrew)* Healer.

**Asenka** *(Hebrew)* Graceful.

**Asha** *(African)* Life.
  *Variant:* Aisha.

**Ashleigh** *(English)* Of the ash tree.
  *Variants:* Ashley, Ashlee.

**Ashley** *See* Ashleigh.

**Aspasia** *(Greek)* Welcomed.

**Astra** *(Greek)* A star.
  *See also* Esther.

**Astrid** *(Germanic)* Divine strength.

**Asura** *(Sanskrit)* Spiritual.

**Atai** *(InupiaQ)* Cute; sweet.

**Atalanta** *(Greek)* Swift runner.
  *Variants:* Atalante, Atalanti, Attalanta.

**Atalaya** *(Spanish)* Guardian; watcher.
  *Variants:* Ataliah, Atalya, Talia, Talya.

**Atanbirrun** *(InupiaQ)* Liberty.

**Atara** *(Hebrew)* A crown.

**Athalia** *(Hindu)* God is exalted; the Lord is mighty.

**Athanasia** *(Greek)* Immortal.

**Athena** *(Greek)* Wisdom.
  *Variant:* Athene.

**Atifa** *(Arabic)* Affection.

**Atik** *(Innu)* Caribou.

**Atmaja** *(Hindu)* Daughter.

**Audrey** *(English)* Noble strength.
  *Variants:* Audrea, Audree, Audrie, Audrye, Etheldreda.

**Audun** *(Norwegian)* Deserted.

**August** *(Latin)* A summer month.
  *See also* Augusta.

**Augusta** *(Latin)* The high; honoured; mighty. Feminine form
  of Augustus.
  *Variants:* Augusteen, Augustina, Augustine, Austina,
  Austine, Gus, Gussie, Gusta, Tina; Agostina *(Italian)*.

**Aurelia** *(Latin)* Golden woman.
  *Variants:* Aralie, Aurea, Aurel, Aurelie.

**Aurora** *(Latin)* Dawn.

**Austina**, **Austine** *See* Augusta.

**Autumn** *(Latin)* The season of autumn.

**Ava** *(Greek)* Eagle.

**Avasa** *(Hindu)* Independent.

**Aveline** *(Hebrew)* Pleasant.

**Avena** *(English)* Oats.

**Averil** *(English)* Sacred wild boar.

**Avis** *(Germanic)* Bird-like.
  *Variants:* Aricia, Avice, Avicia.

**Aviva** *(Hebrew)* Springtime.

**Avril** *See* April.

**Axelia** *(Greek)* Protector of mankind.

**Axseenayi** *(Tlingit)* My light.

**Ayaka** *(Japanese)* Colourful fragrance; colourful flower.

**Ayala** *(Hebrew)* Gazelle; goat.

**Ayame** *(Japanese)* Iris.

**Ayesha** *(Persian)* Happy.

**Ayleen** *See* Aileen.

# B

**Azadi** *(Algonquin)* Poplar tree.

**Azalea** *(Germanic)* Of noble cheer; a flower.
*Variant:* Azaleah.

**Azaria** *(Hebrew)* Blessed by God. Feminine form of Azariah.
*Variants:* Azeria, Zaria.

**Aziza** *(African)* Gorgeous.

**Azura** *(Persian)* Sky blue.

**Baako** *(African)* First born.

**Babette** *(French)* Stranger; lovely.
*See also* Barbara.

**Babica** *See* Barbara.

**Bachiko** *(Japanese)* Happy child.

**Baka** *(Hindu)* Crane.

**Bakarne** *(Basque)* Solitude.

**Balbina** *(Latin)* Stammers.

**Bambi** *(Italian)* Child.

**Banan** *(Arabic)* Fingertips.

**Baptista** *(French)* One who baptizes. Feminine form of Baptist.
*Variants:* Baptysta, Batista; Battista *(Greek)*.

**Barakah** *(Arabic)* White one.

# B

**Barbara** *(Greek)* Stranger.
*Variants:* Babica, Barbrischa, Barbro, Varina; Baruska *(Czech)*; Babette, Barbe *(French)*;Varenka, Varvara *(Russian)*.

**Barika** *(Swahili)* Bloom.

**Baruska** *See* Barbara.

**Basilia** *(Greek)* Royal. Feminine form of Basil.
*Variants:* Basia, Basilea, Basilie, Basilla.

**Bassania** *(Greek)* Realm of the sea.

**Bathsheba** *(Hebrew)* Daughter of a vow.
*Variant:* Sheba.

**Batista, Battista** *See* Baptista.

**Beatrice** *(Latin)* Blessed one; she who brings joy.
*Variants:* Beatrix, Beatriz, Beatty, Blaza, Blazena, Trixie.

**Bebe** *(French)* Baby.

**Becca** *See* Beka.

**Becky** *See* Beka, Rebecca.

**Bedelia** *See* Bridget.

**Beka** *(Hebrew)* Half-sister; ensnarer.
*Variants:* Becca, Becky, Bekah, Bekka.
*See also* Rebecca.

**Bel** *(Hindu)* Sacred wood apple tree.

**Bela** *(Czech)* White.

**Belicia** *(Spanish)* Dedicated to God.

**Belinda** *(Germanic)* Wise serpent.
*Variants:* Belynda, Linda, Melinda.

**Belisama** *(Gaelic)* Most brilliant; a goddess in Celtic mythology.

**Belladonna** *(Italian)* Beautiful woman.

**Bellanca** *(Greek)* Stronghold.

**Belle** *(French)* Beautiful.
*Variants:* Annabel, Arrabel, Bell, Bella.
*See also* Elizabeth, Mabel, Mirabelle.

# B

**Belvina** *(Latin)* Blessed one. Feminine form of Benedict.
*Variants:* Benedetta, Benedikta, Benetta, Benicia, Benoite;
Benita *(Spanish)*.

**Belynda** *See* Belinda.

**Benedetta** *See* Belvina.

**Berengaria** *(Latin)* A bear-spear. Feminine form of Berenger.

**Berenice** *(Greek)* Bringer of victory.
*Variants:* Berneice, Bernice, Berniz, Berrice.

**Beret** *See* Bridget.

**Bernadette** *(Germanic)* As brave as a bear. Feminine form of
Bernard.
*Variants:* Bernadina, Bernadine, Bernadot, Bernadotte,
Bernetta, Burnette, Bernita.

**Bertha** *(Germanic)* The bright one.
*Variants:* Berit, Berta, Berthe, Bertilia, Bertina, Bertine.

**Beryl** *(Greek)* Precious jewel.
*Variants:* Beryle, Berylla.

**Bethany** *(Hebrew)* Worshipper of God; consecrated to God.
*Variants:* Beth, Bethanie, Bettina.

**Bethia** *(Hebrew)* Daughter of Jehovah.

**Beulah** *(Hebrew)* To be married.
*Variants:* Beula, Buelie.

**Beverley** *(English)* Beaver's stream.
*Variants:* Beverlie, Beverly.

**Bian** *(Vietnamese)* Secretive; hidden.

**Bianca** *See* Blanche.

**Bibiana** *(Latin)* Full of life.
*Variants:* Bibi, Viviana.

**Bijanka** *See* Blanche.

**Bijou** *(French)* Jewel.

# B

**Binty** *(Swahili)* Daughter.
*Variant:* Binti.

**Birget** *(Norwegian)* Protecting.

**Birkita** *(Celtic)* Strength.

**Blanche** *(French)* White.
*Variants:* Blanch; Bluinse *(Irish)*; Bianca, Blanca *(Italian)*; Blanka *(Polish)*; Branca *(Spanish)*.

**Blasia** *(Latin)* The babbler.

**Blaza, Blazena** *See* Beatrice.

**Bliss** *(English)* Felicity; happiness.

**Blodwen** *(Welsh)* White flower.

**Blossom** *(English)* Flower; lovely.

**Bluinse** *See* Blanche.

**Bluma** *(Germanic)* Flower; bloom.
*See also* Anthea.

**Bly** *(Native American)* High; tall.

**Blythe** *(English)* Happy and filled with joy.
*Variant:* Blithe.

**Bo** *(Chinese)* Precious.

**BoBae** *(Korean)* Treasure, precious.

**Bobbette** *See* Roberta.

**Bohdana** *(Russian)* From God.

**Bonnie** *(Latin)* Good.
*Variants:* Bona, Bonita, Bonny.

**Bracha** *(Hebrew)* A blessing.

**Branca** *See* Blanche.

**Branwen** *(Welsh)* Dark-haired beauty.
*Variant:* Branwyn.

**Breanna** *See* Bryony.

# B

**Bree** *(Celtic)* Broth.

**Brenda** *(English)* Firebrand; sword.

**Brenna** *(Celtic)* Dark-haired.
*Variants:* Brianna, Brienne.

**Bretta** *See* Brittany.

**Brianna** *(English)* Strong; powerful. Feminine form of Brian.
*Variants:* Breanna, Brianne.

**Bridget** *(Celtic)* The highest strength.
*Variants:* Bedelia, Beret, Bride, Bridgid, Brie, Bries, Brietta, Briganti, Brigid, Brigide, Brigita, Brischia, Brit, Brita, Britta; Brigette, Brigitte *(French)*; Birget *(Germanic)*; Bridie, Brighid, Brigit *(Irish)*; Brigida *(Italian)*; Brigyta *(Lithuanian)*; Birgitta, Brigitta, Britt *(Scandinavian)*.

**Brier** *(French)* Heather.
*Variant:* Briar.

**Brietta** *(Celtic)* Strong.
*Variant:* Brites.

**Briony** *See* Bryony.

**Brina** *(Celtic)* Protector.
*See also* Sabrina.

**Brittany** *(Latin)* From England; strong; industrious.
*Variant:* Bretta *(Celtic)*.

**Brontë** *(Greek)* Thunder.

**Bronwen** *(Celtic)* The white breast.
*Variant:* Bronwyn.

**Brooke** *(English)* At the brook.

**Bryony** *(Greek)* The name of a plant; to swell or grow.
*Variant:* Briony.

**Buffy** *(Hebrew)* God's promise.

**Bunny** *(English)* Little rabbit.

# C

**Cacilia** *See* Cecilia.

**Caddie** *See* Caroline.

**Cadence** *(Latin)* Melodious; to fall.

**Caimile** *(African)* A figure in an African proverb.

**Cairine** *See* Catherine.

**Cairistine, Cairistiona** *See* Christine.

**Caitlin, Caitlyn, Caitrin** *See* Catherine.

**Cala** *(Arabic)* Castle.

**Calandra** *(Greek)* Lark.

**Calantha** *(Greek)* Beautiful blossoms.

**Caledonia** *(Latin)* From Scotland.

**Caley** *(Gaelic)* Slender.

**Calida** *(Latin)* Ardent; warm and loving.

**Calista** *(Greek)* Most beautiful.
    *Variants:* Callia, Callidora, Kallista, Kallisti.

**Calliope** *(Greek)* Beautiful voice.

**Caltha** *(Latin)* The name of a yellow flower.

**Calypso** *(Greek)* Concealer.

**Cam** *(English)* Sweet; beloved; referring to the sun;
    *(Vietnamese)* Orange fruit.

**Camellia** *(Latin)* The name of a flower.

# C

**Camilla** *(Etruscan)* Attendant at a religious ceremony.
   *Variants:* Camellia, Kamilla; Camila *(Czech)*; Camille
   *(French)*; Kamilia *(Polish)*; Kamila *(Slavic)*.

**Candace** *(Greek)* White-hot; glowing; glittering.
   Variants: Candice, Candide; Candida *(Latin)*.

**Candra** *(Latin)* Luminescent.

**Cantara** *(Arabic)* Small bridge.

**Caoimhe** *(Celtic)* Gentleness; beauty; grace.

**Capri** *(Anglo-Saxon)* The goat.

**Caprice** *(Italian)* Fanciful; unpredictable.

**Capucine** *(French)* Capuchin.

**Cara** *(Latin)* Dearest one; diamond.
   *Variants:* Carina, Carita, Kara; Caresse *(French)*.
   *See also* Caroline.

**Caren** *See* Catherine.

**Carha** *(Latin)* A pillar stone.

**Cari** *(Turkish)* Flows like water.

**Carin** *See* Catherine.

**Carine** *(Armenian)* Friend.

**Carissa** *(Latin)* Artful; skilful.
   *Variants:* Carisa, Chrissa.

**Carita** *See* Cara.

**Carla** *(English)* Strength.
   *See also* Carly, Caroline, Charlotte.

**Carleen** *See* Charlotte.

**Carlina** *See* Caroline, Charlotte.

**Carline** *See* Caroline.

**Carling** *(English)* Hill where old women or witches gather.

**Carlita** *See* Carly, Caroline, Charlotte.

# C

**Carlotta** *(Italian) See* Charlotte.

**Carly** *(Germanic)* Freeholder; free woman; *(Latin)* Little; womanly.
*Variants:* Carla, Carley, Carlita, Karla.

**Carma** *(Sanskrit)* Destiny.

**Carmel** *(Hebrew)* Woodland; garden; vineyard.
*Variants:* Carmela, Carmelina, Carmeline, Carmelita, Melina.

**Carmen** *(Spanish)* Songstress.
*Variants:* Carmena, Carmencita, Carmia, Carmina, Carmine, Carmita; Charmain, Charmaine *(Greek)*.

**Carna** *(Arabic)* Horn.

**Carnelian** *(Latin)* A red gem.

**Carol** *(French)* To sing joyously.
*Variants:* Carola, Carole, Caroll, Karel, Karol.

**Caroline** *(Latin)* Strong and virile. Feminine form of Charles or Carolus.
*Variants:* Caddie, Cara, Carla, Carline, Carlita, Carolina, Carolyn, Carrie, Charleen, Charlene, Karla, Karoly, Sharleen, Sharlene; Karolyn *(Germanic)*; Carlina *(Italian)*; Karolina *(Polish)*; Karoline *(Scandinavian)*.

**Caron** *(French)* Pure.

**Carrie** *See* Caroline.

**Carrington** *(English)* Beautiful.

**Cary** *(Celtic)* Honest one; shy.

**Casandra** *See* Cassandra.

**Casey** *(Celtic)* Brave; *(Gaelic)* Watchful.

**Casilda** *(Latin)* Of the home; *(Spanish)* Solitary one.
*Variants:* Casilde, Cassilda.

**Casimira** *(Latin)* Bearer of peace.

# C

**Cassandra** *(Greek)* Prophet of doom; entangler of men; one who excites love.
*Variants:* Casandra, Cassandre, Cassie, Kassandra, Sandra, Sandrine.

**Cassia** *(Greek)* Champion.
*See also* Kezia.

**Cassiel** *(Latin)* Angel of Saturday; earth mother.

**Castalia** *(Greek)* A nymph in Greek mythology whom Apollo transformed into a fountain at Delphi.

**Catava** *(African)* A figure in an African proverb.

**Catherine** *(Greek)* Pure.
*Variants:* Katetin *(Abenaki)*; Cara, Cateline, Catharine, Cathelina, Catherina, Catheryn, Cathren, Cattarina, Kady, Kalina, Kara, Karia, Kate, Kateryn, Katherine, Kathryn, Kathy, Katie, Katren, Katy, Kitty; Kata, Katerine, Katharine *(Czech, Germanic)*; Caren, Kaatje *(Dutch)*; Caterine *(French)*; Katchen *(Germanic)*; Katalin *(Hungarian)*; Cairine, Caitlin, Caitlyn, Caitrin, Cathleen, Catlin, Catriona, Kathleen, Katrina, Katrine *(Irish)*; Caterina *(Italian)*; Kasia, Kassia, Katarzyna, Katatzyna *(Polish)*; Katerina, Katinka, Katka, Katya *(Russian)*; Carin, Kaarina, Kajsa, Karen, Karin, Karina, Karna, Katina, Katri *(Scandinavian)*; Catalina *(Spanish)*; Catrin *(Welsh)*.
*See also* Kay.

**Cayleigh** *(Gaelic)* Party.
*Variants:* Ceilidh, Ceili.

**Cecania** *(Germanic)* Free.

**Cecilia** *(Latin)* Blind. Feminine form of Cecil.
*Variants:* Cacilia, Cecily, Sheelagh, Sheilah, Shelagh, Sileas, Sycily; Celia, Cicely *(English)*; Cecile, Célie *(French)*; Cecilie *(Germanic)*; Sheila *(Irish)*; Cecilija, Cilka *(Slovenian)*.

**Ceilidh** *See* Cayleigh.

# C

**Celandia** *(Greek)* The swallow.

**Celeste** *(Latin)* Heavenly.
*Variants:* Celesta, Celestina, Celestine.

**Celine** *See* Selena.

**Cerdwin** *(Celtic)* A goddess in Celtic mythology.

**Cerelia** *(Latin)* Of the spring.

**Chaitra** *(Hindu)* The first month of the year in the Hindu calendar, associated with the coming of spring.

**Chana, Chanah** *See* Anne.

**Chanda** *(Sanskrit)* Destroyer of evil.

**Chandra** *(Sanskrit)* Eminent; illustrious; moon.

**Chanel** *(French)* A canal.

**Channa** *See* Anne.

**Chantal** *(French)* A song or singer.
*Variants:* Chantalle, Chantel, Chantelle, Shantelle.

**Charity** *(Greek, Latin)* Affection, love, and grace.
*Variants:* Charis, Charissa, Charita, Cherry.

**Charleen, Charlene** *See* Caroline, Charlotte.

**Charlotte** *(French)* Virile and strong. Feminine form of Charles.
*Variants:* Sallot *(Abenaki)*; Carla, Carleen, Carlina, Charleen, Charlene, Karla, Lola; Charlotta *(Germanic, Scandinavian)*; Karlotta *(Greek)*; Carlotta *(Italian)*; Carlita, Lolita *(Spanish)*.

**Charmain, Charmaine** *See* Carmen.

**Charmian** *(Greek)* A little joy.
*Variant:* Charmion.

**Chastity** *(Latin)* Purity; chastity.

**Chaya** *(Hebrew)* Life.

**Chelsea** *(English)* River landing; port.
*Variant:* Chelsey.

# C

**Chen** *(Chinese)* Precious and rare.

**Cherise** *(Greek)* Grace.

**Cherry** *(French)* A fruit.
*See also* Charity.

**Cheryl** *(French)* Beloved; dear one.
*Variants:* Cher, Cheri, Cherie, Sharyl, Sherrill, Sherry, Sheryl.

**Chesna** *(Slavic)* Peaceful.

**Chiang** *(Chinese)* The last queen of the Yin dynasty.

**Chiara, Chiaris** *See* Clare.

**Chika** *(Japanese)* Near.

**Chinatsu** *(Japanese)* Thousand summers.

**Chipo** *(African)* A gift.

**Chiquita** *(Spanish)* Little.

**Chispa** *(Spanish)* A spark.

**Chitra** *(Hindu)* Portrait.

**Chloe** *(Greek)* Blooming; a fresh young shoot.

**Chloris** *(Germanic)* Name of a pale flower; fresh and blooming.
*Variants:* Chloras, Clorita, Loris.

**Cho** *(Japanese)* Butterfly.

**Chris** *See* Christabel, Christine.

**Chrissa** *See* Carissa.

**Chrissie, Chrissy, Christa** *See* Christine.

**Christabel** *(Greek)* Beautiful, bright-faced Christian.
*Variant:* Chris.

**Christel** *See* Crystal.

**Christine** *(Greek)* A Christian. Feminine form of Christian.
*Variants:* Chris, Chrissie, Chrissy, Christie, Christinha, Christophine, Christy, Cristin, Cristina, Cristiona, Gristin,

Kristiana, Kristin, Tina; Krista *(Czech)*; Christa, Christina *(French)*; Christiane *(Germanic)*; Christiana *(Italian)*; Kirsten, Kristina *(Scandinavian)*.

**Chruse** *(Greek)* Golden; the golden one.

**Chrystal** *See* Crystal.

**Chu** *(Chinese)* Pearl.

**Chyou** *(Chinese)* Autumn.

**Ciannait** *(Irish)* Ancient.

**Cicely, Cilka** *See* Cecilia.

**Cilla** *See* Priscilla.

**Cinta** *See* Cynthia.

**Circe** *(Greek)* Witch-goddess; seductive female.

**Claiborne** *(English)* Born of the earth.

**Clair, Claire, Clairette, Clara** *See* Clare.

**Clarabelle** *(Latin)* Clear, bright, and beautiful.
*Variants:* Clarabella, Claribel.

**Clare** *(Latin)* Clear and bright.
*Variants:* Klalis *(Abenaki)*; Chiaris, Claresta, Clareta, Clarine, Clariss, Clarisse, Clarita; Clair, Claire, Clarice *(French)*; Klara, Klarissa *(Germanic)*; Kara *(Greek)*; Klarika *(Hungarian)*; Chiara, Clara, Clarissa *(Italian)*; Clarinda *(Spanish)*.

**Clarimond** *(French)* Bright protector.
*Variant:* Clairemond.

**Clarinda, Clarine, Clariss, Clarissa, Clarisse, Clarita, Clarona** *See* Clare.

**Claudia** *(Latin)* The lame. Feminine form of Claude or Claudius.
*Variants:* Claude, Claudette, Claudina, Claudine, Clause, Klaudia.

# C

**Claver** *See* Clover.

**Cleine** *(Greek)* Renowned.

**Clematis** *(Greek)* Name of a flower; clinging.

**Clémence** *See* Clementine.

**Clementine** *(Latin)* The merciful one. Feminine form of
Clement.
*Variants:* Clementa, Cleti, Tina; Clemency *(English)*;
Clémence, Clemente *(French)*; Clementia, Clementina
*(Italian)*; Clemenza, Klementyna *(Polish)*.

**Cleopatra** *(Greek)* Glory; fame.
*Variant:* Cleo.

**Cleti** *See* Clementine.

**Cliantha** *(Greek)* Flower of glory.

**Clio** *(Greek)* Praise; the muse of history.

**Clodagh** *(Irish)* Name of a river in Ireland.

**Clorinda** *(Persian)* Renowned.

**Clorita** *See* Chloris.

**Clover** (English) Name of a plant.
*Variants:* Claver, Clovis.

**Coleen, Colene** *See* Colleen.

**Colette** *(French)* A small collar or necklace; *(Greek)*
Victory of the people.
*Variants:* Coletta, Collette.

**Colleen** *(Irish)* Girl.
*Variants:* Coleen, Colene.

**Colombe** *(French)* A dove.
*Variants:* Columba, Columbia *(English)*.

**Columbia** *See* Colombe.

**Columbine** *(Latin)* Name of a flower.
*Variants:* Columbia, Columbina.

# C

**Conception** *(Spanish)* Fertile one; mother of nations; the beginning.
*Variants:* Concepcion, Concetta *(Italian)*.

**Concettina** *See* Constance.

**Concha** *(Latin)* Shell.
*Variant:* Conchita.

**Constance** *(Latin)* Steadfast in faith. Feminine form of Constantine.
*Variants:* Constanta, Constantia; Constantina *(English)*; Konstancia *(Hungarian)*; Concettina, Constanzia *(Italian)*; Kostka *(Polish)*; Constancia, Constanza *(Spanish)*.

**Consuelo** *(Latin)* Consolation.
*Variant:* Consuela.

**Cora** *(Greek)* Young maiden.
*Variants:* Corella, Corenna, Corenne, Coretta, Corette, Corianna, Corinna, Corinne, Corrie, Corry, Kora.

**Coral** *(Latin)* Charm.
*Variants:* Coralie, Coralina, Coraline.

**Corazon** *(Filipino)* Heart.

**Cordelia** *(Latin)* Heart; a sea jewel.
*Variants:* Cordelie, Delia.

**Corella, Corenna, Corenne, Coretta, Corette, Corianna, Corinna, Corinne** *See* Cora.

**Corliss** *(English)* Cheerful and generous.

**Cornelia** *(Latin)* Horn. Feminine form of Cornelius.

**Corrie, Corry** *See* Cora.

**Cosette** *(French)* Pet lamb.
*Variant:* Cosetta.

**Cosima** *(Greek)* Order and harmony.

**Cottina** *(Greek)* Crown of wild flowers.

**Courtney** *(English)* From the court.

# D

**Crescent** *(French)* Creator.

**Cressa** *(Germanic)* Water cress.

**Cressida** *(Greek)* Gold.

**Cristin, Cristina, Cristiona** *See* Christine.

**Crystal** *(Latin)* Clear; bright; ice.
 *Variants:* Christel, Chrystal, Krystal.

**Cuc** *(Vietnamese)* Chrysanthemum.

**Cybele** *(Latin)* An Asiatic goddess.

**Cynara** *(Greek)* Thistle.

**Cynthia** *(Greek)* Moon; a Greek god.
 *Variants:* Cinta, Cynta, Cynthie.

**Cyrene** *(Greek)* A nymph in Greek mythology.

**Cyrilla** *(Greek)* Lordly lady; proud; high born. Feminine form
 of Cyril.
 *Variant:* Cyrille.

**Cytheria** *(Latin)*Venus; from Cythera.
 *Variant:* Cythera.

**Cyzarine** *(Russian)* Royalty.

**Czenzi** *(Hungarian)* Increasing.

**Daba** *(Hebrew)* Kind words.

**Dabria** *(Latin)* Name of an angel.

**Dacey** *(Gaelic)* Southerner.
 *Variants:* Dacie, Dacy, Daycie.

# D

**Dacia** *(Latin)* From the district of Dacia.

**Dacie, Dacy** *See* Dacey.

**Dae** *(Korean)* Great.

**Dael** *See* Dale.

**Daffodil** *(Greek)* Name of a flower.

**Dagmar** *(Germanic)* Joyous day; bright; joy of the Danes.
Variants: Dagna; Dagny *(Norwegian)*.

**Dahlia** *(Scandinavian)* Name of a flower.

**Dahna** *(Arabic)* Of the desert.

**Dai** *(Japanese)* Great.

**Daisy** *(Latin)* Day's eye; name of a flower.

**Dakota** *(Native American)* Friend.

**Dale** *(Norse, English)* Valley.
Variants: Dael, Dail, Dayle.

**Dalila** *(Kenyan)* Gentle.
See also Delilah.

**Damali** *(Arabic)* Beautiful.

**Damara** *(Greek)* Gentle girl.
Variants: Dama, Damaris.

**Dame** *(Germanic)* Lady.

**Damia** *(Greek)* The goddess of nature in Greek mythology.

**Damiana** *(Greek)* Tame. Feminine form of Damian or Damon.

**Damini** *(Hindu)* Lightning.

**Damita** *(Spanish)* Little princess.

**Dana** *(Celtic)* The goddess of fertility in Irish mythology;
*(Swedish)* From Denmark. Variants: Danna, Dayna.

**Danella, Danelle, Danette, Dani** *See* Danielle.

**Danica** *(Slavic)* The morning star.
Variant: Danika.

# D

**Danielle** *(Hebrew)* God is my judge. Feminine form of Daniel.
*Variants:* Danni, Daniela *(Czech)*; Danya *(English)*; Danette
*(French)*; Danella, Danelle, Dani, Daniella, Danita, Danny
*(Italian)*.

**Danna** *See* Dana.

**Danni, Danny, Danya** *See* Danielle.

**Daphne** *(Greek)* Laurel or bay tree; victory.

**Dara** *(Hebrew)* Compassionate; *(Persian)* Angel of rains
and rivers.

**Daralis** *(English)* Beloved.

**Darby** *(Gaelic)* Free woman; without envy.
*Variant:* Derby.

**Darcy** *(Gaelic)* Dark-haired; from the castle.
*Variants:* Darcey, Darci, Darcie.

**Darel, Darelle** *See* Daryl.

**Daria** *(Persian)* Queen; wealthy protector. Feminine form of
Darius.

**Darlene** *(Anglo-Saxon)* Tenderly beloved; little darling.
*Variant:* Darleen.

**Darlita** *(Armenian)* Young girl.

**Darnelle** *(Irish)* Feminine form of Darren.
*Variants:* Daron, Daryn.

**Darra** *(Gaelic)* Small wealthy one.

**Darrelle** *See* Daryl.

**Darryl** *See* Daryl.

**Darva** *(Slavic)* Honeybee.

**Daryl** *(French)* Beloved.
*Variants:* Darel, Darelle, Darrelle, Darryl.

**Daschenka** *See* Dorothy.

**Dasha** *(Greek)* Gift from God.

# D

**Davida** *(Hebrew)* Beloved. Feminine form of David.
  *Variants:* Dava, Davene, Davina, Davinia, Davita, Vida, Vita.

**Daw** *(Thai)* Stars.

**Dawn** *(English)* Daybreak.

**Daya** *(Hebrew)* Tiny bird.

**Daycie** *See* Dacey.

**Dayla** *(Hebrew)* To draw water; branch or bough.

**Dayle** *See* Dale.

**Dayna** *See* Dana.

**Deandra, Deanna, Deanne** *See* Diana.

**Deborah** *(Hebrew)* Bee; prophetess.
  *Variants:* Debbie, Debra, Debrah, Devora, Devra.

**Decla** *(Gaelic)* Goodness.

**Dee** Short form of any name starting with the letter *D*.

**Deena** *See* Diana, Dinah.

**Deepika** *(Hindu)* A little light.

**Dehlia** *See* Delia.

**Deianira** *(Greek)* Husband destroyer; the third wife of
  Heracles in Greek mythology.

**Deiene** *(Basque)* Religious holiday.

**Deirdre** *(Celtic)* Sorrowful; brokenhearted; the most beautiful
  woman in the world in Celtic mythology.
  *Variants:* Deirdra, Deirdriu, Dierdre.

**Deja** *(French)* Before.

**Deka** *(Somali)* Pleasing.

**Del, Dela** *See* Della.

**Delaine** *See* Delaney.

**Delana** *(Germanic)* Noble protector.

**Delaney** *(Gaelic)* Descendent of the challenger.
  *Variant:* Delaine *(French)*.

# D

**Delanna** *(Italian)* Soft as wool.

**Delfa, Delfina, Delfine** *See* Delphine.

**Delia** *(Greek)* From the island of Delos.
*Variant:* Dehlia.
*See also* Adelaide, Cordelia.

**Delicia** *(Latin)* Delightful one.
*Variants:* Delica, Delice, Delissa; Delysee *(French)*; Delizia
*(Italian)*.

**Delilah** *(Hebrew)* Delicate; amorous.
*Variants:* Dalila, Delila.
*See also* Dalila.

**Delissa, Delizia** *See* Delicia.

**Della** *(Germanic)* Of nobility.
*Variants:* Del, Dela.
*See also* Adèle, Ella.

**Delma** *(Spanish)* From the sea.

**Delphine** *(French)* From the town of Delphi; *(Greek)*
Dolphin; like a delphinium flower.
*Variants:* Delfa, Delfina, Delfine, Delphina, Delvene, Delvine.

**Delta** *(Greek)* The fourth letter of the Greek alphabet;
fourth child.
*Variant:* Deltora.

**Delvene, Delvine** *See* Delphine.

**Delwyn** *(Welsh)* Neat.
*Variant:* Delwen.

**Delysee** *See* Delicia.

**Delyth** *(Welsh)* Pretty.

**Dembe** *(Ugandan)* Peace.

**Demelza** *(English)* Fort on a hill.

**Demetria** *(Greek)* The goddess of fertility and agriculture in
Greek mythology.
*Variants:* Demeter, Demetre.

# D

**Demi** *(French)* Half; small.

**Dena** *(Hebrew)* Vindicated; *(Native American)* Valley.

**Denise** *(Greek)* From the city of Dionysus.

**Dep** *(Vietnamese)* Beautiful.

**Derby** *See* Darby.

**Desdemona** *(Greek)* Ill-fated one; misery.

**Desiree** *(Latin)* Long hoped for; desired.

**Desta** *(Ethiopian)* Happiness.

**Destinee** *(French)* Destiny.

**Destry** *(French)* War horse.

**Deva** *(Sanskrit)* Divine.

**Devaki** *(Hindu)* Black; the mother of Krishna in Hindu mythology.

**Devi** *(Hindu)* Resides in heaven.

**Devin** *(Gaelic)* Poet.
*Variant:* Devnet.

**Devon** *(English)* Defender.

**Devora, Devra** *See* Deborah.

**Diamanta** *(French)* Like a diamond.

**Diana** *(Latin)* Divine; the goddess of chastity, hunting, and the moon in Roman mythology.
*Variants:* Deandra, Deanna, Deanne, Deena, Diandra, Diane, Dianna, Dianne, Dyan, Dyanna.

**Dianthe** *(Greek)* Divine flower.

**Dido** *(Latin)* Wanderer.
*See also* Elissa.

**Diella** *(Latin)* One who worships God.

**Dikranouhi** *(Armenian)* Queen.

# D

**Dillian** *(Latin)* Worshipped one.

**Dilys** *(Welsh)* Genuine.

**Dinah** *(Hebrew)* Vindicated; judgement.
*Variant:* Deena.

**Dione** *(Greek)* The mother of Aphrodite in Greek mythology.

**Dionne** *(Greek)* Divine queen.

**Disa** *(Norwegian)* Active spirit.

**Dita** *See* Edith.

**Divya** *(Hindu)* Heavenly; brilliant.

**Djamila** *See* Jamilah.

**Dodie** *See* Dorothy.

**Dolores** *(Spanish)* Pains; lady of sorrows.

**Dominique** *(French)* Belonging to God.
*Variants:* Domini, Dominica; Domenica *(Italian)*; Dominga *(Spanish)*.

**Dona** *See* Donna.

**Donata** *(Italian)* Gift from God.

**Donna** *(Italian)* Lady.
*Variants:* Dona, Dondi, Donella, Donia, Donnica.

**Dooriya** *(English)* The sea.

**Dora** *(Greek)* Gift.
*Variants:* Dorah, Dore, Doretta, Dorinda.
*See also* Isadora.

**Doreen** *(French)* Golden.
*Variant:* Dorinne.

**Doretta** *See* Dora.

**Dorette** *See* Dorothy.

**Dori** *(French)* Golden-haired.
*Variant:* Dorée.
*See also* Dory.

# D

**Doria** *(Greek)* A place name.
*See also* Doris.

**Dorice** *See* Doris.

**Dorinda** *See* Dora.

**Doris** *(Greek)* A Dorian woman; of the sea.
*Variants:* Dorice, Dorise.

**Dorothy** *(Greek)* God's gift.
*Variants:* Toloti *(Abenaki)*; Dodie, Dot *(English)*; Dorette,
Dorothee *(French)*; Dorota, Dorothea, Thea *(Greek)*;
Dorotea *(Italian, Spanish)*; Dorosia, Dorota *(Polish)*;
Daschenka, Dorka *(Russian)*.

**Dory** *(English)* Golden-haired.
*See also* Dori.

**Dot** *See* Dorothy.

**Dreama** *(Greek)* Joyous music.

**Drew** *(Welsh)* Wise.
*Variants:* Dru, Drue.

**Drina** *(Spanish)* Helper and defender of mankind.

**Drisana** *(Hindu)* Daughter of the sun.

**Dru** *See* Drew.

**Drucilla** *(Greek)* Dewey eyes; *(Latin)* Mighty; strong; from the
family name Drusus, belonging to one of the wives of
Roman Emperor Augustus.
*Variants:* Druscilla, Drusilla.

**Drue** *See* Drew.

**Druscilla, Drusilla** *See* Drucilla.

**Duena** *(Spanish)* Loyal; protector of friends.
*Variant:* Duenna.

**Dulcea** *(Latin)* Sweetness.
*Variants:* Dulce, Dulcie, Dulcy; Dulcinea *(Spanish)*.

**Durene** *(Latin)* Everlasting.

# E

**Dusha** *(Russian)* Soul; sweetheart.
   *Variant:* Duscha.

**Dustine** *(English)* Dark stone. Feminine form of Dustin;
   *(Germanic)* Valiant fighter.
   *Variants:* Dustina, Dusty.

**Duvessa** *(Irish)* Dark beauty.

**Duyen** *(Vietnamese)* Charming.

**Dyan** *See* Diana.

**Dyani** *(Native American)* Deer.

**Dyanna** *See* Diana.

**Dyllis** *(Welsh)* Sincere.

**Dymphna** *(Gaelic)* Suitable one; virgin saint.
   *Variant:* Dympna.

**Dyna** *(Greek)* Powerful.

**Dysis** *(Greek)* Sunset.

**Earla** *(English)* Pledge.

**Earnesta, Earnestine** *See* Ernestine.

**Eartha** *(English)* Of the earth.
   *Variant:* Ertha.
   *See also* Hertha.

**Easter** *(English)* Born at Easter time.

**Eavan** *(Celtic)* Fair one.

**Ebba** *(Germanic)* Strength; return of the tide.

# E

**Ebere** *(African)* Mercy.

**Ebony** *(English)* Dark beauty; *(Greek)* Strength.
*Variants:* Eboni, Ebonie.

**Ebrilla** *(Welsh)* April.
*Variant:* Ebrel *(Cornish)*.

**Echo** *(Greek)* A nymph in Greek mythology.

**Eda** *(English)* Wealthy.
*Variants:* Edalene, Edda, Edsel.
*See also* Ada.

**Edana** *(Celtic)* Zealous; fiery; an Irish saint.
*Variant:* Eidan.
*See also* Edna.

**Edda** *See* Eda.

**Edeline** *(Germanic)* Noble; good cheer.
*Variants:* Edelyn, Edla, Edlin; Edlyn, Edlynne *(English)*.
*See also* Adelaide.

**Eden** *(Hebrew)* Delightful; paradise.

**Edie** *See* Edith.

**Edila** *See* Adèle.

**Edina** *See* Edna.

**Edith** *(Germanic)* Rich gift; happy; prosperous.
*Variants:* Edie; Dita *(Czech, Spanish)*; Edita *(Italian, Spanish)*; Editha, Edithe, Ediva *(Polish)*.

**Edla** *See* Adèle, Edeline.

**Edlin, Edlyn, Edlynne** *See* Edeline.

**Edme** *See* Esme.

**Edmonda** *(English)* Wealthy protector.
*Variant:* Edmunda.

**Edna** *(Hebrew)* Pleasure; delight.
*Variants:* Edana, Edina.
*See also* Eithne.

# E

**Edolie** *(English)* Noble.

**Edony** *See* Idona.

**Edria** *(Hebrew)* Mighty.

**Edsel** *(English) See* Eda.

**Edwina** *(Germanic)* Prosperous friend; heir's axe.
*See also* Edith.

**Eereenia** *See* Irene.

**Effie** *(Greek)* Sweet voice.
*See also* Euphemia.

**Efia** *(Ghanaian)* Born on Tuesday.

**Efrosini** *(Hebrew)* A fawn; a bird.

**Efterpi** *(Greek)* Pretty.

**Eglantine** *(French)* The name of a flower.

**Eidan** *See* Edana.

**Eileen** *(Irish)* Light.
*Variants:* Aileen, Ayleen.
*See also* Evelyn, Helen.

**Eilis** *(Gaelic)* God is my oath.
*Variants:* Ailis, Ailish, Eilish.
*See also* Alice.

**Eira** *(Welsh)* Snow.
*Variant:* Eirawan.

**Eirena, Eirene** *See* Irene.

**Eirian** *(Welsh)* Silver.
*Variants:* Eirianedd, Eirianell.

**Eirlys** *(Welsh)* Snowdrop.

**Eithne** *(Irish)* Fiery; the mother of sun god Lugh in Irish
mythology.
*Variants:* Aithne, Edna, Ena, Enya.

**Ekata** *(Hebrew)* Unity.

# E

**Elain** *(Welsh)* Fawn.

**Elaine** *See* Helen.

**Elan** *(Welsh)* To push; the name of several Welsh rivers.

**Elana** *(Latin)* Light.
*Variant:* Elani *(Greek)*.

**Elata** *(Latin)* Happy.

**Elberta** *See* Alberta.

**Eldora** *(Spanish)* Gilded; golden.

**Eldoris** *(Greek)* Of the sea.

**Eleanor** *See* Helen.

**Elecia** *See* Elisha.

**Electra** *(Greek)* Bright; the shining one; a mythological Greek figure who killed her mother.
*Variant:* Elektra.

**Elen, Elena, Eleni** *See* Helen.

**Eleora** *(Hebrew)* The lord is my light.

**Elesha** *See* Elisha.

**Elexis** *See* Alexandra.

**Elfrida** *(English)* Noble; strong.
*Variants:* Alfreda, Elfreda.

**Elga** *(Anglo-Saxon)* Elfin spear.

**Eliane** *(Latin)* Sunshine.
*Variant:* Eliana.

**Elicia** *(Hebrew)* Jehovah is God.
*See also* Elisha.

**Elin** *(Scandinavian)* Light.

**Elina** *(Greek)* Intelligent; *(Hindu)* Pure.

**Elinor** *(English)* Light.

**Elinora** *(Hebrew)* Light of God.

# E

**Elisa** *(Spanish)* Dedicated to God.
*See also* Eliza.

**Elisabeth, Elise** *See* Elizabeth.

**Elisha** *(Greek)* Wise.
*Variants:* Elecia, Elesha; Elicia *(Hebrew)*.
*See also* Alice.

**Eliska** *(Czech)* Truthful.
*See also* Eliza.

**Elissa** *(Greek)* The queen of Carthage (also known as Dido) in Greek and Roman mythology.
*See also* Alice, Elizabeth.

**Elita** *(French)* Special one.

**Eliza** *(Latin)* The chosen one.
*Variants:* Eliska *(Czech)*; Elisa *(French, Italian, Latvian)*.

**Elizabeth** *(Hebrew)* God's oath; God's satisfaction; a relative of the Virgin Mary and mother of John the Baptist.
*Variants:* Alizbat *(Abenaki)*; Eliska *(Czech)*; Bess, Bessie, Beth, Betsy, Betty, Elisabeth, Eliza, Libby, Lis, Lisa, Lisabet, Lisbet, Liz, Lizzie *(English)*; Belle, Elise, Isabel, Isobel, Lisette *(French)*; Elisabet, Elisabeth, Elsbeth, Ilse, Lise, Liesel *(Germanic)*; Elissa, Elyssa *(Greek)*; Elisabeth, Lisbet, Liza *(Hebrew)*; Liszka, Zizi, Zoska *(Hungarian)*; Bettina, Elisa, Elisabetta, Lisettina, Tina *(Italian)*; Alzbeta, Beta, Betuska, Lissie *(North American)*; Elzunia, Ela, Elka *(Polish)*; Elisavetta, Lisenka, Elisabete, Lizka *(Russian)*; Elspeth *(Scottish)*.

**Elke** *(Germanic, Hebrew)* Owned by God.
*Variant:* Elkie.

**Ella** *(English)* Beautiful fairy woman.
*See also* Della.

**Elle** *(French)* Woman; girl.

# E

**Ellen** *(Hebrew)* Light; mercy.
*Variants:* Ellie, Elly, Nellie, Nelly.
*See also* Helen.

**Elly** *See* Ellen.

**Elma** *(Greek)* Amiable; *(Turkish)* Apple.

**Elmira** *(English)* Noble.
*See also* Almira.

**Élodie** *(French)* Fragile blossom.

**Eloisa** *See* Louisa.

**Eloise** *(French)* Wise; intelligent.
*Variants:* Eloisa, Heloise, Louise.
*See also* Louisa.

**Eloisia** *See* Louisa.

**Elon** *(African)* Loved by God.

**Elora** *(Greek)* Light.

**Elpida** *(Greek)* Hope.

**Elsa** *See* Ailsa.

**Else** *See* Elizabeth.

**Elsie** *(Anglo-Saxon)* Gaiety.

**Elvina** *(English)* Friend of elves.

**Elvira** *(French)* Fair; blond one; *(Spanish)* Impartial
judgment.
*Variants:* Alvira, Elvire.

**Elwyne** *(Welsh)* Pale; fair.

**Elysia** *(Latin)* Sweetly blissful.

**Ema** *(Polynesian)* Beloved.
*See also* Emma.

**Emalia** *(Latin)* Flirt.

**Eman** *(Arabic)* Faithful.

**Emanuela** *(Hebrew)* God is with us.
*Variants:* Emmanualle; Emanuelle *(French)*.

# E

**Ember** *(English)* Ember.

**Emele, Emelina, Emeline** *See* Emily.

**Emerald** *(Spanish)* A bright green gemstone.

**Emiko** *(Japanese)* Blessed.

**Emily** *(Latin)* Industrious; eager.
Variants: Emilia, Milly, Emilka *(Czech)*; Amelie, Emele, Emeline, Emilee, Emilia, Emilie, Emmaline, Emmeline *(French)*; Emiliya *(Latvian)*; Milka *(Slavic)*; Amelita, Emelina, Emilaina *(Spanish)*.

**Emlyn** *(Welsh)* A place name.

**Emma** *(Germanic)* Universal; all-embracing.
Variants: Emme; Emmelina, Emmeline *(French)*; Ema *(Spanish)*.

**Emmaline** *See* Emily.

**Emme, Emmelina** *See* Emma.

**Émeline, Emmeline** *See* Emily, Emma.

**Emogene** *See* Imogen.

**Emuna** *(Arabic)* Faith.

**Ena** *(English)* Wife; soul.
*See also* Eithne.

**Ena** *(Irish)* Little fire. Feminine form of Aidan.

**Endora** *(Hebrew)* Fountain.

**Engel, Engelchen** *See* Angela.

**Enid** *(Welsh)* Quiet woman; soul.

**Enola** *(English)* Solitary; alone.

**Enrica** *See* Henrietta.

**Enya** *See* Eithne.

**Enye** *(Hebrew)* Grace.

**Eolanda** *See* Violet.

# E

**Epifania, Epiphanie** *See* Tiffany.

**Eranthe** *(Greek)* Spring flower.

**Erasma** *(Greek)* Amiable.

**Erasto** *(East African)* Bringer of peace.

**Erena** *See* Irene.

**Erianthe** *(Greek)* Sweet as many flowers.

**Erica** *(Scandinavian)* Powerful, honourable ruler;
the botanical name for heather. Feminine form of Eric.
*Variants:* Arica, Erika.

**Erin** *(Celtic)* Peace; *(Gaelic)* Ireland; west.
*Variants:* Erina, Erinne, Errin, Eryn, Erynn, Erynne.

**Erlina** *(Celtic)* Girl from Ireland.
*See also* Erline.

**Erline** *(Anglo-Saxon)* The elfin.
*Variant:* Erlina.

**Erma** *(Germanic)* Whole; universal.
*Variants:* Ermina.
*See also* Irma.

**Ermina, Erminia** *See* Irma.

**Ermintrude** *(Germanic)* Strength.
*Variant:* Ermyntrude.

**Ernestine** *(Germanic)* Earnest; vigorous.
*Variants:* Earnesta, Earnestine.

**Errin** *See* Erin.

**Ertha** *See* Eartha.

**Eryn, Erynn, Erynne** *See* Erin.

**Erzsebet** *(Hebrew)* Devoted to God.

**Eshana** *(Sanskrit)* One who searches.

**Esiban** *(Algonquin)* Raccoon.

# E

**Eskarne** *(Spanish)* Merciful.

**Esme** *(Latin)* Esteem.
Variants: Esmee *(French)*; Edme *(Scottish)*.
See also Amy.

**Esmé, Esmée** See Amy.

**Esmeralda** *(English)* Green gemstone.
Variant: Ezmeralda.

**Esperanza** *(Spanish)* Hope.
Variant: Esperance.

**Esta** *(Italian)* From the east.

**Estaphania** See Stephanie.

**Estelle** *(Latin, Persian)* Star.
Variants: Estee, Estella *(French)*; Stella *(Latin)*;
Estrella *(Spanish)*.

**Esther** *(Hebrew, Persian)* Myrtle; the heroine in the biblical
Book of Esther.
Variants: Astra, Ester, Hadassa, Hester; Stella *(Latin)*.

**Estra** *(Anglo-Saxon)* Goddess of spring.

**Estralita** *(Spanish)* Little star.

**Etain** *(Celtic)* Shining; a fairy princess in Irish mythology.
Variants: Edain, Etan.

**Etana** *(Hebrew)* Dedication.

**Etania** *(Native American)* Wealthy.

**Ethel** *(Germanic)* Noble.

**Etheldreda** See Audrey.

**Ethene, Ethne** See Aithne.

**Etienette** See Stephanie.

**Etoile** *(French)* Star.

**Etsu** *(Japanese)* Delight.
Variant: Etsuko.

# E

**Etta** *See* Ada, Henrietta.

**Ettie** *See* Henrietta.

**Ettienette** *See* Stephanie.

**Euadne** *See* Evadine.

**Eucaria** *(Greek)* Happy helper.
*Variants:* Euchar *(Germanic)*; Eucharya *(Polish)*.

**Euclea** *(Greek)* Glorious.

**Eudocia** *(Greek)* Esteemed.

**Eudokhia** *See* Eudoxia.

**Eudora** *(Greek)* Delightful gift.

**Eudoxia** *(Greek)* Happy glory; the daughter of Roman
emperor Valentinian III.
*Variants:* Eudocie, Eudoxie *(French)*; Eudossia *(Italian)*;
Eudokhia *(Russian)*.

**Eufamie, Eufrayza** *See* Euphemia.

**Eugenia** *(Greek)* Well born, noble. Feminine form of
Eugene.
*Variants:* Eugena, Eugenie, Eugina, Gina.

**Eulalia** *(Greek)* Fair of speech; a fourth century saint.

**Eunice** *(Greek)* Good or happy victory.

**Euphemia** *(Greek)* Of fair fame; one who speaks sweetly.
*Variants:* Euphemie *(French)*; Effie *(Greek)*; Eufemia *(Italian,*
*Spanish)*; Eufrayza *(Polish)*; Eufamie *(Scottish)*.

**Euphrosyne** *(Greek)* Joy; delight.

**Europa** *(Greek)* A beautiful Phoenician princess in Greek
mythology.

**Eustacia** *(Greek)* Fruitful; plentiful; *(Latin)* Tranquil.

**Eva** *See* Eve.

**Evadine** *(Greek)* Fortunate one; a water nymph in Greek
mythology.
*Variants:* Euadne, Evadne.

**Evangelia** *(Greek)* Bringer of good news.
*Variants:* Evangelique *(French)*; Evangelina, Evangeline *(Greek)*.

**Evania** *(Greek)* Tranquil; peaceful.

**Evanthe** *(Greek)* Flower.

**Eve** *(Hebrew)* Life giving; the first woman created by God, according to the Bible. *Variants:* Eva, Evie *(French)*; Evelina, Evelyn *(Hebrew)*; Evita *(Spanish)*.

**Evelyn** *(Celtic)* Lively; pleasant.
*Variants:* Eileen, Evalina, Eveleen, Evelina, Eveline.
*See also* Eve.

**Evette** *See* Yvette.

**Evie, Evita** *See* Eve.

**Evonne** *See* Yvonne.

**Ewa** *(Polish)* Life.

**Eyota** *(Native American)* Greatest one.

**Ezmeralda** *See* Esmeralda.

**Fabia** *(Latin)* An ancient Roman family name derived from "the bean grower." Feminine form of Fabian.
*Variants:* Fabian, Fabiana, Fabienne, Fabiola, Fabyan.

**Faiga** *(Germanic)* A bird.

**Faina** *(Anglo-Saxon)* Joyful.
*Variants:* Faine, Fayna, Fayne.

# F

**Fainche** *(Celtic)* The name of a saint.

**Faine** *See* Faina.

**Fairlee** *(English)* Beautiful forest.
*Variant:* Fairleigh.

**Fairuza** *(Turkish)* Turquoise.

**Faith** *(Latin)* Trust; faith.
*Variant:* Fay.

**Faizah** *(African)* Victorious.

**Fala** *(Native American)* Crow.

**Fallon** *(Celtic)* Grandchild of the ruler; in charge.

**Fameuse** *See* Fayme.

**Fannie, Fanny** *See* Frances.

**Fantine** *(French)* Childlike.

**Fanya** *See* Frances.

**Fara** *See* Farrah.

**Farfalla** *(Italian)* Butterfly.

**Farica** *See* Frederika.

**Fariishta** *(Urdu)* Angel.

**Farrah** *(English)* Beautiful; *(Latin)* Wild ass.
*Variant:* Fara.

**Fascienne** *(Latin)* Black.

**Fatima** *(Arabic)* The daughter of Islamic prophet Muhammad.

**Fatin** *(Arabic)* Captivating.

**Faustine** *(Latin)* Fortunate.

**Fawne** *(French, Latin)* Young deer.
*Variant:* Fawn.

**Fay** *See* Faith.

**Fayar** *(Polynesian)* Dawn.

**Faye** *(French)* Fairy.

# F

**Fayina** *(Russian)* Free one.

**Fayme** *(English)* Held in high esteem; famed.
*Variant:* Fameuse.

**Fayna, Fayne** *See* Faina.

**Fayola** *(African)* Walks with honour.

**Fedellas** *See* Fidella.

**Fedora** *See* Theodora.

**Felicity** *(Latin)* Happy. Feminine form of Felix.
*Variants:* Felicianna, Felicidad, Felicitas, Felicitia, Felis,
Felise; Felicite *(French)*; Felicie *(Germanic)*; Felicita *(Italian)*;
Felice, Felicia *(Spanish)*.

**Felipa** *See* Philippa.

**Femi** *(African)* Love me.

**Fenella** *See* Fiona.

**Feodora** *See* Theodora.

**Fern** *(English)* Wing; feather; a leafy plant.

**Feronia** *(Latin)* The goddess of springs and woods in Roman
mythology.

**Fidella** *(Latin)* Faithful. Feminine form of Fidel.
*Variants:* Fedellas, Fidela, Fidelia, Fidelle, Fidellia, Fidellis.

**Fiedricke** *See* Frederika.

**Fifi** *See* Fifine, Josephine.

**Fifine** *(Hebrew)* He shall add.
*Variant:* Fifi.
*See also* Josephine.

**Filippa** *See* Philippa.

**Fillis** *See* Phyllis.

**Fiona** *(Gaelic)* White; fair.
*Variants:* Fenella, Fia, Finella, Fionna, Phia, Phio, Phiona,
Phionna.

# F

**Fionnuala** *(Gaelic)* White-shouldered; swan maiden in Irish mythology.
*Variants:* Finola, Fionnoula, Fionuala, Nuala.

**Fiora, Fiorella, Fiorenza** *See* Florence.

**Flannery** *(French)* Sheet of metal; flat land.

**Flavia** *(Latin)* Blonde or golden-haired.
*Variant:* Flavie.

**Fleta** *(English)* Swift; fleet.

**Fleur** *(French)* Flower.
*Variant:* Fleurette.

**Flora** *(Latin)* The goddess of flowers in Roman mythology.
*See also* Florence.

**Florence** *(Latin)* Blooming flower; flourishing.
*Variants:* Fiora, Fiorella, Flora, Flore, Florene, Florentia, Florentina, Florentine, Florentyna, Floria, Florice, Florinda, Florine, Floris; Florette *(French)*; Florenz *(Hungarian)*; Fiorenza, Firenze *(Italian)*.

**Flos** *(Norse)* Chieftain.

**Fola** *(African)* Honour.

**Frances** *(Latin)* From France; free. Feminine form of Francis.
*Variants:* Fannie, Fanny, Fran, Francella, Franchon, Francyne, Rania; Francine, Francoise *(French)*; Franzchen, Franziska *(Germanic)*; Franca, Francesca, Francisca *(Italian)*; Fanya, Franka *(Russian)*; Francisquita, Frasquita *(Spanish)*.

**Francoise** *(French)* Frenchwoman; free.
*See also* Frances.

**Frea** *See* Freya.

**Freda** *(Germanic)* Peaceful.
*Variants:* Frida, Frieda.

**Frederika** *(Germanic)* Peaceful ruler. Feminine form of Frederick.

# G

*Variants:* Farica, Fiedricke, Frederica, Fredericka, Fredrica, Fredrika; Frederique *(French)*.

**Freya** *(Scandinavian)* Noble woman; lady; the goddess of fertility, love, and beauty in Norse mythology.
*Variants:* Frea, Freja, Freyja.

**Frida, Frieda** *See* Freda, Halfrida.

**Fruma** *(Hebrew)* One who is religious.

**Fuensanta** *(Spanish)* A holy fountain; a municipality in Spain.

**Fuiju** *(Japanese)* Winter.

**Fujita** *(Japanese)* Field.

**Fulvia** *(Latin)* Blond.

**Fuscienne** *(Latin)* Black.

**Fung** *(Chinese)* Bird.

**Gabrielle** *(Hebrew)* Woman of God; God is my strength.
*Variants:* Gavriella, Garvilla; Gabbie, Gabby, Gabriele *(Germanic)*; Gabriella *(Italian, Spanish)*; Gabriela *(Polish)*.

**Gada** *(Hebrew)* Lucky; fortunate.

**Gae** *See* Gay.

**Gaea** *(Greek)* Earth; the goddess of earth in Greek mythology.
*Variants:* Gaia, Gaya.

**Gaenor** *See* Guinevere.

**Gai** *See* Gay.

# G

**Gail** *(English)* Gay; lively.
  *Variants:* Gael, Gale, Gayle, Gayleen.
  *See also* Abigail.

**Gaines** *(English)* Increase in wealth.

**Gajendra** *(Hindu)* The king of all elephants in Hindu
  mythology (also known as Airavata).

**Gala** *(Italian)* Finery; *(Swedish)* Singer.

**Galatea** *(Greek)* Milk-white; a sea nymph in Greek
  mythology.

**Gale** *(Irish)* Stranger.
  *See also* Abigail, Gail.

**Galena** *See* Galina.

**Gali** *(Hebrew)* Spring; fountain.

**Galia** *(Hebrew)* Wave.

**Galiana** *(Germanic)* Supreme one.

**Galina** *(Greek)* Calm; *(Russian)* Light.
  *Variant:* Galena *(Greek)*; Halina *(Polish)*.
  *See also* Helen.

**Galinka** *See* Helen.

**Galla** *(Scottish)* Stranger.

**Galya** *(Hebrew)* God is redeemed.

**Gamada** *(African)* Pleased.

**Gana** *(Hebrew)* Garden.
  *Variant:* Ganya.

**Ganesa** *(Hindu)* Good luck.

**Ganya** *See* Gana.

**Garance** *(French)* Dark red.

**Garda** *(Germanic)* Protected.

**Gari** *(Germanic)* Feminine form of Gary.

**Garland** *(French)* Garland or posy of flowers.

# G

**Garnet** *(English)* A red gemstone.
*Variants:* Garnetta, Garnette.

**Garvilla** *See* Gabrielle.

**Gasha** *(Russian)* Good.

**Gauri** *(Hindu)* The golden; she who is shining and brilliant; the goddess of marital felicity and longevity in Hindu mythology (also known as Dakshayani).

**Gavriella** *See* Gabrielle.

**Gavrilla** *(Hebrew)* Heroine.

**Gay** *(French)* Cheerful; merry; lighthearted.
*Variants:* Gae, Gai, Gaye.

**Gaya** *See* Gaea.

**Gayatri** *(Hindu)* A goddess in Hindu mythology.

**Gaye** *See* Gay.

**Gayle, Gayleen** *See* Gail.

**Gaylor** *(French)* Brave.

**Gaynor** *See* Guinevere.

**Gazella** *(Latin)* Gazelle-like.

**Geela** *(Hebrew)* Joyful.

**Geena** *See* Gina.

**Geeta** *(Sanskrit)* Song.

**Gelasia** *(Greek)* Predisposed to laughter.

**Gella** *(Hebrew)* Golden-haired.

**Gelsey** *(Persian)* Little flower.

**Gemina** *(Greek)* From the astrological sign Gemini.

**Gemma** *(Latin)* Jewel.
*Variant:* Jemma.
*See also* Jemima.

**Gena** *(French)* Nobility.
*Variants:* Gene, Genna.

# G

**Genesis** *(Hebrew)* Origin.

**Geneva** *(French)* Juniper berry.
*Variants:* Geneve; Ginevre *(Italian)*.

**Geneviève** *(French)* White wave; the patron saint of Paris.

**Genista** *(Italian, Spanish)* A yellow flower.

**Genji** *(Chinese)* Gold.

**Genna** *See* Gena, Jennifer.

**Gennifer** *See* Jennifer.

**Georgeanna** *See* Georgia.

**Georgette** *(Greek)* Feminine form of George.
*See also* Georgia.

**Georgia** *(Greek)* Farmer; to work the earth.
*Variants:* Georgeanna, Georgianna, Georgianne, Georgie, Gina *(English)*; Georgette, Georgiana, Georgine, Gigi *(French)*; Georgetta *(Italian)*; Georgina *(Latin)*.

**Geraldine** *(Germanic)* Ruler with the spear.
*Variants:* Jeraldine, Jerry *(English)*; Geraldene *(French)*; Geralda, Geraldina, Giralda, Giraldina *(Italian)*.

**Gerda** *(Germanic)* Protection.

**Gerlinde** *(Germanic)* Spear; the name of a saint.

**Germaine** *(French)* From Germany; to sprout; *(Germanic)* Armed.
*Variant:* Jermaine.

**Gertrude** *(Germanic)* Spear maiden.

**Gessica** *See* Jessica.

**Geva** *(Hebrew)* Hill.

**Ghada** *(Arabic)* Graceful; young girl.

**Ghila** *See* Gilana.

**Ghislaine** *(French)* Sweet pledge.
*Variant:* Ghislane.

# G

**Ghita** *(Greek)* Pearl.

**Giacinta** *See* Hyacinth.

**Giacobba** *(Italian)* Feminine form of Jacob.

**Gianina** *(Italian)* God is gracious.
 *Variants:* Gianna, Giovanna.

**Gianna** *See* Jane.

**Gigi** *See* Georgia.

**Gilana** *(Hebrew)* Joy.
 *Variants:* Ghila, Gila.

**Gilberta** *(Germanic)* Feminine form of Gilbert.
 *Variants:* Gilbertina, Gilbertine.

**Gilda** *(Celtic)* God's servant.

**Gilen** *(Germanic)* Industrious pledge.

**Gillian** *(Latin)* Downy-haired.
 *Variants:* Gill, Jill, Jillian, Juliana.
 *See also* Juliana.

**Gin** *(Japanese)* Silver.

**Gina** A short form for any name ending in *-gina*: Georgina,
 Eugina, etc.; *(Japanese)* Silvery.
 *See also* Eugenia, Georgia.

**Ginita** *(Italian)* Flower.

**Ginger** *(Latin)* Ginger-haired; the name of a plant.

**Gioconda** *(Italian)* Jocular; happy.

**Giolla** *(Italian)* Servant.

**Giovanna** *See* Gianina, Jane, Joanne, Jovanna.

**Giralda, Giraldina** *See* Geraldine.

**Giselle** *(Germanic)* A pledge.
 *Variants:* Gisela, Jizelle; Giselda, Gisella, Gizelle *(Italian)*;
 Gisele *(French)*.

# G

**Gitana** *(Spanish)* Gypsy.

**Gitel** *(Hebrew)* Goodness.
*Variant:* Gittel.

**Githa** *(Anglo-Saxon)* Gift.

**Gittel** *See* Gitel.

**Giuda, Giuditta** *See* Judith.

**Giulia** *See* Julia.

**Giulietta** *See* Juliet.

**Giuseppina** *See* Josephine.

**Giustina** *See* Justine.

**Gizane** *(Basque)* Christ's incarnation.

**Gizela** *(Polish)* Promise; pledge.
*Variant:* Gizi *(Hungarian)*.

**Gizelle** *See* Giselle.

**Gizem** *(Turkish)* Mysterious.

**Gizi** *See* Gizela.

**Gladys** *(Latin)* Lame.

**Gleda** *(English)* To make happy.

**Glenda** *(Welsh)* Of the glen; pure and good.
*Variants:* Glen, Glenn, Glenna.

**Glenys** *(Welsh)* Of the glen; holy; pure.
*Variants:* Glenice, Glenis, Glennis, Glynis, Glynnis.

**Gloria** *(Latin)* Glory.
*Variants:* Glora, Gloriane, Glorianne, Glory.

**Godiva** *(English)* Gift of God; an English lady who rode naked through the streets of Coventry to shame her husband.

**Gogo** *See* Margaret.

**Golda** *(French)* Gold.
*Variants:* Goldi, Goldie, Goldy.

# G

**Gonnilda** *See* Gunhilda.

**Gordana** *(Serbian)* Proud.

**Gotzone** *(Basque)* Angel; messenger.

**Grace** *(Latin)* Grace; blessing.
Variants: Gracielle *(Dutch)*; Gracie *(English)*; Gratia, Gratiana, Grazia, Graziella *(Italian)*; Gracia, Graciosa *(Spanish)*.

**Graeae** *(Greek)* Grey one.

**Grainne** *(Irish)* Fruitfulness; grain; a mythical Irish princess.
Variants: Grania, Granya.

**Gratia, Gratiana, Grazia, Graziella** *See* Grace.

**Grear** *(Scottish)* Watchful; vigilant mother.
Variants: Greer, Grier.

**Gregoria** *(Greek)* Watchful. Feminine form of Gregory.

**Greer, Grier** *See* Grear.

**Gret, Greta, Gretchen, Grethel, Grette, Griet**
*See* Margaret.

**Griselda** *(Germanic)* Stone heroine; woman of battle.
Variants: Grisel, Grizel.

**Gristin** *See* Christine.

**Grizel** *See* Griselda.

**Guadalupe** *(Spanish)* River of the wolf.
*See also* Lupe.

**Gudrun** *(Norse)* Divine wisdom; wise in battle.

**Guenevere, Guenivere** *See* Guinevere.

**Guglielma** *See* Wilhelmina.

**Guida** *(Italian)* Feminine form of Guy.

**Guilema** *See* Wilhelmina.

**Guilette, Guilia, Giulietta** *See* Juliet.

**Guillelmina, Guillelmine** *See* Wilhelmina.

**Guinevere** *(Welsh)* White; fair; white wave; the wife of King Arthur and lover of Sir Lancelot.
*Variants:* Gaenor, Gaynor, Guenevere, Guenivere, Jennifer.
*See also* Jennifer.

**Gülay** *(Turkish)* Rose moon.

**Gunhilda** *(Norse)* Maiden of battle.
*Variants:* Gonnilda, Gunda, Gunnhild.

**Gurit** *(Hebrew)* Innocent.

**Gus, Gussie, Gusta** *See* Augusta.

**Gustava** *(Scandinavian)* Rod of the gods.

**Gwen** *(Celtic)* White; fair.
*Variants:* Gwendoline, Gwendolyn, Gwynne.

**Gweneth, Gwenith, Gwennan** *See* Gwyneth.

**Gwylan** *(Welsh)* Seagull.

**Gwyneth** *(Welsh)* Happiness; blessed.
*Variants:* Gweneth, Gwenith, Gwennan, Gwyn, Gwynneth.

**Gytha** *(English)* A gift.

**Habeeba** *(Arabic)* Beloved; dear one.
*Variants:* Habiba, Habibah.

**Habika** *(African)* Sweetheart.

**Hadara** *(Hebrew)* Bedecked in beauty.

**Hadassa** *(Hebrew)* Flowering myrtle.
*Variant:* Hadassah.
*See also* Esther.

# H

**Hadiya** *(Arabic)* Guide to righteousness; gift.

**Hadley** *(English)* Field of heather.
*Variant:* Hadleigh.

**Hadriane** *See* Adriana.

**Hafwen** *(Welsh)* Beautiful like a summer's day.

**Hagar** *(Hebrew)* Stranger; forsaken one.
*Variant:* Hajar (Arabic).

**Haidee** *(Greek)* Modest.

**Haifa** *(Arabic)* Slender.

**Hailee** *See* Hayley.

**Hailey** *See* Hale, Hayley.

**Haimi** *(Hawaiian)* The seeker.

**Hajar** *See* Hagar.

**Halcyon** *(Greek)* Kingfisher.
*Variant:* Halcyone.

**Haldis** *(Germanic)* Spirit of stone; *(Norse)* Reliable helper.

**Hale** *(English)* Hero; army ruler.
*Variants:* Hailey, Halie, Haliegh; Haley *(Scandinavian)*.

**Haleigha** *(Hawaiian)* House of the rising sun.

**Haley** *See* Hale, Hayley.

**Halfrida** *(Germanic)* Peaceful one.
*Variants:* Frida, Frieda.

**Hali** *(Greek)* Sea; *(Hebrew)* Necklace; a place name.

**Halie** *See* Hale.

**Halima** *(African)* Gentle; *(Arabic)* Kind.

**Halina** *See* Galina, Helen.

**Hallie** *(Greek)* Thinking of the sea.

**Halona** *(Native American)* Fortunate.

**Hana** *(Arabic)* Happiness; bliss; *(Japanese)* Flower; blossom.
*See also* Anne, Hannah.

# H

**Hanan** *(Arabic)* Mercy.

**HaNeul** *(Korean)* Sky.

**Hang** *(Vietnamese)* Moon.

**Hanicka** *See* Anne, Hannah.

**Hannah** *(Hebrew)* Grace of God; the mother of Samuel the prophet in the Bible.
*Variants:* Anna; Hanicka, Hanka *(Czech)*; Hanni *(Estonian)*; Hannelore *(Germanic)*; Hana, Hanna *(Hebrew)*; Hanne *(Scandinavian)*.
*See also* Anne.

**Hannette** *See* Anne.

**Hanni** *See* Hannah.

**Haralda** *(English)* Ruler of the army. Feminine form of Harold.
*Variants:* Harolda, Haroldina; Harelda *(Germanic)*.

**Harika** *(Turkish)* Wonderful.

**Harley** *(English)* Hare meadow.

**Harmonia** *(Greek)* In harmony; the daughter of Aphrodite, goddess of love in Greek mythology.
*Variants:* Harmonie; Harmony *(English)*.

**Harolda, Haroldina** *See* Haralda.

**Harper** *(English)* Harp player.

**Harriet** *(English)* Home ruler.
*Variants:* Harriett, Harrietta.
*See also* Henrietta.

**Harsha** *(Sanskrit)* Happiness.

**Haruka** *(Japanese)* Far away.

**Harva** *(English)* Army warrior.

**Hasna** *(Arabic)* Beautiful.
*Variants:* Haseena, Hasina.

# H

**Hattie** *(Germanic)* Mistress of the home.

**Hava** *(Hebrew)* Life.

**Havana** *(Spanish)* Place of refuge.
Variants: Havanna, Havannah.

**Haya** *(Japanese)* Quick; light.

**Hayley** *(English)* Hay meadow.
Variants: Hailee, Hailey, Haley, Haylee.

**Hazel** *(English)* Commander; the name of a nut tree.

**Hea** *(Korean)* Grace.

**Heather** *(English, Scottish)* The name of a plant.

**Heba** *(Hebrew)* Gift from God.

**Hebe** *(Greek)* Youth; the name of a plant; the daughter of
Zeus and Hera in Greek mythology.

**Hecate** *(Greek)* The goddess of the underworld in Greek
mythology.

**Hedda** *(Germanic)* War.
Variants: Heda, Hede.

**Hedia** *(Hebrew)* Voice of the Lord.

**Hedva** *(Hebrew)* Joy.

**Heidi** *(Swiss)* Noble; kind.
Variants: Hedy *(English)*; Heide, Heidie, Hilde *(Germanic)*;
Hedya *(Hebrew)*.

**Helen** *(Greek)* Bright one; light; the mother of Greek emperor
Constantine.
Variants: Eleni, Ellen, Helaine, Narella, Narelle, Nell,
Nella, Nellie, Nelly, Yalena; Jelena, Lenka *(Czech)*; Elaine
*(English)*; Helena, Helene *(English, French, Spanish)*; Alienor
*(French)*; Ilona *(Hungarian)*; Aileen, Eileen, Eleanor,
Honora, Nora, *(Irish)*; Halina, Helenka, Helka *(Polish)*;
Alenka, Galina, Galinka, Olena, Yelena *(Russian)*; Jalena
*(Slavic)*; Elena *(Spanish)*; Elen *(Welsh)*.

# H

**Helga** *(Scandinavian)* Holy; faithful.

**Helia** *(Greek)* Sun.

**Helianthe** *(Greek)* The name of a flower.

**Heliotrope** *(Latin)* The name of a flower.

**Helka** *See* Helen.

**Héloïse** *See* Eloise, Louisa.

**Hema** *(Hindu)* Snow; Himalayas.

**Henka** *(Germanic)* Ruler of an estate.

**Henna** *(Hindu)* An orange dye.

**Henrietta** *(Germanic)* Ruler of the home.
*Variants:* Etta, Ettie, Harriet, Henriette, Hetty, Netta; Yetta *(English)*; Enrica *(Italian, Spanish)*.

**Hera** *(Greek)* Queen of the gods; the wife of Zeus in Greek mythology.

**Hermelinda** *(Spanish)* Shield of power.

**Hermia, Hermina, Hermine** *See* Hermione.

**Herminia** *(Spanish)* Lady of the earth.
*See also* Hermione.

**Hermione** *(Greek)* Eloquence; the daughter of Menelaus and Helen in Greek mythology. *Variants:* Hermia, Hermina; Hermine *(French)*; Herminia *(Spanish)*.
*See also* Irma.

**Hermosa** *(Spanish)* Beautiful.

**Hernanda** *(Spanish)* Feminine form of Ferdinand.

**Hertha** *(Germanic)* Goddess of the earth.
*Variants:* Eartha, Herta.

**Hesper** *(Greek)* Evening star.
*Variants:* Hespera, Hesperia.

**Hester** *See* Esther.

# H

**Hestia** *(Greek)* Goddess of the hearth.

**Hetty** *(Persian)* A star.
  *See also* Henrietta.

**Hibernia** *(Latin)* From Ireland.

**Hibiscus** *(Greek)* A tropical flower.

**Hide** *(Japanese)* Excellent.

**Hilary** *(Latin)* Cheerful.
  *Variants:* Hilery, Hillary; Hilaire *(French)*; Ilaria *(Italian)*;
  Hilaria *(Spanish)*.

**Hilda** *(Scandinavian)* Protector.
  *Variants:* Hildie *(English)*; Hilde, Hildegard *(Germanic)*.

**Hilde** *See* Heidi, Hilda.

**Hilery, Hillary** *See* Hilary.

**Hinda** *(Hindu)* Female deer.

**Hiroko** *(Japanese)* Generous.

**Hisa** *(Japanese)* Long-lasting.
  *Variant:* Hisako.

**Hoa** *(Vietnamese)* Flower.

**Holly** *(English)* A plant with red berries; holly grove.
  *Variants:* Hollee, Holley, Hollie.

**Honey** *(English)* Honey.

**Hongvi** *(Hopi)* Strong.

**Honora** *See* Helen.

**Honoria** *(Latin)* Honour.
  *Variants:* Honorine, Honoure *(French)*; Onora *(Irish)*;
  Honor, Honorata *(Italian)*.

**Hope** *(English)* Trust; faith; one of the daughters of Saint Sophia.

**Horatia** *(Latin)* Feminine form of Horace.

**Hortense** *(Latin)* Garden lover.
  *Variants:* Hortensia, Ortense.

**Hosanna** *(Latin)* Praise God.
*Variant:* Hosana.

**Hoshi** *(Japanese)* Star.
*Variant:* Hoshiko.

**Hua** *(Chinese)* Flower.

**Huberta** *(Germanic)* Bright mind.
*Variant:* Hubertha.

**Hue** *(Vietnamese)* Lily.

**Huette** *(French)* Of the heart and mind.
*Variants:* Huguette; Huela *(Germanic)*.

**Huyana** *(Native American)* Rain falling.

**Hyacinth** *(Greek)* The name of a flower.
*Variants:* Jacinta, Jacinthe; Hyacintha, Hyacinthe *(French)*;
Hyacymthe, Jacenta, Jacinthe *(Greek)*; Gia, Giacinta
*(Italian)*; Jacinta, Jakinda *(Spanish)*.

**Hypatia** *(Greek)* Highest one.

**Ianthe** *See* Violet.

**Ida** *(English)* Prosperous; *(Germanic)* Happy.
*Variants:* Idaka, Idda, Idetta, Idette; Idalia *(Italian)*.

**Idala** *(Hebrew)* One who goes softly.

**Idalia, Idda** *See* Ida.

**Ideh** *(Hebrew)* Praise.

# I

**Idetta, Idette** *See* Ida.

**Idola** *(Greek)* Idolized.

**Idona** *(Norse)* The goddess of eternal youth in Norse mythology.
*Variants:* Edony, Idonea; Idonia *(Germanic)*.

**Iggabri** *(InupiaQ)* Black bear.

**Ignatia** *(Latin)* Fiery; ardent. Feminine form of Ignatius.
*Variants:* Igna, Ignazia, Ingezia, Iniga.

**Ikniq** *(InupiaQ)* Fire.

**Ila** *(French)* Isle.

**Ilana** *(Hebrew)* Sunshine.

**Ilaria** *See* Hilary.

**Ildiko** *(Hungarian)* A fierce warrior.

**Ilisapesi** *(Tongan)* Blessed one.

**Ilka** *(Scottish)* Each and every one; *(Slavic)* Flattering.
*Variant:* Milka.

**Ilona** *See* Helen.

**Ilsa** *See* Ailsa, Alice.

**Ilse** *See* Elizabeth.

**Imagina** *See* Imogen.

**Iman** *(Arabic)* Faith; belief.

**Imogen** *(Latin)* Image of her mother.
*Variants:* Imagina, Imelda, Imogene, Imogine, Imojean; Emogene *(Germanic)*.

**Ina** *(Filipino)* Mother.

**Inari** *(Japanese)* Keeper of the rice.

**Inayat** *(Hindu)* Kindness.

**India** *(English)* From India; *(Sanskrit)* River.

**Indira** *(Hindu)* India.

# I

**Indra** *(Hindu)* An important god in Hindu mythology.
*Variant:* Indred.

**Indrina** *(Hindu)* Deep.

**Ines, Inesita** *See* Agnes.

**Inez** *(Spanish)* Gentle.
*Variants:* Ines, Inesita; Inès *(French)*.
*See also* Agnes.

**Inga, Ingar, Inge, Ingeberg, Inger** *See* Ingrid.

**Ingezia, Iniga** *See* Ignatia.

**Ingrid** *(Germanic)* Hero's daughter; a meadow.
*Variants:* Inga, Ingar, Inge, Ingeberg, Inger, Ingria, Ingrida, Ingunna.

**Iola** *(Greek)* Dawn cloud.
*Variant:* Iole.

**Iolana** *(Hawaiian)* To soar like an eagle.

**Iolanda, Iolanthe** *See* Violet.

**Iona** *(Greek)* The name of a flower; purple jewel; *(Indigenous Australian)* The name of a tree.

**Ira** *(Hindu)* Watchful; descendant.

**Irem** *(Turkish)* Gardens in heaven.

**Irene** *(Greek)* Peace.
*Variants:* Arina, Irena, Irène, Irénée, Irenka, Irina.

**Iris** *(Greek)* Rainbow; a play of colours.

**Irma** *(Germanic)* Strong; *(Latin)* Noble.
*Variants:* Ermina, Erminia, Irme, Irmina, Irmine.
*See also* Erma, Hermione.

**Iruka** *(African)* The future is supreme.

**Isa** *(Germanic)* Iron-like.

**Isabel** *See* Elizabeth.

**Isabulik** *(InupiaQ)* Angel.
*Variant:* Israbulik.

# I

**Isadora** *(Greek)* Gift of the moon goddess Isis. Feminine form of Isidore.
*Variants:* Isadore, Isidora.
*See also* Dora.

**Isaura** *(French)* God is bountiful.

**Ishana** *(Hindu)* Rich.

**Ishkode** *(Algonquin)* Fire.

**Isidora** *See* Isadora.

**Isis** *(Egyptian)* Supreme goddess.

**Isleta** *(Spanish)* Little island.

**Ismenis** *(Greek)* Learned.
*Variant:* Ismena.

**Isoke** *(African)* Satisfying gift.

**Isolde** *(Celtic)* Beautiful.
*Variant:* Isolda *(Germanic)*.

**Israt** *(Arabic)* Affection.

**Istas** *(Native American)* Snow.

**Ita** *(Gaelic)* Desire for truth.

**Iva** *(Hebrew)* God's great gift; *(Japanese)* Yew tree.

**Ivana, Ive** *See* Ivy.

**Ivette** *See* Yvonne.

**Ivis** *See* Ivy.

**Ivory** *(Latin)* White as ivory.

**Ivy** *(Greek)* A vine.
*Variants:* Ivana, Ive, Ivis.

**Ixchel** *(Mayan)* The Mayan goddess of earth and moon.

**Jacaline** *See* Jacqueline.

**Jacinda** *(Greek)* Beautiful.
*Variant:* Jacenda.

**Jacinta** *(Greek)* Lovely.
*See also* Hyacinth.

**Jacinthe** *See* Hyacinth.

**Jackie, Jacklyn, Jaclyn** *See* Jacqueline.

**Jacoba** *(Hebrew)* To conquer.
*Variants:* Jacobella *(Italian)*; Jacobina, Jakoba, Jakuba *(Polish)*;
Jacovina *(Russian)*.

**Jacqueline** *(Hebrew)* Supplanter; one who takes over.
Feminine form of Jacques or Jacob.
*Variants:* Jackie, Jacklyn, Jaclyn, Jacquelina, Jacquelyn;
Jacaline *(English)*; Jacquette, Jacqui *(French)*; Jacquetta
*(Latin)*.

**Jada** *(Hebrew)* Wise.

**Jade** *(Spanish)* A green gemstone.
*Variant:* Jayde.

**Jadzia** *(Polish)* Princess.

**Jael** *(Hebrew)* One who ascends the mountain.
*Variant:* Yael.

**Jaen** *(Hebrew)* Ostrich.

**Jaffa** *(Hebrew)* Beautiful; lovely.

**Jaimica** *(Spanish)* Supplanter; one who takes over.

**Jaimie** *(French)* I love.

# J

**Jaine** *See* Jane.

**Jaina** *(Hindu)* Good character.

**Jaione** *(Basque)* Nativity.

**Jakinda** *See* Hyacinth.

**Jakoba, Jakuba** *See* Jacoba.

**Jala** *(Arabic)* Charity.

**Jaleela** *(Arabic)* Honour; glory.
*See also* Jalila.

**Jalena** *See* Helen.

**Jalila** *(Arabic)* Great one.
*See also* Jaleela.

**Jamari** *(French)* Great girl warrior.

**Jamee** *(Hebrew)* Supplanter; one who takes over.

**Jamesina** *(Hebrew)* Feminine form of James.
*Variants:* Jamesetta, Jamesette; Jamie *(English)*.

**Jamilah** *(Arabic)* Beautiful.
*Variant:* Djamila.

**Jamima** *See* Jemima.

**Jan** *See* Jane.

**Jana** *(Arabic)* A harvest of fruit.
*See also* Jane.

**Jane** *(Hebrew)* Gracious; merciful; God is gracious.
*Variants:* Janeen, Janina, Janique, Jayne, Jeanine, Joan, Joanna, Johanna, Johanne; Jana *(Czech, Polish)*; Jan, Janelle, Janet, Janice, Janine *(English)*; Jeanette, Jeanne, Jehane, Jehanne, Netta *(French)*; Shauna, Sinead, Siobhan *(Irish)*; Gianna, Giovanna *(Italian)*; Zanna *(Latvian)*; Jaine, Jania, Janina *(Polish)*; Jean, Sheena, Sheenah, Shena, Shona *(Scottish)*; Juana, Juanita *(Spanish)*; Siân *(Welsh)*.

# J

**Janna** *(Hebrew)* Flourishing.

**January** *(Latin)* After the month.

**Japonica** *(Latin)* Of Japan; the name of a tree.

**Jara** *(Slavic)* The season of spring.

**Jardena** *(Hebrew)* To flow downward.

**Jarmila** *(Sanskrit)* The season of spring.

**Jarrita** *(Sanskrit)* Bird.

**Jarvia** *(Germanic)* Spear-keen.

**Jarvinia** *(Germanic)* Keen intelligence.

**Jasmine** *(Persian)* A flower; gift from God.
*Variants:* Jess, Jessamy, Jessamyn, Jazmin; Yasmeen, Yasmin, Yasmina, Yasmine *(Arabic)*; Jessamine *(French)*; Jasmin, Jasmina, Jasmyn, Yasmin *(Persian)*.
*See also* Jessica, Mali.

**Jaya** *(Sanskrit)* Victory.
*Variant:* Jayanti.

**Jayde** *See* Jade.

**Jayne** *(Hindu)* Victorious.

**Jazmin** *See* Jasmine.

**Jazz** *(English)* After the style of music.

**Jean, Jeanette, Jeanine, Jeanne** *See* Jane.

**Jehan** *(Arabic)* Beautiful flower.

**Jehane, Jehanne** *See* Jane.

**Jelena** *(Russian)* Shining light; pretty girl.
*See also* Helen.

**Jemima** *(Hebrew)* Dove; fair one; Job's daughter in the Bible.
*Variants:* Jamima, Jemimah, Jemmie; Jemma *(English)*.

**Jemma** *See* Gemma, Jemima.

**Jemmie** *See* Jemima.

# J

**Jena** *(Arabic)* Paradise.

**Jenay** *(French)* The name of a plant.

**Jendayi** *(African)* Give thanks.

**Jenell** *(Germanic)* Knowledge; understanding; kindness.

**Jenica** *(Romanian)* God is gracious.

**Jenifer** *See* Jennifer.

**Jenna** *(English)* Small bird.
*See also* Jennifer.

**Jennifer** *(Welsh)* White wave; white spirit; white-cheeked.
*Variants:* Genna, Gennifer, Guinevere, Jenifer, Jenna, Jennie, Jenny.
*See also* Guinevere.

**Jeno** *(Greek)* Heaven sent; well born.

**Jensine** *(Hebrew)* God is gracious.

**Jeovana, Jeovanna** *See* Jovanna.

**Jeraldine** *See* Geraldine.

**Jereni** *(Slavic)* Peace.

**Jeroma** *(Greek)* Feminine form of Jerome.

**Jermaine** *See* Germaine.

**Jerry** *See* Geraldine.

**Jess** *See* Jasmine, Jessica.

**Jessamine, Jessamy, Jessamyn** *See* Jasmine.

**Jesse** *See* Jessica.

**Jessenia** *(Arabic)* Flower; bloom.

**Jessica** *(Hebrew)* God's grace; God beholds.
*Variants:* Jess, Jesse, Jessie, Jesslyn, Jessy; Gessica *(Italian)*.
*See also* Jasmine.

**Jet** *(Latin)* Black; a semi-precious stone.
*Variant:* Jetta *(English)*.

# J

**Jewel** *(French)* Jewel; gem.

**Jezebel** *(Hebrew)* Follower of idols; wicked; harlot; a Biblical figure of disrepute.

**Jiera** *(Lithuanian)* Living.

**Jihan** *(Turkish)* Universe.

**Jillian** *(Latin)* Girl; young child.
*Variants:* Jill, Jillianne.
*See also* Gillian.

**Jina** *(Greek)* Farmer; *(Swahili)* Named child.

**Jinny** *See* Virginia.

**Jinx** *(Latin)* A charm.

**Jizelle** *See* Giselle.

**Joakima** *(Hebrew)* The Lord will judge.
*See also* Joaquina.

**Joan** *(French)* Feminine form of John or Jean; *(Hebrew)* God is gracious.
*Variants:* Joanie, Joni.
*See also* Jane.

**Joanna** *See* Jane, Joanne.

**Joanne** *(Hebrew)* God is gracious. Feminine form of Johannes.
*Variants:* Joanna, Jo Anne, Jovanna, Yohannah; Johana *(Czech)*; Johanne, Jonna *(Danish)*; Johanna *(Germanic)*; Giovanna, Vanna *(Italian)*.

**Joaquina** *(Spanish)* Feminine form of Joachim.
*See also* Joakima.

**Jobeth** *(English)* A combination of the names Jo and Beth.

**Jobey** *(Hebrew)* Persecuted.
*Variants:* Jobie, Jobina, Joby.

**Jocasta** *(Greek)* Scorned; the daughter of Menocenes in Greek mythology who unwittingly married her son, Oedipus.

# J

**Jocelyn** *(English)* Just; *(Latin)* Happy; joyful.
*Variants:* Joscelyn, Josselyn, Josslyn; Jocelin, Josselin
*(French)*; Jocunda *(Italian)*.

**Jocosa** *(Latin)* Gleeful; playful.

**Jocunda** *See* Jocelyn.

**Jodie** *(English)* Form of Judith.
*Variants:* Jodene, Jodi, Jody.
*See also* Judith.

**Joelle** *(French)* The Lord is willing; *(Hebrew)* Jehovah
is God.
*Variants:* Joella, Joelliane, Joelly, Joely.

**Johana** *See* Joanne.

**Johanna** *(Hebrew)* God's gracious gift.
*See also* Jane, Joanne.

**Johanne** *See* Jane, Joanne.

**Johari** *(African)* Jewel; precious.

**Joice, Joie** *See* Joyce.

**Jola** *(Greek)* Pretty.

**Jolan, Jolanda, Jolande, Jolandi** *See* Violet.

**Jolene** *(English)* He will increase.
*Variants:* Joleen, Joline.

**Joletta** *See* Violet.

**Jolie** *(French)* Pretty; merry.

**Joline** *See* Jolene.

**Joni** *See* Joan, Jonina.

**Jonina** *(Hebrew)* Dove.
*Variants:* Joni; Jonita *(Latin)*.

**Jonna** *See* Joanne.

**JooEun** *(Korean)* Silver pearl.

**Jora** *(Hebrew)* Autumn rain.

# J

**Jordane** *(Hebrew)* Descendant; flowing down.
*Variants:* Jordain, Jordan, Jordana, Jordanna, Jorden, Jordin.

**Joscelyn** *See* Jocelyn.

**Josephine** *(Hebrew)* God will increase.
*Variants:* Josie *(English)*; Fifi, Fifine, Josee, Josepha,
Josephina, Josetta, Josette *(French)*; Guiseppina *(Italian)*;
Jozefina *(Polish)*; Josefa, Pepita *(Spanish)*.

**Josselin, Josselyn, Josslyn** *See* Jocelyn.

**Josette** *See* Josephine.

**Jovanna** *(Latin)* Majestic.
*Variants:* Giovanna, Jeovana, Jeovanna.
*See also* Joanne.

**Joy** *(English)* Joy.

**Joyce** *(Latin)* Rejoicing.
*Variants:* Joice, Joie.

**Jozefina** *See* Josephine.

**Juana, Juanita** *See* Jane.

**Juci** *See* Judith.

**Jucinda** *(Spanish)* A fifth-century saint.

**Judith** *(Hebrew)* Praised; woman from Judea.
*Variants:* Jude, Judee, Judi, Judie, Judy; Judita *(Czech)*;
Juditha, Judithe *(French)*; Yehudit *(Hebrew)*; Juci, Judit, Jutka
*(Hungarian)*; Giuda, Giuditta *(Italian)*.
*See also* Jodie.

**Julia** *(Latin)* Soft-haired; youthful; gentle. Feminine form of Julius.
*Variants:* Julie *(French)*; Giulia *(Italian)*; Julene *(Latin)*; Jula,
Julcia, Julka *(Polish)*; Julya, Yulia, Yulinka *(Russian)*.

**Juliana** *(Latin)* Youthful. Feminine form of Julian.
*Variants:* Julian, Julianna, Jullianne; Gillian *(English)*;
Julienne *(French)*.
*See also* Gillian.

# K

**Julie** *See* Julia.

**Julienne** *See* Juliana.

**Juliet** *(French)* Little.
 *Variants:* Juilette, Juliette *(French)*; Guilia, Giuletta, Julitta *(Italian)*; Julieta *(Portuguese)*; Julietta *(Spanish)*.

**Julinka** *(Latin)* Youthful.

**Julitta** *See* Juliet.

**Julka** *See* Julia.

**July** *(Latin)* The month.

**Julya** *See* Julia.

**Jun** *(Chinese)* Truth.

**June** *(Latin)* The month.
 *Variants:* Juna, Junella, Junelle, Junette, Junia.

**Juniper** *(Latin)* A fragrant evergreen.

**Justine** *(Latin)* Just; true.
 *Variants:* Justa, Juste, Justina; Guistina *(Italian)*.

**Jutka** *See* Judith.

**Jyoti** *(Hindu)* Light.

**Kaarina, Kaatje** *See* Catherine.

**Kacey** *(Irish)* Eagle-eyed.
 *Variants:* Kacie, Kacy.

**Kadija** *(African)* The prophet's wife.

**Kadisha** *(Hebrew)* Holy.

# K

**Kady** *See* Catherine.

**Kaeda** *(Japanese)* Maple.

**Kaelyn** *(English)* Meadow.

**Kai** *(Hawaiian)* Sea; *(Maori)* Food; *(Native American)* Willow tree; *(Scottish)* Fire; *(Welsh)* Keeper of the keys.

**Kaia** *(Greek)* Earth.

**Kaie** *(Celtic)* Combat.

**Kaii** *(Gwich'in)* Willow.

**Kaimi** *(Polynesian)* The seeker.

**Kairos** *(Greek)* The right or opportune moment; one of Zeus' daughters in Greek mythology.

**Kaitlyn** *(Celtic)* Little darling.

**Kaiya** *(Indigenous Australian)* A type of spear; *(Japanese)* Forgiveness.

**Kajsa** *See* Catherine.

**Kakra** *(Ghanaian)* Younger of twins.

**Kala** *(Hindu)* Time; black; *(Indigenous Australian)* Fire.
*Variant:* Kalama.
*See also* Kalama, Kali.

**Kalama** *(Hawaiian)* Flaming torch.

**Kalanit** *(Hebrew)* The name of a flower.

**Kalare** *(Latin)* Bright; clear.

**Kalea** *(Hawaiian)* Bright.

**Kali** *(Hindu)* Energy; dark goddess; the evil companion of the god Shiva in Hindu mythology.
*Variant:* Kala.

**Kalia** *(Hawaiian)* Beauty.

**Kalika** *(Greek)* Rosebud.

**Kalila** *(Arabic)* Beloved.

**Kalina** *See* Catherine.

# K

**Kalinda** *(Indigenous Australian)* A lookout; *(Sanskrit)* The sun; a mythical mountain range.

**Kalonice** *(Greek)* Beauty's victory.

**Kama** *(Sanskrit)* Love.

**Kamala** *(Hindu)* Lotus.

**Kamali** *(Rhodesian)* Spirit protector.

**Kamaria** *(Swahili)* Like the moon.
*Variant:* Kamania.

**Kambo** *(African)* Must work for everything.

**Kameko** *(Japanese)* Tortoise-child; symbol for long life.
*Variant:* Kameka.

**Kamila** *See* Camilla.

**Kamilah** *(Arabic)* The perfect one.

**Kamilia, Kamilla** *See* Camilla.

**Kamna** *(Hindu)* Desire.

**Kane** *(Gaelic)* Tribute; warrior; *(Hawaiian)* The eastern sky; *(Japanese)* The doubly-accomplished; golden; *(Welsh)* Beautiful.

**Kanene** *(African)* A little thing in the eye is big.

**Kanika** *(Kenyan)* Black cloth.

**Kaniq** *(InupiaQ)* Frost.

**Kanna** *See* Kennis.

**Kara** *See* Cara, Catherine, Clare.

**Karel** *See* Carol.

**Karen** *See* Catherine.

**Karensa** *See* Kerensa.

**Kari** *(Turkish)* Flows like water.

**Karia** *See* Catherine.

**Karida** *(Arabic)* Untouched; virginal.

# K

**Karimah** *(African)* Generous.

**Karina** *See* Catherine.

**Karissa** *(Greek)* Love; grace.

**Karla** *See* Caroline, Carly, Charlotte.

**Karli** *(Turkish)* Covered with snow.

**Karlotta** *See* Charlotte.

**Karma** *(Sanskrit)* Destiny.

**Karna** *See* Caroline.

**Karol** *See* Carol.

**Karolina, Karoline, Karoly, Karolyn** *See* Caroline.

**Karyan** *(Armenian)* The dark one.

**Kasia** *See* Catherine.

**Kasinda** *(African)* Born to a family with twins.

**Kasmira** *(Slavic)* Demands peace.

**Kassandra** *See* Cassandra.

**Kassia, Kata, Katalin, Katarzyna, Katchen, Kate, Katerina, Katerine, Kateryn, Katharine, Katherine**
*See* Catherine.

**Kathleen** *(Celtic)* Little darling.
*See also* Catherine.

**Kathryn, Kathy, Katie, Katina, Katinka, Katka, Katren, Katri, Katrina, Katrine, Katti, Katy, Katya**
*See* Catherine.

**Kaula** *(Polynesian)* Prophet.

**Kavindra** *(Hindu)* Mighty poet.

**Kay** *(Greek)* To rejoice.
*Variant:* Kaya.

**Kaya** *(Japanese)* Place of rest or peace.

**Kayla** *(Hebrew)* Crown of laurel.

**Kayley** *(English)* Bright; beautiful.

# K

**Kazia** *See* Kezia.

**Keara** *(Irish)* The name of a saint.

**Keeley** *See* Keely.

**Keelin** *(Celtic)* Slender; fair.

**Keely** *(Gaelic)* Beautiful and graceful.
*Variants:* Keeley, Keelin.
*See also* Kelly.

**Kefira** *(Hebrew)* Young lioness.

**Kei** *(Japanese)* Rapture; reverence.

**Keiko** *(Japanese)* Adored one.

**Keilana** *(Hawaiian)* Adored one.

**Keisha** *(African)* Favourite.

**Kekona** *(Hawaiian)* Second-born.

**Kelda** *(Scandinavian)* Clear mountain spring.

**Kellan** *(Gaelic)* Warrior princess.

**Kelly** *(Gaelic)* Church; warrior; wood; holly; *(Germanic)* Farm
by the spring.
*Variants:* Keely, Kelli, Kellie.

**Kelsey** *(English)* Beautiful island; from the ship's island;
shipping harbour.
*Variants:* Kelcey, Kelsie.

**Keme** *(Algonquin)* Secret.

**Kendall** *(Celtic)* Ruler of the valley.
*Variants:* Kendal, Kendel, Kendell.

**Kendra** *(Anglo-Saxon)* Understanding, knowledge.

**Kennis** *(Gaelic)* Beautiful.
*Variants:* Kanna, Kenice, Kenise, Kennice, Kennise.

**Kenyangi** *(Ugandan)* White egret.

**Kepa** *(Basque)* Stone.

**Kerani** *(Hindu)* Sacred bells.

# K

**Kerensa** *(Cornish)* Love.
  *Variants:* Karensa, Kerenza.

**Kerri** *(Gaelic)* Dark-haired.
  *See also* Kerry.

**Kerry** *(Gaelic)* Descendants of Ciar; a place name; dark eyes.
  *Variants:* Kerri, Kerrie.

**Kesare** *(Spanish)* Long-haired.

**Kesi** *(Swahili)* Born when father was in trouble.

**Kesia** *(African)* Favourite.

**Kessie** *(Ghanaian)* Fat at birth.

**Keturah** *(Hebrew)* Fragrance.

**Kezia** *(Hebrew)* Cassia tree; cinnamon; one of Job's daughters.
  *Variants:* Cassia, Kazia, Ketzia, Ketziah, Kezi, Keziah.

**Khaii** *(Gwich'in)* Winter.

**Khalidah** *(Arabic)* Immortal.

**Khorshed** *(Persian)* The sun.

**Kiana** *(Hawaiian)* Moon goddess.

**Kichi** *(Japanese)* Fortunate.

**Kiele** *(Hawaiian)* Gardenia; fragrant blossom.

**Kim** *(English)* Chief.

**Kimatra** *(Hindu)* Seduce.

**Kimberley** *(English)* Land belonging to Cyneburg; royal
  fortress meadow.
  *Variants:* Kimberlea, Kimberlee, Kimberlie, Kimberly.

**Kineta** *(Greek)* Active one.

**Kiona** *(Native American)* Brown hills.

**Kira** *(Latin)* Light; sun.

**Kiran** *(Hindu)* Ray.

**Kirby** *(Anglo-Saxon)* Church town.
  *Variant:* Kirbie.

# K

**Kirgavik** *(InupiaQ)* Peregrine falcon.

**Kirima** *(Inuit)* A hill.

**Kirsten** *(English)* Stone church.
  *See also* Christine.

**Kirstyn** *(Scandinavian)* Anointed one.

**Kirti** *(Hindu)* Fame.

**Kisa** *(Russian)* Kitty.

**Kisina** *(Algonquin)* Cold weather.

**Kiska** *(Russian)* Pure.

**Kismet** *(English)* Fate, destiny.

**Kissa** *(Ugandan)* Born after twins.

**Kit-Ming** *(Cantonese)* Vessel of honour.

**Kita** *(Japanese)* North.

**Kitty** *See* Catherine.

**Klara, Klarika, Klarissa** *See* Clare.

**Klaudia** *See* Claudia.

**Klavdia** *(Slavic)* Lame one.

**Klementyna** *See* Clementine.

**Kohana** *(Japanese)* Little flower.

**Koko** *(Native American)* Night.

**Kolina** *(Greek)* Pure.

**Konstancia** *See* Constance.

**Koren** *(Greek)* Maiden.

**Kostancia, Kostka** *See* Constance.

**Kotone** *(Japanese)* Sound of the harp.

**Krista** *See* Christine.

**Kristen** *(Latin)* Follower of Christ.
  *Variants:* Kristin, Kristyn.

**Kristiana, Kristin, Kristina** *See* Christine.

**Kriti** *(Hindu)* A work of art.

**Krystal** *See* Crystal.

**Kshama** *(Hindu)* Forgiveness; patience.

**Kunik** *(InupiaQ)* Kiss.

**Kuwakei** *(Tlingit)* Good weather.

**Kyla** *(Gaelic)* Narrow; straight. Feminine form of Kyle;
    *(Hebrew)* Lovely.
    *Variants:* Kyleigh, Kylene, Kyle.

**Kylie** *(Indigenous Australian)* Boomerang.
    *Variant:* Kylee.

**Kyna** *(Gaelic)* Wise.

**Kynthia** *(Greek)* Born under the sign of Cancer.

**Kyoko** *(Japanese)* Mirror.

**Kyra** *(Persian)* Sun.

**Lacey** *(Russian)* Cheerful one.
    *Variants:* Lace, Lacie, Lacy.

**Lacy** *(French)* A place name.

**Lae** *(Laos)* Dark.

**Laeta, Laetitia** *See* Letitia.

**Lailie** *(Hebrew)* Born during light.

**Laine** *See* Lane.

**Lainey** *(English)* Sun ray.

**Lakeisha** *(Swahili)* Favourite one.

# L

**Lala** *(Slavic)* Tulip.

**Lalasa** *(Hindu)* Love.

**Lalo** *(Latin)* To sing a lullaby.

**Lamar** *(Germanic)* Land.

**Lan** *(Vietnamese)* The name of a flower.

**Lana** *(Polynesian)* To float.
   *See also* Alana.

**Lane** *(English)* Narrow road.
   *Variants:* Laine, Lanette.
   *See also* Alana.

**Lani** *(Hawaiian)* Sky; heaven.

**Lanikai** *(Hawaiian)* Heavenly sea.

**Lanna** *See* Alana.

**Lara** *(Latin)* Protector.
   *See also* Larissa.

**Laraine** *(Latin)* Sea bird.
   *Variant:* Larina.

**Lari** *(English)* Crowned with laurel.

**Laria** *(Greek)* The stars are mine.

**Larina** *See* Laraine.

**Larissa** *(Greek)* The name of a Greek city; a nymph in Greek
   mythology; *(Russian)* Cheerful one.
   *Variants:* Lara, Laricia, Larisa.
   *See also* Lara.

**Lark** *(English)* The name of a bird; *(Indigenous Australian)* Cloud.

**Lateefah** *(African)* Gentle; pleasant.
   *Variants:* Latifa, Latifah.

**Lateesha, Latesha, Latisha** *See* Letitia.

**Laura** *(Latin)* Laurel leaves; honour; fame; spirit.
   *Variants:* Lauri, Lora, Lori; Lauraine, Laurie *(English)*;

# L

Lauren *(French)*; Lauretta, Lorene, Loretta, Lori, Lorie, Lorna, Lorretta *(Italian)*.

**Laurel** *(Latin)* A laurel garland.
*Variant:* Laurelie.

**Lauren, Lauretta, Lauri, Laurie** *See* Laura.

**Laurinda** *(Latin)* Crowned with laurel; praise.

**Lavani** *(Hindu)* Grace.

**Laveda** *(Latin)* Innocent one.

**Lavena, Lavenia** *See* Lavinia.

**Laverne** *(French)* Alder grove; spring-like.

**Lavinia** *(Latin)* Lady; pure.
*Variants:* Lavena, Lavenia, Lavina, Livinia.

**Layna** *(Greek)* Light; truth.

**Léa** *See* Leah, Lee.

**Leah** *(Assyrian)* Mistress; ruler; *(Greek)* Glad tidings; *(Hebrew)* Cow; weary one.
*Variants:* Léa *(French)*; Lea *(Hebrew)*; Lia, Liah *(Italian)*.

**Leala** *(French)* Loyal one.

**Leandra** *(Greek)* Lion woman. Female form of Leander.

**Leanne** *(English)* Combination of Lee and Anne.

**Leba** *(Hebrew)* Beloved.

**Ledah** *(Hebrew)* Birth.

**Lee** *(English)* Meadow.
*Variant:* Lea, Leigh.

**Leena** *See* Lena.

**Leigh** *See* Lee.

**Leiko** *(Japanese)* Arrogant.

**Leila** *(Arabic)* Dark as the night.

**Lemuela** *(Hebrew)* Dedicated to God. Female form of Lemuel.

# L

**Lena** *(Latin)* Alluring; temptress; light.

Variants: Leena, Leni, Lina.

**Lene** *(Norwegian)* Illustrious.

**Leni** *See* Lena.

**Lenice** *See* Leonie.

**Lenita** *(Latin)* Gentle.

**Lenka** *See* Helen.

**Leonie** *(Latin)* The lioness.

Variants: Leonelle, Leonice, Leonne *(French)*; Lenice, Leoni, Leona *(Germanic)*; Leola, Leonita, Leontine *(Italian)*; Leonida *(Russian)*; Leonarda *(Spanish)*.

**Leonora** *(Greek)* Light.

Variants: Lennora, Lenore, Leonore, Leora.

**Leontine** *See* Leonie.

**Leopolda** *(Germanic)* Bold leader.

**Leslie** *(English)* Small meadow; *(Scottish)* Dweller in the grey castle.

**Leta** *(Latin)* Joy.

**Letha** *(Greek)* Forgetful; oblivion.

**Letitia** *(Latin)* Joy.

Variants: Lateesha, Latesha, Latisha, Lettice *(English)*; Laetitia *(French)*; Letizia *(Italian)*; Leticia *(Spanish)*.

**Levana** *(Latin)* Rising sun.

Variants: Levania, Levanna, Livana.

**Lexine** *(Hebrew)* Helper and defender of mankind.

**Leyna** *(Germanic)* Little angel.

**Lia** *(Hebrew)* Dependence.

*See also* Leah.

**Liadan** *(Irish)* Grey lady.

**Liah** *See* Leah.

**Lian** *(Chinese)* The graceful willow.

# L

**Liana** *(French)* Vine; to bind; youth.

**Liannaka** *(Dutch)* Bringer of peace; hope.

**Liberty** *(English)* Freedom.

**Lien** *(Chinese)* Lotus flower.

**Liese** *(Germanic)* Beloved by God.

**Lila** *(Arabic)* Night.

**Lilah, Lili, Lilia** *See* Lily.

**Lilian, Lilias** *See* Lillian.

**Lilith** *(Assyrian)* Storm goddess; *(Hebrew)* Spirit of the night; *(Sumerian)* Ghost.
  *Variants:* Lillith, Lillitu.

**Lillian** *(Greek)* The lily flower.
  *Variants:* Lilian, Lillias; Lilias *(Scottish)*.

**Lily** *(Latin)* The name of a flower.
  *Variants:* Lillie, Lilly *(English)*; Lilia, Lilie *(Germanic)*; Lilah *(Greek)*; Lili *(Welsh)*.

**Lilybell** *(Latin)* Fair lily.

**Limber** *(African)* Joyfulness.

**Lina** *(Arabic)* Tender.
  *See also* Lena.

**Linda** *(Spanish)* Pretty.
  *See also* Belinda.

**Lindsay** *(English)* Pool island; linden island.
  *Variants:* Lindsey, Linsey, Lynsey.

**Linette** *(French)* Linnet bird; flaxen.
  *Variant:* Linne *(Scandinavian)*.

**Linnea** *(Norwegian)* Lime tree; the national flower of Sweden.

**Linsey** *See* Lindsay.

**Lisa, Lisabet, Lisbet** *See* Elizabeth.

**Litsa** *(Greek)* Bearer of good news.

**Liv** *(Norwegian)* Life.

# L

**Livana** *(Greek)* Goddess.

> *See also* Levana.

**Livia** *(Latin)* The olive; a famous Roman empress.

**Liz, Lizzie** *See* Elizabeth.

**Lobelia** *(Latin)* The name of a flower.

**Locke** *(English)* Stronghold.

**Logan** *(Scottish)* Little hollow.

**Lois** *(Greek)* Desirable. Feminine form of Louis.

**Lokelani** *(Hawaiian)* Small red rose.

**Lola** *See* Charlotte.

**Londiwe** *(Zulu)* Protected; kept safe.

**Lora** *See* Laura.

**Lore** *(Basque)* Flower.

**Lorelei** *(Germanic)* From the Rhine River.

**Lorena** *(Latin)* The laurel.

**Loretta, Lori, Lorie** *See* Laura.

**Loris** *See* Chloris.

**Lorna** *(Celtic)* Of Lorne.

> *See also* Laura.

**Lorraine** *(Germanic)* Where Lothar dwells.

> *Variants:* Laraine, Laurain, Lauraine, Laureen, Loraine.

**Lorretta** *See* Laura.

**Lotus** *(Greek)* Dreamlike; the name of a flower.

**Louisa** *(French)* Famous in battle; warrior maiden.

> *Variants:* Aloise, Eloise, Heloise *(French)*; Aloisa, Aloysia, Louise, Luise, Lulu *(Germanic)*; Eloisia *(Greek)*; Eloisa, Luisa, Luiza *(Italian, Spanish)*; Lovisa *(Swedish)*.

**Lourdes** *(French)* A French place name; site of a miracle in Catholic tradition.

> *Variant:* Lurdes (Portuguese).

# L

**Love** *(English)* Loved one.

**Loveday** *(English)* Fine, good day.
*Variant:* Lovette.

**Lovisa** *See* Louisa.

**Lucia** *(Latin)* Light.
*Variants:* Lucille *(French)*; Luca, Luciana *(Italian)*; Luzia *(Portuguese)*.

**Lucinda** *(Latin)* Bringer of light.

**Lucine** *(Armenian)* Moon.

**Lucretia** *(Latin)* Riches.
*Variants:* Lucrece *(French)*; Lacrecia, Lucrezia *(Italian)*.

**Lucy** *(Latin)* Light; a Sicilian saint.
*Variants:* Luce, Lucette; Lucie, Lucienne, Lucille *(French)*; Luca *(Hungarian)*; Lucetta, Lucia, Lucilla *(Italian, Spanish)*.

**Luella** *(English)* Elfin.

**Luisa, Luise, Luiza** *See* Louisa.

**Lukina** *(Ukrainian)* Graceful and bright.

**Lulu** *See* Louisa.

**Luna** *(Latin)* The goddess of the moon in Roman mythology.
*Variants:* Luneta, Lunetta, Lunette.

**Lungile** *(Zulu)* Kind; good.

**Lupe** *(Latin)* Wolf.
*Variant:* Lupita.
*See also* Guadalupe.

**Lydia** *(Greek)* Woman from Persia; beauty.

**Lykaios** *(Greek)* Wolf-like.

**Lynn** *(Anglo-Saxon)* A cascade.

**Lynsey** *See* Lindsay.

**Lyris** *(Greek)* Player of the lyre.
*Variant:* Lyra.

M

**Mab** *(Gaelic)* Joy.
  *See also* Maeve.

**Mabel** *(French)* My fair maid; lovely.
  *Variants:* Belle, Mabella, Mabelle, Maybelle, Maybelline.

**Macaria** *(Greek)* Daughter of Heracles and Deianira in Greek mythology.
  *Variant:* Makaria.

**Macawi** *(Sioux)* Female coyote.

**Machi** *(Japanese)* Ten thousand.

**Machiko** *(Japanese)* Child of Machi.

**Mackenzie** *(Gaelic)* Daughter of the wise leader.
  *Variant:* Meckenzie.

**Madalena** *See* Madeline.

**Madeira** *(Spanish)* A sweet wine; a place name.

**Madeline** *(Hebrew)* Woman from Magdala; one who is elevated; a high tower.
  *Variants:* Maddie, Maddy, Magda, Magdalene; Magdalena *(Czech, Russian)*; Madelaine, Madeleine, Madelon, Magdalaine *(French)*; Magdalini *(Greek)*; Maighlin *(Irish)*; Maddalena *(Italian)*; Madalena *(Spanish)*.

**Madge** *See* Margaret.

**Madhu** *(Hindu)* Honey.

**Madhur** *(Sanskrit)* Sweet.

**Madison** *(Germanic)* Daughter of a mighty warrior.
  *Variant:* Maddison.

# M

**Madra** *(Spanish)* Mother.

**Mae** *See* May.

**Maegan** *See* Megan.

**Maëlle** *(French)* Princely.

**Maeve** *(Irish)* Joyful one; a mythical Irish fairy queen. *See also* Mab.

**Mafalda** *See* Mathilda.

**Magan** *(Germanic)* Power.

**Magda, Magdalaine, Magdalena, Magdalene, Magdalini** *See* Madeline.

**Magena** *(Hebrew)* A covering or protection; *(Native American)* The coming moon.

**Maggie** *See* Margaret.

**Magna** *(Latin)* Large.

**Magnolia** *(French)* The name of a flower.

**Mahala** *(Arabic)* Marrow; *(Hebrew)* Tenderness. *Variants:* Mahalah, Mahalia.

**Mahalia** *(Hebrew)* Affection.

**Mai** *(French)* The month of May; *(Japanese)* Dance. *See also* May.

**Maia** *(Greek)* Nurse; good mother; a daughter of Atlas in Greek mythology; *(Latin)* Great.

**Maida** *(English)* A maiden.

**Maighlin** *See* Madeline.

**Maikan** *(Innu)* Wolf.

**Maire** *See* Mary.

**Maisie** *(Scottish)* Child of light. *See also* Margaret.

**Maitane** *(English)* Beloved.

# M

**Maitryi** *(Hindu)* Friendship.

**Maizah** *(African)* Discerning.

**Maj** *(Swedish)* Pearl.

**Makayla** *See* Michaela.

**Makwa** *(Algonquin)* Bear.

**Mala** *(English)* Meeting hall; *(French)* Bad one.

**Malati** *(Hindu)* The name of a small fragrant flower.

**Malaya** *(Filipino)* Free.

**Malca** *(Hebrew)* Queen.

**Mali** *(Thai)* Jasmine flower; *(Welsh)* Beloved.

**Malibuaqti** *(InupiaQ)* Disciple; learner.

**Maliha** *(Hindu)* Strong; beautiful.

**Malika** *(African)* Queen; princess.

**Malila** *(Native American)* Salmon going quickly upstream.

**Malina** *(Hebrew)* Tower; *(Hindu)* Dark.

**Malissa** *See* Melissa.

**Malka** *(Hebrew)* Queen.

**Mallory** *(Germanic)* Army counsellor; without good fortune.

**Malu** *(Hawaiian)* Peacefulness.

**Malva** *(Greek)* Soft.

**Malvina** *(Gaelic)* Smooth snow.

**Mamta** *(Hindu)* Maternal love.

**Manami** *(Japanese)* Love and beauty.

**Manda** *See* Amanda.

**Mandara** *(Hindu)* The name of a mythical mountain.

**Mandeep** *(Hindu)* Light of heart.

**Mandisa** *(African)* Sweet.

**Mandi** *See* Amanda.

# M

**Mandy** *(Spanish)* Harmony.
*See also* Amanda.

**Mangena** *(Hebrew)* Melody.

**Manisha** *(Hindu)* Sharp intellect; genius; sagacious.

**Manjusha** *(Sanskrit)* A box of jewels.

**Manon** *(French)* Bitter; diminutive form of Marie.
*See also* Mary.

**Manuela** *(Spanish)* God is with us. Female form of Manuel.

**Mara** *(Hebrew)* Sorrowful.

**Marcella** *(French)* A fourth-century saint.
*Variants:* Marcela, Marceline, Marcellina, Marcelline *(Czech)*; Marcelia, Marcelle *(French)*.

**Marcia** *(Latin)* War-like.
*Variants:* Marci, Marcie, Marcy, Marsha.

**Mared** *See* Margaret.

**Maren** *(Latin)* Sea.

**Margaret** *(Greek)* Pearl.
*Variants:* Malgelit *(Abenaki)*; Gredel, Margaretta, Margherita, Margherite, Margred, Marguetta, Marjorie; Marjeta *(Czech)*; Grette, Maret, Margarete, Mette *(Danish)*; Griet, Margriet, Marika *(Dutch)*; Madge, Maggie, Margo, Meg, Peg, Pegeen, Peggy, Rita *(English)*; Gogo, Margerie, Margery, Margory, Margot, Marguerite, Marjory *(French)*; Margareta, Margarethe, Gretchen, Grethel, Marghet *(Germanic)*; Mariah *(Hebrew)*; Margita *(Hungarian)*; Marget *(Italian)*; Margarida *(Portuguese)*; Maisie *(Scottish)*; Margarita *(Spanish)*; Gret *(Swedish)*; Mared, Marge, Meagan, Megan *(Welsh)*.
*See also* May.

**Maria** *See* Mary.

**Mariabella** *(Italian)* My beautiful Mary.

**Mariah** *See* Margaret.

# M

**Mariam** *See* Mary, Miriam.

**Marian** *See* Mary.

**Mariana, Marianna** *See* Miriam.

**Marianne** *(French)* Little Mary.
   *See also* Mary, Miriam.

**Mariasha** *(Egyptian)* Perfect one; *(Hebrew)* Bitter; with sorrow.

**Maribel** *(Latin)* Mary the beautiful.
   *Variants:* Maribella, Maribelle.
   *See also* Mary.

**Maricel** *(Latin)* Full of grace.

**Maridel, Marie, Mariel** *See* Mary.

**Marie** *See* Mary.

**Marigold** *(Greek)* The name of a flower.

**Marika** *See* Margaret.

**Marilla** *See* Amaryllis.

**Marilyn** *See* Mary.

**Marina** *(Latin)* Sea maiden.
   *Variants:* Maris, Marisa, Marissa, Marnia; Marnie *(English)*;
   Marita *(Spanish)*; Mareena, Marna, Marny *(Scandinavian)*.

**Marion** *See* Mary, Miriam.

**Marionne** *See* Miriam.

**Mariposa** *(Spanish)* Butterfly.

**Marisa** *(Hindu)* Mother of Hindu sun god Daksa.
   *See also* Marina.

**Marissa** *See* Marina.

**Marjani** *(African)* Coral.

**Marjeta, Marjorie, Marjory** *See* Margaret.

**Marlene** *(Germanic)* Child of light; bitter.

**Marmara** *(Greek)* Radiant.

# M

**Marna** *(Hebrew)* Rejoice.

**Marnia** *See* Marina.

**Marnina** *(Hebrew)* Cause of joy.

**Marny** *See* Marina.

**Marsha** *See* Marcia.

**Martha** *(Arabic)* Lady; mistress.
   *Variant:* Marta *(Aramean)*.

**Martina** *(Latin)* Warlike.
   *Variant:* Tina.

**Marvela** *(Latin)* Marvelous.

**Marvelle** *(French)* Miracle.

**Mary** *(Hebrew)* Bitter; star of the sea; the mother of Jesus Christ.
   *Variants:* Mali *(Abenaki)*; Marieke *(Dutch)*; Marian, Marilyn,
   Marion *(English)*; Maillard, Manette, Maree, Mari, Maria,
   Marianne, Marie, Marielle, Maryse, Mimi *(French)*; Marla,
   Mieke *(Germanic)*; Mariam, Marika *(Greek)*; Mara *(Hebrew)*;
   Mair, Maire, Maureen, Miriam, Moira, Molly, Moyra *(Irish)*;
   Mariel, Mariella, Marietta *(Italian)*; Maria *(Latin)*; Maika
   *(Russian)*; Minnie *(Scottish)*; Marica, Marieta, Marisa, Marita
   *(Spanish)*; Mair *(Welsh)*.

**Masako** *(Japanese)* Elegant child; flourishing child.

**Matana** *(Arabic)* Gift.

**Mathea** *(Hebrew)* Gift of God.

**Mathilda** *(Germanic)* Battle maiden; strength.
   *Variants:* Matilda; Mathilde, Tilly *(French)*; Matilde *(Italian)*;
   Mafalda, Matuxa *(Spanish)*.

**Matrika** *(Hindu)* Mother; a band of goddesses in Hindu
   mythology.

**Matuxa** *See* Mathilda.

**Maude** *(Germanic)* Mighty in battle.
   *Variant:* Maud.

# M

**Maura** *(Latin)* Dark.

**Maureen** *(Latin)* Great; little Mary; dark-haired.

**Maxine** *(Latin)* The greatest.
*Variants:* Maxene, Maxie, Maxime, Maxina.

**May** *(Hebrew)* A form of Margaret; the month of the year.
*Variants:* Mae, Mai, Maybelle, Maybelline.

**Maya** *(Hindu)* Divine creative force in everything; *(Sanskrit)* Illusion.

**Maybelle, Maybelline** *See* May, Mabel.

**Mayu** *(Japanese)* True reason.

**Meagan** *See* Margaret, Megan.

**Meaghan** *See* Megan.

**Meckenzie** *See* Mackenzie.

**Meda** *(Hindu)* Good house.

**Medea** *(Greek)* Ruling; *(Latin)* Middle child; a vengeful figure in Greek mythology.

**Medha** *(Hindu)* Intelligence.

**Meena** *(Hindu)* Precious stone.
*See also* Mina.

**Meg** *See* Margaret.

**Megan** *(Gaelic)* Able; *(Greek)* Mighty; *(Welsh)* Pearl.
*Variants:* Maegan, Meagan, Meaghan, Meghan.
*See also* Margaret.

**Megara** *(Greek)* Wife of Hercules.

**Meghan** *See* Megan.

**Meghana** *(Hindu)* Rain cloud.

**Mei** *(Latin)* Great one.

**Meira** *(Hebrew)* Light.

**Meirion** *See* Miriam.

**Mela** *(Hindu)* Religious gathering.

# M

**Melanie** *(Greek)* Dark-haired.
  *Variants:* Melaine, Melania, Melony, Mellony; Melany,
  Melonie *(English)*; Melania *(Italian)*; Melana *(Russian)*.

**Melantha** *(Greek)* Black flower.

**Melba** *(Greek)* Slender; soft; *(Latin)* The name of a mallow
  flower.

**Melia** *(Greek)* Meliae were nymphs in Greek mythology,
  daughers of Oceanus.

**Melina** *(Latin)* Canary yellow.
  *See also* Carmel, Melissa.

**Melinda** *(Greek)* Gentle one.
  *See also* Belinda.

**Melisenda** *(Spanish)* Honest; diligent.

**Melissa** *(Greek)* Bee, honey.
  *Variants:* Malissa, Melina, Melita, Melitta, Millissa; Missy
  *(English)*; Milice *(French)*.
  *See also* Carmel.

**Melody** *(Greek)* Song.

**Melonia, Melonie** *See* Melanie.

**Melosa** *(Spanish)* Gentle; sweet.

**Melusine** *(French)* A mysterious, serpentine figure in French
  mythology.
  *Variant:* Melusina.

**Melvina** *(Celtic)* Handmaiden.

**Mena** *(Hindu)* The mother of Menaka, a spirit in Hindu
  mythology.
  *See also* Mina.

**Menaka** *(Hindu)* One of the Apsaras (female spirits of clouds
  and waters) in Hindu mythology.

**Mercedes** *(Latin)* Merciful.
  *Variants:* Mercy, Sadie; Mercede *(Italian)*.

# M

**Meredith** *(Welsh)* Protector of the sea.

**Merion** *See* Miriam.

**Meris** *(Latin)* Sea born.

**Merit** *(Latin)* Deserving.

**Merle** *(Latin)* Blackbird.

**Merry** *(English)* Joyful.

**Messina** *(Latin)* Middle child.

**Meta** *(Latin)* Ambitious.

**Mette** *See* Margaret.

**Mia** *(Italian)* Mine.
*See also* Michaela.

**Michaela** *(Hebrew)* Like God. Feminine form of Michael.
*Variants:* Micaela, Michelina, Michella, Mikaela, Mikala,
Mikayla; Makayla, Midge *(English)*; Michel, Michele,
Micheline, Michelle, Mishelle *(French)*; Micah, Michala
*(Hebrew)*; Mia, Michaella *(Italian)*; Misha *(Russian)*.

**Michi** *(Japanese)* Righteous.

**Michiko** *(Japanese)* Child of Michi.

**Midge** *See* Michaela.

**Midori** *(Japanese)* Green.
*Variants:* Mido.

**Mignon** *(French)* Dainty; petite; sweet.
*Variants:* Mignonne, Mignonette.

**Mihku** *(Maliseet)* Squirrel.

**Miho** *(Japanese)* Beautiful crest of the wave.

**Mika** *(Japanese)* New moon; *(Omaha, Osage)* Raccoon;
*(Russian)* God's child.

**Mikaela, Mikala, Mikayla** *See* Michaela.

**Miki** *(Indigenous Australian)* The moon; *(Japanese)*
Beautiful tree.

# M

**Mildred** *(Anglo-Saxon)* Gentle strength.

**Milice** *See* Melissa.

**Milka** *See* Emily, Ilka.

**Millicent** *(Germanic)* Industrious; strong.
  *Variant:* Milicent.

**Millissa** *See* Melissa.

**Milly** *See* Emily.

**Mily** *(Hawaiian)* Beautiful.

**Mimi** *(Germanic)* Strong opponent.

**Min** *(Korean)* Clever.

**Mina** *(Japanese)* South.
  *Variants:* Meena, Mena, Minna.
  *See also* Wilhelmina.

**Minako** *(Japanese)* Child of Mina.

**Minda** *(Native American)* Knowledge.

**Mindel** *(Hebrew)* Sea of bitterness.

**Mine** *(Japanese)* A resolute protector.

**Minerva** *(Greek)* Power; *(Latin)* Thinker; the goddess of
  wisdom and the arts in Roman mythology.

**Mingmei** *(Chinese)* Smart; beautiful.

**Minka** *(Germanic)* Strong; resolute.

**Minna** *(Germanic)* Love; *(Hebrew)* Bitterness; *(Scottish)* Mother.
  *See also* Mina.

**Minta** *(Greek)* Mint.

**Minush** *(Innu)* Cat.

**Mira** *(Latin)* Wonder; aim; light of God.
  *Variant:* Mirah.
  *See also* Almira, Miranda.

# M

**Mirabelle** *(Latin)* Wonderful; beautiful to look upon.

   *Variants:* Belle, Mirabel, Mirabella *(French)*; Mirella *(Italian)*.

**Mirah** *See* Mira.

**Miranda** *(Latin)* Extraordinary; to be admired.

**Mireille** *(French)* Wonder; marvel.

   *Variants:* Mireye, Mireilla; Mireya *(Spanish)*.

   *See also* Mirabelle.

**Mirella** *See* Mirabelle.

**Miremba** *(Ugandan)* Peace.

**Mireya** *See* Mireille.

**Miriam** *(Hebrew)* Good; full; sea of bitterness; wished-for child; the wife of King Herod in Jewish history.

   *Variants:* Meriem *(Arabic)*; Mariam, Miryam; Marianne, Marion, Marionne *(French)*; Mariana, Marianna *(Italian, Spanish)*; Meirion, Merion *(Welsh)*.

**Miryam** *See* Miriam.

**Misaki** *(Japanese)* Beautiful bloom.

**Misha, Mishelle** *See* Michaela.

**Missy** *(English)* Young girl.

   *See also* Melissa.

**Misty** *(English)* Covered by mist.

**Mitiq** *(InupiaQ)* Duck.

**Miyoko** *(Japanese)* Beautiful child.

**Mizuki** *(Japanese)* Beautiful moon.

**Modesty** *(Latin)* Modest one.

   *Variants:* Modestine *(French)*; Modesta, Modeste, Modestia *(Italian, Spanish)*.

**Mohini** *(Hindu)* Most beautiful.

**Moira** *(Celtic)* Great; *(Irish)* Bitter.
   *Variants:* Moire, Maire.
   *See also* Mary.

# M

**Molly** *See* Mary.

**Mona** *(Latin)* Peaceful; individual; noble one; my lady.
*See also* Shimona.

**Monica** *(Latin)* Adviser.
*Variants:* Monique *(French)*; Monika, Monike *(Germanic)*.

**Montague** *(French)* Steep mountain.

**Moon** *(Korean)* Letters.

**Mora** *(Spanish)* Blueberry.

**Morgan** *(Gaelic)* White sea; *(Welsh)* Bright; dweller by the sea.
*Variants:* Morgaine, Morgana, Morgance, Morgane *(Celtic)*.

**Morgandy** *(Celtic)* Little one from the edge of the sea.

**Morgen** *(Germanic)* Morning.

**Moria** *(Hebrew)* My teacher is God.

**Moselle** *(Hebrew)* Taken from water.

**Muriel** *(Greek)* Myrrh; *(Irish)* Sea-bright; *(Latin)* Angel
of June.

**Musetta** *(French)* A ballad.

**Muwin** *(Maliseet)* Bear.

**Mya** *(Burmese)* Emerald.

**Mychau** *(Vietnamese)* Great.

**MyDuyen** *(Vietnamese)* Beautiful.

**Myfanwy** *(Welsh)* Sweet woman; my fine one.

**Myiesha** *(Arabic)* Life's blessing.

**Myra** *(Latin)* Wonderful; quiet song.

**Myrna** *(Gaelic)* Polite one; gentle.

**Myrtle** *(Greek)* The name of a flower; symbol of victory.

**Nabelung** *(African)* Beautiful one.

**Nada** *See* Nadia.

**Nadège** *(French)* Hope

**Nadezda** *(Czech)* One with hope.

**Nadia** *(Russian)* Hope.
 *Variants:* Nada, Nadine, Natejda.

**Nafeeza** *(Arabic)* Precious thing.

**Nahmana** *(Dakota)* Secretive; sly.

**Naia** *(Greek)* Flowing.

**Naiad** *(Greek)* Water nymph.

**Nailah** *(African)* Succeeding.

**Naimah** *(Arabic)* Living an easy, enjoyable life.

**Naina** *(Hindu)* Eyes.

**Nairn** *(Scottish)* Narrow river glade.

**Nakal** *(Gwich'in)* Cloudberry.

**Nalani** *(Hawaiian)* Calm skies.

**Naledi** *(Sotho)* Star.

**Nalini** *(Sanskrit)* Lovely.

**Nami** *(Japanese)* Wave.

**Namiko** *(Japanese)* Child of Nami.

**Nan** *See* Anne.

**Nanami** *(Japanese)* Seven seas.

# N

**Nancy, Nanette, Nanna, Nanny** *See* Anne.

**Nanuk** *(InupiaQ)* Polar bear.
*Variants:* Nanook, Nanuq.

**Naomi** *(Hebrew)* Pleasant one; *(Japanese)* Above all, beauty.
*Variants:* Naoma, Noami, Noemi, Nomi.

**Napea** *(Latin)* Of the valley.

**Nara** *(English)* Joyous; *(Indigenous Australian)* Companion;
*(Norse)* Nearest to.

**Narcissa** *(Greek)* Self-loving.

**Narda** *(Latin)* Fervently anointed.

**Narella, Narelle** *See* Helen.

**Narkeasha** *(African)* Pretty.

**Narmada** *(Hindu)* The name of a river.

**Nashwa** *(Egyptian)* Wonderful feeling.

**Nasiche** *(Ugandan)* Born during locust season.

**Nastassia, Nastassja, Nastasya, Nastaya, Nastya,
Nastyenka** *See* Anastasia.

**Natalie** *(Latin)* Child born at Christmas.
*Variants:* Nataline, Natica, Tally, Tasha; Nathalia, Nathalie
*(French)*; Nollaig *(Irish)*; Natale *(Italian)*; Natalia, Natalka,
Natasha, Natika *(Russian)*; Natala *(Slavic)*.
*See also* Noeline.

**Natane** *(Native American)* Daughter.

**Nataniella** *(Hebrew)* Gift of God. Feminine form of Nathaniel.

**Natasha** *See* Natalie.

**Natassia** *See* Anastasia.

**Natejda** *See* Nadia.

**Nathalia, Nathalie** *See* Natalie.

**Natica, Natika** *See* Natalie.

**Natsu** *(Japanese)* Summer.

# N

**Natsuko** *(Japanese)* Child of Natsu.

**Naysa** *(Hebrew)* Miracle of God.

**Nazirah** *(Arabic)* Equal; like.

**Neala** *(Gaelic)* Champion. Feminine form of Neal.

**Neci** *(Latin)* Intense; fiery.

**Neda** *(English)* Sanctuary; *(Slavic)* Born on Sunday.

**Nediva** *(Hebrew)* Noble and generous.

**Neelam** *(Hindu)* Sapphire.

**Neerja** *(Hindu)* Lotus flower.

**Nefertiti** *(Egyptian)* The beautiful one has come; the wife of
Pharaoh Amenhotep IV.

**Neha** *(Hindu)* Rain.

**Nelda** *(English)* Elder tree.

**Nell** *See* Helen.

**Nelleke** *(Dutch)* A horn.

**Nellie, Nelly** *See* Ellen, Helen.

**Neola** *(Greek)* Youthful.

**Neoma** *(Greek)* New moon.
*Variant:* Neomah.

**Neria** *(Hebrew)* Lamp of God; angel.

**Nerilee** *See* Nerolie.

**Nerine** *(Latin)* From the sea; nereids are sea nymphs in Greek
mythology.
*Variants:* Nerice, Nerissa, Nerita.

**Neroli** *(Italian)* Orange blossom.

**Nerolie** *(Italian)* Black. Feminine form of Nero.
*Variant:* Nerilee.

**Nessa** *(Greek)* Pure; *(Norse)* Headland.
*Variant:* Nessia.
*See also* Vanessa.

**Nesta** *See* Agnes.

**Netta** *(Latin)* Pure and tidy.
*See also* Antonia, Henrietta, Jane.

**Netti, Netty** *See* Antonia.

**Neva** *(Spanish)* Covered with snow.

**Nevada** *(Latin)* Snowy.

**Neysa, Neza** *See* Agnes.

**Nezhoni** *(Navajo)* Beautiful.

**Ngaio** *(Maori)* A tree.

**Ngaire** *(Maori)* Flax.
*Variant:* Nyree.

**Ngoc Lan** *(Vietnamese)* Magnolia.

**Nhu** *(Vietnamese)* Everything according to one's wishes.

**Nia** *(Swahili)* Purpose.

**Nicia** *(Greek)* Victorious army.

**Nicole** *(Greek)* The people's victory. Feminine form of
Nicholas.
*Variants:* Nichola *(English)*; Nicolette, Nicoline *(French)*;
Nicola, Nicoletta, Nicolina *(Italian)*.

**Nidra** *(Hindu)* Sleep; a goddess in Hindu mythology.

**Nika** *(Algonquin)* Goose; *(Russian)* Born on Sunday.

**Nike** *(Greek)* Victory.

**Nilini** *(Hindu)* Perpetuator of the Kuru race.

**Nimah** *(Arabic)* Blessing; loan.

**Nina, Ninette** *See* Anne.

**Niobe** *(Greek)* Fern.

**Nipi** *(InupiaQ)* Voice; sound.

**Nira** *(Hebrew)* Of the loom.

**Nirvana** *(Hindu)* Deep silence; ultimate bliss.

**Nisha** *(Hindu)* Night.

# N

**Nissa** *(Scandinavian)* Elf fairy who can only be seen by lovers.

**Nita** *(Native American)* Bear.
See also Anne.

**Nitara** *(Hindu)* Deeply rooted.

**Nitya** *(Hindu)* A name for the goddess Parvati in Hindu mythology.

**Nitzana** *(Hebrew)* Blossom.

**Nixie** *(Germanic)* Water sprite.

**Niyati** *(Hindu)* Fate.

**Noami** *See* Naomi.

**Nobantu** *(Zulu)* Mother of people.

**Noelani** *(Hawaiian)* Beautiful girl from heaven.

**Noeline** *(Germanic)* Born at Christmas. Feminine form of Noel.
*Variants:* Noelie, Noelita, Noella, Noelle; Nollaig *(Gaelic)*.
See also Natalie.

**Nola** *(Celtic)* Noble; famous.

**Noleta** *(Latin)* The unwilling.

**Nomalanga** *(Zulu)* The mother of sun/sunshine.

**Nomandla** *(Zulu)* The mother of strength.

**Nomi** *See* Naomi.

**Nomzamo** *(Zulu)* She who will endure trials.
*Variant:* Zami.

**Nona** *(Latin)* The ninth child.
*Variant:* Nonie.

**Nora** *(Irish) See* Helen.

**Norberta** *(Germanic)* Blond heroine.

**Nordica** *(Germanic)* From the north.

**Noreen** *(Gaelic)* Little Nora.
*Variants:* Noreena, Norene.
See also Nora.

**Nori** *(Japanese)* Doctrine.

**Noriko** *(Japanese)* Child of Nori.

**Norine** *(Latin)* Honour.

**Norma** *(Latin)* Model; the norm or rule.

**Nova** *(Latin)* New.

**Noya** *(Arabic)* Beautiful; ornamented.

**Nozumi** *(Japanese)* Hope.

**Nuna** *(InupiaQ)* Land; earth.

**Nuray** *(Turkish)* White moon.

**Nutabaq** *(InupiaQ)* Fresh snow.

**Nydia** *(Latin)* Refuge; nest.

**Nyree** *See* Ngaire.

**Nyx** *(Greek)* Night.

**Obelia** *(Greek)* Pillar of strength.

**Océane** *(French)* Ocean.

**Octavia** *(Latin)* Eighth child. Feminine form of Octavius.
   *Variants:* Octavie *(French)*; Ottavia *(Italian)*.

**Oda** *(Norse)* Small pointed spear.

**Odala** *See* Odette.

**Odelette** *(French, Greek)* Little song.

**Odelia** *(Germanic)* Little wealthy one; *(Hebrew)* Praise God.
   *See also* Odette.

# O

**Odella** *See* Odette.

**Odera** *(Hebrew)* Plough.

**Odessa** *(Greek)* Odyssey, journey, voyage.

**Odette** *(French)* Wealthy.
   *Variants:* Odelia, Odella, Odetta, Odila, Odilla, Odille, Othilia; Odala *(Germanic)*.

**Ofelia, Ofeliga, Ofilia** *See* Ophelia.

**Ohanna** *(Armenian)* God's gracious gift.

**Okelani** *(Hawaiian)* From heaven.

**Oksana** *(Russian)* Glory be to God.

**Oktavija** *See* Octavia.

**Olena** *See* Helen.

**Olesia** *(Polish)* Helper and defender of mankind.

**Olethea** *(Latin)* Truth.

**Olga** *(Russian)* Holy.
   *See also* Helga.

**Olimpia, Olimpias** *See* Olympia.

**Olinda** *(Germanic)* Protector of property.

**Olive** *(French)* Peace; *(Latin)* Olive tree; *(Norse)* Kind one.
   *Variant:* Olivia.

**Olympia** *(Greek)* Of Mount Olympus; heavenly.
   *Variants:* Olimpia, Olimpias, Olympias, Olympie, Pia; Olympe *(French)*.

**Omega** *(Greek)* Great; the last letter of the Greek alphabet.

**Ona** *See* Una.

**Onatah** *(Iroquois)* Corn goddess; fertility goddess.

**Ondine** *See* Undine.

**Onora** *See* Honoria.

**Oona, Oonagh** *See* Una.

**Opal** *(Sanskrit)* Jewel.

# O

**Ophelia** *(Greek)* Useful; wise; a serpent.
*Variants:* Ofelia, Ofilia, Phelia; Ophelie *(French)*.

**Ophira** *(Greek)* Gold.

**Oprah** *(Hebrew)* Fawn.

**Ora** *(Latin)* Sea coast.

**Oralia** *(Latin)* Golden; light.
*Variants:* Oralie, Oriel.

**Orane** *(French)* Rising.

**Orianna** *(Latin)* Golden; dawning.
*Variants:* Oriana, Oriande, Oriante.

**Oribel** *(Latin)* Golden beauty.

**Oriel** *(English)* A window.
*See also* Oralia.

**Orinda** *(Germanic)* Fire serpent.

**Oriole** *(Latin)* Fair-haired.

**Orla** *(Latin)* Golden woman.
*Variant:* Orlaith *(Gaelic)*.

**Orlanda** *(Latin)* Bright sun. Feminine form of Orlando.

**Orlantha** *(Germanic)* From the land.

**Orlena** *(Latin)* The golden one.

**Orsa, Orsola** *See* Ursula.

**Ortense** *See* Hortense.

**Ortensia** *(Latin)* Gardener; farmer.

**Orva** *(Anglo-Saxon)* Courageous friend.

**Othilia** *See* Odette.

**Ottavia** *See* Octavia.

**Ove** *(Norse)* Awe; the spear's point.

**Owethu** *(Zulu)* "She is ours."

# P

**Pablan** *(InupiaQ)* Welcome; greeting.

**Padma** *(Hindu)* A river in Bangladesh; a goddess in Hindu mythology.

**Pagan** *(Latin)* Villager.

**Page** *(English)* Attendant.
*Variant:* Paige.

**Paikea** *(Maori)* Whale.
*Variant:* Pai.

**Pakma** *(InupiaQ)* Heaven.

**Palma** *(English)* Palm-bearing pilgrim.

**Paloma** *(Spanish)* Dove.

**Pamela** *(Greek)* Honeyed; sweetness.
*Variants:* Pam, Pamelina, Pamella.

**Pandora** *(Greek)* Talented; gifted.

**Paniga** *(InupiaQ)* My daughter.

**Pansophia** *(Greek)* All wisdom.
*Variant:* Pansofia.
*See also* Sophia.

**Pansy** *(French)* Thought; *(Greek)* The name of a fragrant flower.

**Panya** *(Latin)* Crowned with laurel; mouse; small child.

**Panyin** *(Ghanaian)* Older of twins.

**Paola, Paolina** *See* Paula.

**Papillon** *(French)* Butterfly.

# P

**Parisa** *(Persian)* Angelic face.

**Parnel** *See* Petrina.

**Parnika** *(Hindu)* An auspicious spirit in Hindu mythology.
*Variant:* Parnita.

**Parvani** *(Hindu)* Full moon.

**Parvati** *(Hindu)* A goddess in Hindu mythology.

**Pascale** *(French)* Easter child.
*Variants:* Paschale, Pasquette; Pascha *(English)*.

**Patia** *(Spanish)* Leaf.

**Patience** *(Latin)* Suffering; endurance.

**Patricia** *(Latin)* Noble one. Feminine form of Patrick.
*Variants:* Patreeza, Patrice, Patrizia, Patsy, Patty, Trish,
Trisha, Tricia.

**Paula** *(Latin)* Petite.
*Variants:* Paule, Paulina; Paulette, Pauline *(French)*; Paola,
Paolina *(Italian)*; Pavla, Pavlinca *(Russian)*; Paulita
*(Spanish)*.

**Payal** *(Hindu)* Anklet.

**Payton** *(English)* Warrior's estate.

**Pazia** *(Hebrew)* Golden.

**Peace** *(Latin)* Peace.

**Pearl** *(English)* Pearl.
*Variants:* Pearla, Perle.
*See also* Margaret.

**Peg, Pegeen, Peggy** *See* Margaret.

**Pelagia** *(Greek)* From the sea.

**Pemba** *(African)* The force of present existence.

**Penda** *(Swahili)* Love.

**Penelope** *(Greek)* Weaver; faithful.
*Variants:* Pennie, Penny.

# P

**Penina** *(Hebrew)* Jewel; coral.

**Pennie, Penny** *See* Penelope.

**Penthea** *(Greek)* Fifth child; mourner.

**Peony** *(Greek)* The name of a flower.

**Pepin** *(Germanic)* Perseverance.

**Pepita** *See* Josephine.

**Pepper** *(English)* The name of a plant.

**Perdita** *(Latin)* Lost.

**Perizada** *(Persian)* Persian woman.

**Perle** *See* Pearl.

**Perouze** *(Armenian)* Turquoise.

**Perri** *(English)* Wanderer.

**Persephone** *(Greek)* Bearer of death; the goddess of the underworld in Greek mythology.

**Persis** *(Greek)* Woman from Persia.

**Petrina** *(Greek)* A rock or stone. Feminine form of Peter. *Variants:* Peta, Petra, Petrea; Petronella *(English)*; Perrine *(French)*; Parnel *(Irish)*; Petronilla, Petronille *(Italian)*; Petronia *(Spanish)*.

**Petula** *(Latin)* Impatient; seeker.

**Petunia** *(Indian)* The name of a flower.

**Phaedora** *(Greek)* Gift from God.

**Phaedra** *See* Phedra.

**Phanessa** *See* Vanessa.

**Phebe** *See* Phoebe.

**Phedra** *(Greek)* Shining one. *Variant:* Phaedra.

**Phelia** *See* Ophelia.

**Philadelphia** *(Greek)* Brotherly love; place name.

# P

**Philana** *(Greek)* Adoring.

**Philippa** *(Greek)* Horse lover. Feminine form of Philip.
*Variants:* Felipa, Filippa, Phillipa.

**Phillida** *See* Phyllis.

**Phillipa** *See* Philippa.

**Philomena** *(Greek)* Song lover; nightingale who sings to the moon.

**Phoebe** *(Greek)* The goddess of the moon in Greek mythology.
*Variant:* Phebe.

**Phoena** *(Greek)* Mystical bird; purple.

**Phoolan** *(Hindu)* Flower.

**Phryne** *(Greek)* Pale and delicate.

**Phuong** *(Vietnamese)* Destiny.

**Phyllis** *(Greek)* Leafy branch; dear one.
*Variants:* Fillis, Phillida, Phillyda, Phyllida, Phyllys.

**Pia** *(Italian)* Devout.
*See also* Olympia.

**Pilar** *(Indigenous Australian)* A spear; *(Spanish)* Pillar.

**Piper** *(English)* Bagpipe player.

**Pixie** *(Celtic)* Small elf; fairy.

**Pixiun** *(InupiaQ)* Blessing; passing of power from a shaman.

**Piyali** *(Hindu)* Tree.

**Placida** *(Latin)* Tranquil; calm.

**Polly** *See* Mary.

**Pooja** *(Hindu)* Prayer.
*Variant:* Puja.

**Poppy** *(English)* The name of a flower.

**Portia** *(Latin)* A gift or offering; safe harbour.

# P

**Prabha** *(Hindu)* Lustrous.

**Prama** *(Hindu)* Knowing truth.

**Pramada** *(Hindu)* Woman.

**Pranati** *(Hindu)* Prayer.

**Prashanti** *(Hindu)* Peace.

**Pratima** *(Hindu)* Image.

**Preeti** *(Hindu)* Love.

**Preita** *(Finnish)* Most loving one.

**Preyasi** *See* Prita.

**Prima** *(Italian)* First child.

**Primavera** *(Latin)* Spring's beginning.

**Primrose** *(English)* Small spring flower; *(Latin)* First rose.

**Priscilla** *(Latin)* From ancient times.
  *Variants:* Cilla, Prisca, Priscella.

**Prita** *(Hindu)* Dear one; beloved.
  *Variants:* Preyasi, Pritika, Priya.

**Prudence** *(Latin)* Foresight; discretion.
  *Variants:* Prudencia, Prudentia, Prue.

**Prunella** *(Latin)* Little plum.

**Psyche** *(Greek)* The soul.

**Purvaja** *(Hindu)* Elder sister.

**Pyrena** *(Greek)* Fiery.

**Pythia** *(Greek)* Prophet.

# Q

**Qadira** *(Arabic)* Powerful.

**Qalukisaq** *(InupiaQ)* Butterfly.

**Qamra** *(Arabic)* Moon.

**Qannik** *(InupiaQ)* Snowflake.

**Qitarah** *(Arabic)* Fragrant.

**Quartilla** *(Latin)* Fourth child.

**Qubilah** *(Arabic)* Agreeable.

**Queenie** *(English)* A pet name for girls called Victoria during Queen Victoria's reign.
*Variants:* Queena, Queeny.

**Quella** *(English)* Pacify.

**Quenby** *(Scandinavian)* Womanly.

**Querida** *(Spanish)* Beloved.

**Questa** *(French)* Searcher.

**Quinn** *(Gaelic)* Wise; *(Greek)* Queen.

**Quintessa** *(Latin)* Essence.

**Quintina** *(Latin)* Fifth child.
*Variants:* Quinta, Quintella.

**Quirita** *(Latin)* Citizen.

**Quitterie** *(French)* Tranquil.

# R

**Rachel** *(Hebrew)* Little lamb; one with purity.
　*Variants:* Rachael, Raechael, Raychela, Shelley; Rachelle, Racquel *(French)*; Rahel *(Germanic)*; Rachele *(Italian)*; Raoghnailt *(Scottish)*; Raquel *(Spanish)*.

**Radella** *(English)* Elfin advisor.

**Radhika** *(Hindu)* The wife of Krishna in Hindu mythology.

**Radinka** *(Slavic)* Active.

**Rae** *(Scandinavian)* Doe.

**Raeka** *(Spanish)* Beautiful; unique.

**Raelin** *(Celtic)* Unknown.

**Ragnhild** *(Norse)* Wise in battle.

**Rahel** *See* Rachel.

**Rai** *(Japanese)* Trust.

**Raimonda** *See* Ramona.

**Rain, Raina** *See* Regina.

**Raissa** *(French)* Thinker.

**Raizel** *(Hebrew)* Rose.
　*Variant:* Raissa *(Greek)*.

**Ralia** *See* Rose.

**Ramla** *(Egyptian)* One who predicts the future.

**Ramona** *(Germanic, Spanish)* Wise protector. Feminine form of Raymond.
　*Variants:* Raimonda, Ramonda.

# R

**Ramya** *(Hindu)* Elegant; beautiful.

**Randi** *(English)* Strong defender. Feminine form of Randall.
*Variant:* Randy.

**Rane** *(Norwegian)* Queen; pure.

**Rani** *(Hindu)* A queen.

**Rania** *(Sanskrit)* Royal.

**Raoghnailt** *See* Rachel.

**Raphaela** *(Hebrew)* Divine healer.
*Variants:* Rafaella, Raphaella.

**Raquel** *See* Rachel.

**Rasche** *See* Rose.

**Rashida** *(African)* Righteous.

**Rasine** *(Polish)* Rose.

**Rata** *(Indigenous Australian)* The name of a plant; *(Polynesian)*
A great Polynesian chief.

**Rati** *(Hindu)* A goddess in Hindu mythology; *(Sanskrit)* Love
and desire.

**Rayna** *(Hebrew)* Pure; clean.

**Raziya** *(African)* Agreeable.

**Rea** *See* Rhea.

**Rebecca** *(Hebrew)* Compliant wife; bound; tied.
*Variants:* Becky, Reba, Rebeca, Rebeccah, Rebekah, Rifke,
Rivkah; Rebekka *(Germanic)*; Rebeka *(Hungarian)*.
*See also* Beka.

**Regina** *(Latin)* Queenly.
*Variants:* Regan *(Gaelic)*; Reina, Reinha *(Portuguese)*; Reyna.

**Rei** *(Japanese)* Gratitude; ceremony.

**Reiko** *(Japanese)* Child of Rei.

**Reinha** *(Portuguese)* Queen; queenly.
*See also* Regina.

# R

**Rekha** *(Hindu)* Straight line.

**Remy** *(French)* From Rheims.

**Ren** *(Japanese)* Water lily; intelligence.

**Rena** *(Greek)* Peace; *(Hebrew)* Joyous song.

**Renata** *(Latin)* Reborn.
*Variants:* Rena, Renate, Rene, Renee.

**Renita** *(Latin)* To be firm.

**Renwien** *See* Rowena.

**Reseda** *(Latin)* Healing.

**Reshma** *(Hindu)* Silky.

**Revati** *(Hindu)* The wife of Balarama, elder brother of Krishna in Hindu mythology.

**Reyna** *See* Regina.

**Rhea** *(Greek)* Stream; *(Latin)* Poppy.
*Variant:* Rea.

**Rhiamon** *(Welsh)* Witch.

**Rhian** *(Welsh)* Maiden.

**Rhiannon** *(Welsh)* A nymph in Welsh mythology.
*Variant:* Riannon.

**Rhoda** *(Greek)* Rose.
*Variants:* Rhodanthe, Rhodeia, Rhodia.

**Rhonda** *(Celtic)* Good spear; a valley in Wales.

**Rhonwen** *(Celtic)* White skirt.
*See also* Rowena.

**Rhoswen** *(Gaelic)* White rose.

**Ria** *(Spanish)* Mouth of a river.
*See also* Mary.

**Riannon** *See* Rhiannon.

**Richelle** *(English)* Brave one; *(Germanic)* Powerful ruler.

# R

**Rihana** *(Arabic)* Sweet basil.
*Variant:* Rihanna.

**Riko** *(Japanese)* Jasmine child.

**Rina** *(Greek)* Pure; *(Hindu)* Queen.

**Rini** *(Japanese)* Little bunny.

**Riona** *(Gaelic)* Queenly.
*Variants:* Rioghnach, Rionagh.

**Risa** *(Latin)* Laughing one.

**Rishona** *(Hebrew)* First.

**Rita** *(Greek)* Pearl; precious; *(Sanskrit)* Order; law.
*See also* Margaret.

**Riva** *(French)* River.

**Rivkah, Rivke** *See* Rebecca.

**Roberta** *(English)* Bright; famous. Feminine form of Robert.
*Variants:* Bobbette, Robertina; Robine, Robinetta, Robinette
*(French)*; Robena, Robina, Robyn *(Gaelic)*; Robin, Ruperta
*(Germanic)*.

**Rochelle** *(French)* Little rock.

**Roderica** *(Germanic)* Famous one. Feminine form of
Roderick.

**Rogan** *(Gaelic)* Red-haired.

**Rohana** *(Sanskrit)* Sandalwood.

**Rohesia** *See* Rose.

**Roisin** *(Irish)* Little dark rose.
*See also* Rose.

**Romana** *(Italian)* From Rome.

**Romilda** *(Germanic)* Glorious battle maid.

**Rona** *(Gaelic)* Covenant; oath.

**Ronalda** *(Norse)* Mighty. Feminine form of Ronald.

# R

**Rosa** *See* Rose.

**Rosabel** *(Latin)* Beautiful rose.
*Variant:* Rosabella.
*See also* Rose.

**Rosalba** *(Latin)* White rose.
*See also* Rose.

**Rosaleen** *See* Rose.

**Rosalia** *(Italian)* Melody.
*See also* Rose.

**Rosalie, Rosalija** *See* Rose.

**Rosalind** *(Germanic)* Horse serpent; *(Spanish)* Pretty rose.
*Variants:* Rosalinde, Rosalynd, Rosalynde.
*See also* Rose.

**Rosalinda, Rosalinde** *See* Rosalind.

**Rosamund** *(Germanic)* Pure rose.
*Variants:* Rosamunde, Rosemund, Rosemunde.

**Rosanne** *(Latin)* Gracious rose.

**Rose** *(Latin)* The name of a flower.
*Variants:* Rosalia, Rosalind, Rosalinda, Rosalinde, Roseanna, Roseanne, Rosel, Roslyn, Royce; Rosie *(English)*; Roesia, Rosalie *(French)*; Rohesia, Royse, Roysia *(Germanic)*; Roisin, Rosaleen *(Irish)*; Rosa, Rosabel, Rosabella, Rosalba, Rosetta, Rosina *(Italian)*; Roseta, Rosita *(Spanish)*.

**Rosemary** *(Latin)* A herb symbolizing remembrance.
*Variants:* Rosemare, Rosemari, Rosemarie, Rose Marie.

**Roseta, Rosetta** *See* Rose.

**Roshni** *(Hindu)* Light.

**Rosie, Rosina, Rosita** *See* Rose.

**Roslin** *(French)* Little red-haired one.

**Roslyn** *See* Rose.

**Rowena** *(English)* Rugged; *(Gaelic)* Red-haired.
  *Variants:* Renwien, Rhonwen.

**Roxanna** *(Persian)* Brilliant one.
  *Variant:* Roxanne.

**Ruby** *(French)* A red gemstone.

**Rudrani** *(Hindu)* One of the wives of the god Shiva in Hindu mythology.

**Rue** *(Latin)* The name of a herb; regret.

**Rumer** *(English)* Gypsy.

**Runa** *(Scandinavian)* Secret lore.

**Ruperta** *See* Roberta.

**Ruth** *(Hebrew)* Compassionate friend.
  *Variants:* Rutha *(Lithuanian)*; Ruthe, Ruthi, Ruthia, Ruthie.

**Ryba** *(Czech)* Fish.

**Saba** *(Greek)* Woman of Sheba.

**Sabah** *(Arabic)* Morning.

**Sabar** *(Hindu)* Patient; enduring.

**Sabiha** *(Hindu)* Beautiful.

**Sabina** *(Latin)* Woman of the Sabine people in ancient Italy.
  *Variants:* Sabin, Sabine *(French)*; Saidhbhin *(Irish)*; Savina *(Italian)*.

**Sabirah** *(Arabic)* Patient.

**Sabra** *(Arabic)* Thorny cactus; *(Hebrew)* To rest.

# S

**Sabrina** *(Hindu)* Princess; *(Latin)* From the borderland; the goddess of the Severn River in Celtic mythology.

*Variant:* Brina.

**Sacha** *See* Alexandra.

**Sachi** *(Hindu)* The goddess of wrath and jealousy in Hindu mythology; *(Japanese)* Bliss-child.

**Sadako** *(Japanese)* Chaste.

**Sade** *(Nigerian)* Honour confers a crown.

**Sadie** *See* Mercedes, Sarah.

**Sadira** *(Arabic)* Ostrich returning from water.

**Saffi** *(Danish)* Wisdom.

**Saffron** *(English)* The name of a flower and a spice.

**Safiya** *(African)* Pure.

**Sagara** *(Hindu)* Ocean.

**Sahara** *(Arabic)* The moon; the world's largest desert.

**Saheli** *(Hindu)* Friend.

**Sahiba** *(Hindu)* Lady.

**Sahila** *(Hindu)* Guide.

**Sai** *(Japanese)* Intelligence.

**Saida** *(Arabic)* Fortunate one.

*See also* Sarah.

**Saidah** *(African)* Happy; fortunate.

**Saika** *(Japanese)* Colourful flower.

**Sajni** *(Hindu)* Beloved.

**Sakinah** *(Arabic)* God-inspired peace of mind; tranquility.

**Sakti** *(Hindu)* Energy; goodness.

**Sakura** *(Japanese)* Cherry blossoms.

**Salaidh** *See* Sarah.

**Salena** *(Greek)* Salt.

*See also* Salina.

# S

**Salihah** *(African)* Correct.

**Salimah** *(Arabic)* Safe; healthy.

**Salina** *(Latin)* By the salt water; solemn.
*See also* Salena.

**Sallie, Sally** *See* Sarah.

**Salome** *(Hebrew)* Peace; asked of God.
*Variant:* Saloma.

**Saloni** *(Hindu)* Dear; beautiful.

**Salwa** *(Arabic)* Solace; comfort.

**Samantha** *(Aramaic)* A good listener.

**Samara** *(Hebrew)* Mountain; outlook; ruled by God; guarded by God; *(Latin)* Seedling.

**Samirah** *(Arabic)* Entertaining companion.

**Samma** *(Arabic)* Sky.

**Samuela** *(Hebrew)* Heard by God. Feminine form of Samuel.

**Sancia** *(Latin)* Holy.

**Sandra, Sandrine** *See* Alexandra, Cassandra.

**Sandya** *(Hindu)* Sunset time; a god in Hindu mythology.

**Sangita** *(Hindu)* Musical.

**Sanjula** *(Hindu)* Beautiful.

**Sapna** *(Hindu)* Dream.

**Sapphire** *(Hebrew)* Precious jewel; a blue gemstone.
*Variant:* Sapphira *(Greek)*.

**Sarah** *(Hebrew)* Princess.
*Variants:* Sade, Sadie, Sadye, Saida, Sallie, Sally, Sarene, Saretta, Sarette, Sarie, Sarine, Sayda, Sirri, Zahra, Zara, Zarah, Zaras, Zaria; Sari *(Finnish)*; Sara *(French, Germanic, Greek)*; Salaidh, Sorcha *(Gaelic)*; Sarka *(Hungarian)*; Morag *(Scottish)*; Sarita *(Spanish)*.

# S

**Sarai** *(Hebrew)* Quarrelsome.

**Saraid** *(Celtic)* Excellent.
*Variant:* Saraidh.
*See also* Sarah.

**Sarasa** *(Sanskrit)* Beautiful; gracious.

**Sarasvati** *(Hindu)* One of the three great goddesses in Hindu mythology.

**Sarea** *(Hebrew)* Name of an angel.

**Saree** *(Arabic)* Most noble.

**Sarene, Saretta, Sarette, Sari, Sarie** *See* Sarah.

**Sarika** *(Hindu)* A thrush.

**Sarine** *See* Sarah.

**Sarisha** *(Hindu)* Charming.

**Sarita** *(Hindu)* Stream; river.
*See also* Sarah.

**Sarka** *See* Sarah.

**Sarkara** *(Sanskrit)* Sugar; sweetness.

**Sashenka** *See* Alexandra.

**Savanna** *(Spanish)* Open plain.
*Variant:* Savannah.

**Savarna** *(Hindu)* Daughter of the ocean.

**Savina** *See* Sabina.

**Savita** *(Hindu)* The sun.

**Saxon** *(Latin)* Large stone; skilled with a sword.

**Sayda** *See* Sarah.

**Scarlet** *(English)* Deep red.
*Variant:* Scarlett.

**Scota** *(Latin)* An Irish woman.

**Seanna** *(Celtic)* God's grace. Feminine form of Sean.
*See also* Jane.

**Sebastianne** *(Latin)* Revered one. Feminine form of Sebastian.

**Seema** *(Hebrew)* Treasure.

**Sela** *(Hebrew)* A rock.

**Selby** *(English)* Of the manor house farm.

**Selena** *(Greek)* The moon.
*Variant:* Selene.

**Selima** *(Arabic)* Peace.

**Selma** *(Scandinavian)* Divinely protected.

**Semele** *(Latin)* Once.

**Semine** *(Danish)* The goddess of the sun, moon, and stars.

**Sennett** *(French)* Wise one.

**Senta** *(Germanic)* Assistant.

**Septima** *(Latin)* Seventh born.

**Seraphina** *(Hebrew)* Afire; angel; seraph.
*Variants:* Sarafina, Serafina, Seraphine.

**Serena** *(Latin)* Peaceful one; calm.

**Serilda** *(Germanic)* Armed maiden of war.

**Sesha** *(Hindu)* "That which remains"; a snake deity that symbolizes time in Hindu mythology.

**Seskiku** *(Maliseet)* "She is beautiful."

**Sevati** *(Hindu)* White rose.

**Sevita** *(Hindu)* Beloved.

**Shaina** *(Hebrew)* Beautiful.
*Variants:* Shana, Shaine.

**Shakira** *(Arabic)* Grateful.

**Shako** *(Native American)* Mint.

**Shalom** *(Hebrew)* Peace.

**Shamita** *(Hindu)* Peacemaker.

# S

**Shana** *See* Shaina.

**Shanata** *(Hindu)* Peaceful.

**Shandy** *(English)* Rambunctious.

**Shane** *See* Jane.

**Shani** *(Swahili)* Marvellous.

**Shannelle** *(French)* Channel.

**Shannon** *(Irish)* Wise one; slow waters; the name of a river.
  *Variant:* Sinann.

**Shantah** *(Hindu)* Peace; a god in Hindu mythology.

**Shantelle** *See* Chantal.

**Sharee** *See* Sharon.

**Sharleen, Sharlene** *See* Caroline.

**Sharon** *(Hebrew)* Princess.
  *Variants:* Sharee, Sharne, Sharolyn.

**Sharyl** *See* Cheryl.

**Shashi** *(Hindu)* The moon; moonbeam.

**Shasmecka** *(African)* Princess.

**Shauna** *See* Jane.

**Shayndel** *(Hebrew)* Beautiful.

**Sheba** *See* Bathsheba.

**Sheelagh** *See* Cecilia.

**Sheena, Sheenah** *See* Jane.

**Sheetal** *(Hindu)* Cool.

**Sheila, Sheilah** *See* Cecilia.

**Shela** *(Celtic)* Musical.

**Shelagh** *See* Cecilia.

**Shelby** *(English)* Sheltered town.

**Shelley** *(English)* Edge of the meadow.
  *See also* Rachel.

# S

**Shena** *See* Jane.

**Sherrill, Sherry, Sheryl** *See* Cheryl.

**Shiloh** *(Hebrew)* Peaceful one.

**Shika** *(Japanese)* Deer.

**Shimona** *(Hebrew)* Little princess.
*Variant:* Mona.

**Shin** *(Gwich'in)* Summer; *(Korean)* Belief.

**Shina** *(Japanese)* Virtue; good.

**Shiori** *(Japanese)* Woven poem.

**Shira** *(Hebrew)* Song.

**Shirley** *(English)* Country meadow.

**Shobi** *(Hebrew)* Glorious.

**Shona** *See* Jane.

**Shoshannah** *(Hebrew)* Rose.

**Shreya** *(Hindu)* Auspicious.

**Shri** *(Hindu)* Lustre.
*Variant:* Shree.

**Siân** *See* Jane.

**Sibil, Sibley** *See* Sybil.

**Sibongile** *(Zulu)* "We are grateful."

**Sidonia** *(Italian)* From the city of Sidonia.

**Sidra** *(Latin)* Like a star.

**Sienna** *(Italian)* Reddish brown colour.

**Sierra** *(Spanish)* Sawtooth mountain range.

**Signe** *(Swedish)* A sign; victorious.
*Variant:* Signy.

**Sigourney** *(French)* From the town of Sigournais.

**Sigrid** *(Norse)* Winning adviser.

# S

**Siku** *(InupiaQ)* Ice.

**Sileas** *See* Cecilia.

**Silvana** *See* Sylvia.

**Silver** *(English)* A precious metal.

**Silvia, Silvie** *See* Sylvia.

**Simba** *(Swahili)* Lion.

**Simcha** *(Hebrew)* Joy in life.

**Simone** *(Hebrew)* One who hears.
   *Variant:* Simona.

**Simoni** *(Hindu)* Obedient.

**Sine, Sinead, Siobhan** *See* Jane.

**Sipala** *(Hopi)* Peach.

**Siphesihle** *(Zulu)* Beautiful gift.

**Siran** *(Armenian)* Alluring.

**Sirena** *(Greek)* Siren; sweet singer.

**Siroun** *(Armenian)* Lovely.

**Sirri** *See* Sarah.

**Sisi** *(African)* Born on a Sunday.

**Sita** *(Sanskrit)* Furrow.

**Sitara** *(Sanskrit)* Morning star.

**Sitembile** *(African)* Trust.

**Siv** *(Norwegian)* Kinship; the wife of Thor, god of thunder in
   Norse mythology.

**Smita** *(Hindu)* Smiling.
   *Variants:* Shusmita, Sushmita.

**Sofi Sofia, Sofie** *See* Sophia.

**Solace** *(Latin)* Comfort.

# S

**Solana** *(Spanish)* Sunshine.

**Solange** *(French)* Rare jewel.

**Soleil** *(French)* Sun.

**Solita** *(Latin)* Alone.

**Somatra** *(Hindu)* Greater than the moon.

**Sona** *(Hindu)* Gold.

**Sonakshi** *(Hindu)* Golden eye.

**Sondra** *See* Alexandra.

**Sonia** *See* Sophia.

**Sonnenschein** *(Germanic)* Sunshine.

**Sonya** *See* Sophia.

**Soo** *(Korean)* Excellence; long life.

**Sophia** *(Greek)* Wisdom; the name of a saint.
  *Variants:* Sopi *(Abenaki)*; Sofi, Sophy; Sofie *(Dutch)*;
  Sophie *(English)*; Zofia, Zosia *(Polish)*; Sonia, Sonya
  *(Russian)*; Sofia *(Scandinavian)*.
  *See also* Pansophia.

**Sophronia** *(Greek)* Foresighted.

**Sophy** *See* Sophia.

**Sorano** *(Japanese)* Of the sky.

**Sorcha** *See* Sarah.

**Sosanna** *See* Susan.

**Sparrow** *(English)* A bird.

**Spica** *(Latin)* Name of a star.

**Spring** *(English)* The season.

**Stacia, Stacie, Stacy** *See* Anastasia.

**Stefanie, Steffanie, Steffie** *See* Stephanie.

**Stella** *See* Esther.

# S

**Stephanie** *(French)* Crown; garland. Feminine form of
Stephen.
*Variants:* Etienette, Ettienette, Stefanie, Steffanie; Steffi
*(Germanic)*; Stepania, Stephana, Stevana, Stevie *(Greek)*;
Stephania *(Latin)*; Estephania *(Spanish)*.

**Stevana, Stevie** *See* Stephanie.

**Stockard** *(English)* Yard of tree stumps. ›

**Storm** *(English)* Stormy weather; tempest.

**Su** *See* Susan.

**Sudevi** *(Hindu)* A wife of Krishna in Hindu mythology.

**Sue, Suisan, Suke, Sukey** *See* Susan.

**Suki** *(Japanese)* Beloved.

**Sukie** *See* Susan.

**Sukutai** *(African)* Hug.

**Sula** *See* Ursula.

**Suluk** *(InupiaQ)* Wing feather.

**Sumehra** *(Arabic)* Beautiful face.

**Sumey** *(Asian)* Flower.

**Sumi** *(Japanese)* Clear; refined.

**Summer** *(English)* The season.

**Sun** *(Korean)* Goodness.

**Sunita** *(Hindu)* A daughter of the god Dharma in Hindu
mythology.

**Surya** *(Hindu)* The sun.

**Susan** *(Hebrew)* Lily.
*Variants:* Su, Suisan, Suzann, Zusanne; Zuza *(Czech)*; Sue,
Suke, Sukey, Sukie, Susanna, Susannah, Suse, Susie, Susy,
Suze, Suzie *(English)*; Zsazsa, Zsuzsa *(Hungarian)*; Susette,
Suzanna, Suzanne, Suzette *(French)*; Sosanna *(Irish)*; Xuxa
*(Portuguese)*; Suska *(Slavic)*; Susana *(Spanish)*.

**Sushanti** *(Hindu)* Peace.

**Sushmita** *See* Smita.

**Susie** *See* Susan.

**Susila** *(Hindu)* Wife of Krishna.

**Suska, Susy, Suzann, Suzanna, Suzanne, Suze, Suzette, Suzie** *See* Susan.

**Svetlana** *(Russian)* Star.

**Sybil** *(Greek)* Wise, prophetic.
*Variants:* Sibil, Sibley, Sibyl.

**Sydelle** *(Hebrew)* Princess.

**Sydney** *(English)* From the city of Saint Denis.

**Sylvia** *(Latin)* From the forest; the mother of Romulus and Remus in Roman mythology.
*Variants:* Silvana, Silvia, Silvie, Sylvaine; Sylvie *(French)*.

**Syna** *(Greek)* Two together.

**Tabitha** *(Hebrew)* Gazelle.

**Tacita** *(Latin)* To be silent.
*Variant:* Tace.

**Tadhaa** *(Gwich'in)* Golden eagle.

**Tahirah** *(Arabic)* Chaste; pure.
*Variant:* Tahira.

**Taimufa** *(InupiaQ)* Forever.

**Taka** *(Japanese)* Tall; honourable.

# T

**Takara** *(Japanese)* Treasure; precious object.

**Takiyah** *(North African)* Pious; righteous.

**Talia** *(Greek)* Blooming; *(Hebrew)* Dew from heaven;
  *(Indigenous Australian)* Near a waterway.
  *See also* Atalaya.

**Talitha** *(Aramaic)* Young woman.

**Tallulah** *(Native Indian)* Leaping water.

**Tally** *See* Natalie.

**Talya** *See* Atalaya.

**Tam** *(Vietnamese)* Heart.

**Tama** *(Native American)* Thunderbolt.

**Tamara** *(Hebrew)* Palm tree; *(Sanskrit)* Spice.
  *Variants:* Tamar, Tammie, Tammy, Thamar.

**Tamasine** *See* Thomasina.

**Tammie, Tammy** *See* Tamara.

**Tamsin, Tamsyn, Tamzin** *See* Thomasina.

**Tanaka** *(Japanese)* Dweller.

**Tania** *See* Titania.

**Tani** *(Japanese)* Sweetheart; *(Melanesian)* Youth.

**Tansy** *(English)* A golden yellow flower.

**Tanis** *(Cree)* Daughter.

**Tanya** *See* Titania.

**Tapanga** *(African)* Sweet; unpredictable.

**Tara** *(Gaelic)* Rocky crag; a place in Ireland, the historic seat
  of high kings; *(Hindu)* Tower.

**Tarn** *(Scandinavian)* Mountain lake.

**Taryn** *(Greek)* Queen.

**Tasha** *See* Natalie.

**Tasia** *See* Anastasia.

# T

**Tate** *(English)* Cheerful one.

**Tatiana** *(Latin)* Silver-haired.
  *Variants:* Tatianna, Tatjana, Tatyana.

**Tatum** *(English)* Cheerful; light-hearted.
  *See also* Tate.

**Tavia** *See* Octavia.

**Tawnie** *(English)* Little one; yellowish brown.

**Taylor** *(English)* Tailor; *(French)* To cut.

**Tegan** *(Celtic)* Doe.

**Tekla** *(Greek)* Divine fame.

**Tema** *(Hebrew)* Righteous; a palm tree.

**Temina** *(Hebrew)* Honest.

**Tempe** *(Greek)* Beautiful; delightful; charming.

**Tempest** *(French)* Storm.

**Templa** *(Latin)* Temple; sanctuary.

**Teodora** *See* Theodora.

**Terena** *(Latin)* Earthly.

**Terentia** *(Greek)* Guardian.

**Teresa, Terese, Teresija, Teresina, Teresita, Tereza, Terry** *See* Theresa.

**Tertia** *(Latin)* The third.

**Tesia** *(Polish)* Loved by God.

**Tessa** *(Italian)* Countess.
  *See also* Theresa.

**Thabang** *(Sesotho)* "Be happy."

**Thadine** *(Hebrew)* Praised.

**Thais** *(Greek)* The bond.
  *Variant:* Thaïs *(French)*.

**Thalente** *(Zulu)* Talent; gift from God.

# T

**Thalia** *(Greek)* Blooming; plentiful.

**Than** *(Greek)* Death; *(Vietnamese)* Brilliant.

**Thana** *(Arabic)* Gratitude.

**Thandeka** *(Zulu)* Lovely.

**Thandi** *See* Thandiwe.

**Thandiwe** *(Zulu)* Beloved.
*Variant:* Thandi.

**Thanh** *(Chinese)* Blue.

**Thank** *(Vietnamese)* Tranquil.

**Thara** *(Arabic)* Wealth.

**Thea** *(Greek)* Goddess; a Titan in Greek mythology.
*See also* Althea, Anthea, Dorothy, Theodora.

**Thecia** *(Greek)* Divine.
*Variant:* Thecie.

**Thelma** *(Greek)* Will; desire.
*Variant:* Thelmai.

**Theodora** *(Greek)* Gift of God.
*Variants:* Tedora, Thea, Theadora, Theodosia; Teodora
*(Italian, Spanish)*; Feodora *(Russian)*.
*See also* Thea.

**Theophania** *See* Tiffany.

**Theophilia** *(Greek)* Loved by God.
*Variant:* Theofilia.

**Thera** *(Greek)* Wild.

**Theresa** *(Latin)* To harvest.
*Variants:* Talaz *(Abenaki)*; Teresa, Terese, Tressa; Tereza
*(Czech)*; Terry, Tessa *(English)*; Therese *(French)*; Theresia,
Tresa *(Germanic)*; Tresca *(Greek)*; Tracie, Tracy *(Irish)*;
Teresina *(Italian)*; Zilya *(Russian)*; Terezija *(Slovenian)*;
Teresita *(Spanish)*.

**Thetis** *(Greek)* Silver-footed; Achilles' mother in Greek mythology.

**Thia** *See* Anthea.

**Thirza** *(Hebrew)* Sweet-natured; cypress tree.

**Thisbe** *(Greek)* Where the doves live.

**Thistle** *(English)* Thistle.

**Thomasina** *(Aramaic)* A twin. Feminine form of Thomas. *Variants:* Tamasine, Tamsin, Tamsyn, Tamzin, Thomasa, Thomasin, Thomasine.

**Thora** *(Norse)* Thunder. Feminine form of Thor.

**Thyrza** *(Greek)* Staff; wand.

**Tia** *(Greek)* Princess; *(Spanish)* Aunt.

**Tiara** *(Greek)* Turban; *(Latin)* The name of a flower.

**Tiegan** *(Aztec)* Little princess in the big valley.

**Tierra** *(Spanish)* Earth; land.

**Tiffany** *(French)* Appearance of God. *Variants:* Epiphanie, Tifanie, Tiffanie, Tiffeny, Tiphanie; Theophania *(Greek)*; Epifania *(Italian)*.

**Tilda** *(Germanic)* Maid of battles. *See also* Mathilda.

**Tilly** *See* Mathilda.

**Timandra** *(Greek)* The daughter of the Spartan king Tyndareus in Greek mythology.

**Timothea** *(Greek)* Honoured by God. Feminine form of Timothy.

**Tina** *See* Augusta, Christine, Clementine, Elizabeth, Martina, Valentina.

**Ting** *(Chinese)* Graceful.

**Tiphanie** *See* Tiffany.

**Titania** *(Greek)* Giantess; name of Shakespeare's fairy queen. *Variants:* Tania, Tanya.

# T

**Titian** *(Greek)* Red-gold.

**Tivona** *(Hebrew)* Lover of nature.

**Toakase** *(Tongan)* Woman of the sea.

**Toinette** *See* Antonia.

**Tokori** *(Hopi)* Screech owl.

**Tola** *(Polish)* Priceless.

**Tomi** *(Japanese)* Rich.

**Tomiko** *(Japanese)* Child of Tomi.

**Toni, Tonya** *See* Antonia.

**Topaz** *(Latin)* A gemstone.

**Tori** *(Japanese)* Bird.

**Toshi** *(Japanese)* Year of plenty.

**Tosia** *(Latin)* Inestimable.

**Tove** *(Hebrew)* Good.

**Toyo** *(Japanese)* Plentiful.

**Tracie** *See* Theresa.

**Tracy** *(English)* Bold; courageous one.
   *See also* Theresa.

**Tresa, Tresca, Tressa** *See* Theresa.

**Treva** *(Celtic)* Prudent.

**Trind** *(Swedish)* Pure.

**Trinity** *(Latin)* The holy three.

**Trish, Trisha** *See* Patricia.

**Trista** *(Latin)* Sorrowful. Female form of Tristan.

**Trixie** *See* Beatrice.

**Troy** *(French)* A place name.

**Trudy** *(English)* Beloved.

**Tryne** *(Dutch)* Pure.

**Tryphena** *(Latin)* Dainty.

# U

**Tshin** *(Gwich'in)* Rain.

**Tsing** *(Chinese)* Pure and subtle.

**Tuesday** *(English)* Day of the week.

**Tullik** *(InupiaQ)* Golden plover.

**Tully** *(Gaelic)* Peaceful one.

**Tusti** *(Hindu)* Peace; happiness.

**Tuyet** *(Chinese)* White as snow.

**Tzipporah** *(Hebrew)* Bird; the wife of Moses.
*See also* Zipporah.

**U** *(Korean)* Gentle.

**Udele** *(Anglo-Saxon)* Rich; prosperous.

**Uhu** *(Innu)* Owl.

**Uiyula** *(InupiaQ)* Whirlwind.

**Ula** *(Celtic)* Jewel of the sea; *(Germanic)* Inherited estate.

**Ulima** *(Arabic)* Astute; wise.

**Ulla** *(English)* To fill up; *(Indigenous Australian)* A well.

**Ulrike** *(Germanic)* Wolf ruler; prosperity and power. Feminine form of Ulrich.
*Variants:* Ulrica *(French)*; Ulrika *(Scandinavian)*.

**Ultima** *(Latin)* The ultimate or last; aloof.

**Ululani** *(Hawaiian)* Heavenly inspiration.

**Ulva** *(Germanic)* Wolf.

# U

**Uma** *(Hebrew)* Nation; *(Hindu)* Mother; *(Japanese)* Horse.

**Umay** *(Turkish)* Hopeful.

**Umeko** *(Japanese)* Plum; blossom; patient.
Variant: Umeka.

**Una** *(Latin)* One.
Variants: Ona; Oona, Oonagh *(Irish)*.

**Undine** *(Germanic)* A water nymph in German mythology.
Variants: Ondine, Undene, Undin.

**Unity** *(English)* Unity.

**Unn** *(Norwegian)* She who is loved.

**Unna** *(Germanic)* Woman.

**Unnati** (Hindu) Progress.

**Unni** *(Norse)* Modest.

**Urania** *(Greek)* The sky; heavenly; the muse of astronomy and astrology in Greek mythology.

**Urbana** *(Latin)* From the city.

**Uriana** *(Greek)* The unknown.

**Urit** *(Hebrew)* Bright.

**Urmila** *(Hindu)* The wife of Lakshmana, daughter of King Janaka in the epic Hindu poem *Ramayana*.

**Ursula** *(Latin)* She-bear.
Variants: Orsa, Sula, Ursa, Ursel, Ursuline; Ursanne, Ursule *(French)*; Orsola *(Italian)*; Ursola, Ursulina *(Spanish)*.

**Urvasi** *(Hindu)* Most beautiful of the Apsaras (female spirits of the clouds and waters) in Hindu mythology.

**Usagi** *(Japanese)* Rabbit.

**Ushi** *(Chinese)* Ox.

**Uta** *(Germanic)* Fortunate maid of battle.

**Uttara** *(Hindu)* The daughter of King Virata, mother of Pariksit in the epic Hindu poem *Mahabharata*.

**Vail** *(French)* Valley.
   *Variant:* Valonia

**Vala** *(English)* Chosen.

**Valda** *(Germanic)* Warrior.
   *Variants:* Valina, Velda.

**Valeda** *(Latin)* Strong; healthy.

**Valentina** *(Latin)* Strong; valiant. Feminine form of Valentine.
   *Variants:* Valencia, Valentia, Valida, Tina.

**Valerie** *(Latin)* Strong and healthy. Feminine form of Valerian.
   *Variants:* Valéry *(French)*; Valeria *(Italian)*.

**Valeska** *(Polish)* Glorious ruler.

**Valida** *See* Valentina.

**Valina** *See* Valda.

**Valisa** *(Unknown)* Wild one.

**Valma** *(Welsh)* Mayflower.
   *Variant:* Valmai.

**Valonia** *See* Vail.

**Valora** *(Latin)* The valorous.

**Vanessa** *(Greek)* Butterfly.
   *Variants:* Nessa, Vanesa.

**Vania** *(Russian)* God's gift.
   *Variant:* Vanya.

**Vanka** *(Russian) See* Anne.

# V

**Vanna** *See* Joanne.

**Vanya** *See* Vania.

**Vara** *(Greek)* The stranger.

**Varda** *(Hebrew)* Rose.

**Varenka, Varina** *See* Barbara.

**Varsha** *(Hindu)* Rain.

**Varuni** *(Hindu)* The goddess of wine and intoxication in Hindu mythology.

**Varvara** *See* Barbara.

**Vashti** *(Persian)* Beautiful.
*Variants:* Vashta, Vashtee, Vashtia.

**Vega** *(Arabic)* Falling star.

**Velda** *(Germanic)* Inspired wisdom.
*Variant:* Veleda.
*See also* Valda.

**Velika** *(Slavic)* Great.

**Velma** *See* Wilhelmina.

**Velvet** *(Latin)* A fleece.

**Venetia** *(Latin)* From Venice.

**Venitia** *(Italian)* Mercy.

**Venus** *(Latin)* The goddess of love and beauty in Roman mythology.

**Vera** *(Latin)* Faithful; true.
*Variants:* Vere, Verene, Verina, Verine, Verla; Verity *(English)*; Verena *(Germanic)*; Verita *(Italian)*; Veridiana *(Spanish)*.
*See also* Veronica.

**Verda** *(Latin)* Spring-like.

**Vere, Verena, Verene, Veridiana, Verity, Verla**
*See* Vera.

# V

**Veronica** *(Latin)* Belonging to an image.
*Variants:* Veronice; Veronique *(French)*; Veronika, Veronike *(Germanic)*.
*See also* Vera.

**Vesna** *(Croatian, Greek)* The goddess of spring in Slavic mythology.

**Vesper** *(Latin)* Evening.

**Vesta** *(Latin)* Guardian of the sacred fire.

**Vevay** *(Welsh)* White wave.

**Vevila** *(Gaelic)* Woman with a melodious voice.

**Vevina** *(Latin)* Sweet lady.

**Victoria** *(Latin)* Victorious conqueror; champion. Feminine form of Victor.
*Variants:* Victoire, Victorine *(French)*; Viktoria *(Germanic)*; Vittoria *(Italian)*; Vitoria *(Spanish)*.
*See also* Queenie.

**Vida** *See* Davida.

**Vidette** *(Hebrew)* The beloved.

**Vidonia** *(Latin)* Vine branch.

**Vidya** *(Hindu)* Wisdom; knowledge.

**Vienna** *(Latin)* Wine country.

**Viktoria** *See* Victoria.

**Vilhelmina, Vilma** *See* Wilhelmina.

**Vinata** *(Hindu)* Humble; mother of the divinity Garudain in Hindu mythology.

**Vinaya** *(Hindu)* Good behaviour.

**Violet** *(Latin)* A purple flower.
*Variants:* Viola, Violante; Iolanthe, Jolande, Violetta, Violette, Yolande, Yolanthe, Yolette *(French)*; Ianthe, Jolandi *(Germanic)*; Yolanda *(Greek)*; Jolan *(Hungarian)*; Iolanda, Jolanda *(Italian)*.

**Virgillia** *(Latin)* A genus of trees.

**Virginia** *(Latin)* Pure; virginal.
  *Variant:* Virginie *(French)*; Ginny, Jinny *(Scottish)*.

**Viridis** *(Latin)* Youthful and blooming.

**Visala** *(Hindu)* One of the Apsaras (female spirits of the clouds and waters) in Hindu mythology.

**Vita** *See* Davida.

**Vitoria, Vittoria** *See* Victoria.

**Viviana** *See* Bibiana, Vivien.

**Vivien** *(Latin)* Vital; alive. Feminine form of Vivian.
  *Variants:* Vivian, Viviana, Vivianne, Vivyan *(English)*;
  Vivienne *(French)*.

**Voleta** *(Greek)* Veiled one.
  *Variant:* Voletta *(French)*.

**Vrinda** *(Hindu)* Virtue and strength.

**Walburga** *(Anglo-Saxon)* Mighty defender; an eighth-century saint.

**Wanda** *(Germanic)* The wanderer.
  *Variants:* Wandis, Wenda, Wendelin, Wendeline, Wendy;
  Vanda *(Italian)*.
  *See also* Vanda.

**Wate** *(Algonquin)* Northern lights.

**Wenda, Wendelin, Wendeline** *See* Wanda.

**Wendy** *(English)* Fair.
  *See also* Gwendolin, Wanda.

**Wenonah** *(Sioux)* Nickname for a first daughter.
  *Variants:* Wenona, Winona.

**Whitney** *(English)* White island.

**Widjan** *(Arabic)* Ecstasy.

**Wilda** *(Anglo-Saxon)* Forest dweller.

**Wilhelmina** *(Germanic)* Resolute protector. Feminine form of
  William.
  *Variants:* Guillelmine, Mina, Velma, Willa, Willamina,
  Willette, Wilma, Wilmette, Wylma; Wilhelmine *(Danish)*;
  Guglielma, Guilema, Guillelmina *(Italian)*; Vilma *(Russian)*;
  Vilhelmina *(Swedish)*.

**Willamina, Willette** *See* Wilhelmina.

**Willow** *(English)* The name of a tree.

**Wilma, Wilmette** *See* Wilhelmina.

**Wilona** *(English)* Desired.

**Winda** *(Swahili)* Hunt.

**Winifred** *(Germanic)* Peaceful friend.
  *Variants:* Winifrid, Winny.

**Winona** *See* Wenonah.

**Winsome** *(English)* Pleasant; attractive.

**Winter** *(English)* The season.

**Woya** *(Cherokee)* Dove.

**Wylma** *See* Wilhelmina.

**Wynne** *(Celtic)* Fair.
  *Variant:* Wynn.

**Xandra, Xandy** *See* Alexandra.

**Xanthe** *(Greek)* Golden-haired.
 *Variant:* Zanthe.

**Xaviera** *(Arabic)* The saviour.

**Xena** *(Greek)* Guest.

**Xenia** *(Greek)* Hospitable.
 *Variants:* Xena, Xene, Zenia.

**Xiang** *(Chinese)* Fragrant.

**Xiu Mei** *(Chinese)* Beautiful plum.

**Xuan** *(Chinese)* Beautiful jade.

**Xuxa** *See* Susan.

**Xylia** *(Greek)* Of the forest.
 *Variants:* Xylina, Xylona.

**Yachne** *(Hebrew)* Gracious.

**Yadira** *(Hebrew)* Friend.

**Yael** *See* Jael.

**Yaffa** *(Hebrew)* Beautiful.

# Y

**Yakei** *(Tlingit)* "It is good."

**Yakira** *(Hebrew)* Precious.

**Yaksha** *(Hindu)* A class of nature spirits in Hindu mythology; the sister of the god Daksha in Hindu mythology.

**Yalena** *See* Helen.

**Yanaba** *(Native American)* Brave.

**Yang** *(Chinese)* Sun.

**Yarkona** *(Hebrew)* Green.

**Yarmilla** *(Slavic)* Merchant.

**Yasmeen, Yasmin, Yasmina, Yasmine** *See* Jasmine.

**Yayoi** *(Japanese)* March.

**Yedda** *(Germanic)* The singer.

**Yehudit** *See* Judith.

**Yei** *(Japanese)* Flourishing.

**Yelena** *See* Helen.

**Yen** *(Chinese)* Beautiful; charming; pretty.

**Yenene** *(Native American)* Medicine man.

**Yesmina** *(Hebrew)* Right hand; strength.

**Yet Kwai** *(Chinese)* Beautiful as a rose.

**Yetta** *(English)* The given.
  *See also* Henrietta.

**Yeva** *(Russian)* Life-giving.

**Ylwa** *(Scandinavian)* She-wolf.

**Ynes, Ynez** *See* Agnes.

**Yohannah** *See* Joanne.

**Yoko** *(Japanese)* Determined woman; positive.

**Yolanda, Yolande, Yolanthe, Yolette** *See* Violet.

**Yomaris** *(Spanish)* I am the sun.

**Yoninah** *(Hebrew)* Dove.

# Z

**Yoshi** *(Japanese)* Respectful.

**Yoshiko** *(Japanese)* Child of Yoshi.

**Yovela** *(Hebrew)* Rejoicing.

**Yulia, Yulinka** *See* Julia.

**Yumi** *(Japanese)* Beauty.

**Yumiko** *(Japanese)* Child of Yumi.

**Yuriko** *(Japanese)* Child of Yuri.

**Yuuka** *(Japanese)* Gentle flower.

**Yvette** *See* Yvonne.

**Yvonne** *(French)* The archer.
Variants: Evonne, Ivette, Yvette.

**Zada** *(Arabic)* Prosperous.
Variant: Zadah.

**Zafina** *(Arabic)* Victorious.

**Zafirah** *(Arabic)* Successful.
Variant: Zarifa.

**Zahara** *(Arabic)* Shining; luminous.

**Zahavah** *(Hebrew)* Golden.

**Zahra** *(Arabic)* White; *(Swahili)* Flowers.
See also Sarah.

**Zaida** *(Arabic)* Fortunate one.

**Zaira** *(Arabic)* Rose.
Variant: Zaria.

# Z

**Zakia** *(Hebrew)* Bright; pure.

**Zalika** *(African)* Well-born.

**Zama** *(Latin)* Came from Zama.

**Zambda** *(Hebrew)* Meditation.

**Zandra** *See* Alexandra.

**Zaneta** *(Hebrew)* God's gracious gift.

**Zanita** *(Greek)* Long teeth.

**Zanna** *See* Jane.

**Zanthe** *See* Xanthe.

**Zara** *(Arabic)* Princess; *(Hebrew)* Dawn.
*Variant:* Zarah.
*See also* Sarah.

**Zarah, Zaras** *See* Sarah.

**Zaria** *See* Azaria, Sarah, Zaira.

**Zarifa** *See* Zafirah.

**Zarina** *(African)* Golden.

**Zawati** *(Swahili)* Gift.

**Zaynah** *(Arabic)* Great.

**Zaza** *(Arabic)* Flowery; *(Hebrew)* Movement.

**Zdenka** *(Czech)* From Sidon; active.

**Zea** *(Latin)* Grain.

**Zebina** *(Greek)* Gifted.

**Zehava** *(Hebrew)* Golden.

**Zelda** *(Germanic)* Grey warrior.

**Zelene** *(English)* Sunshine.

**Zelenka** *(Czech)* Little innocent one.

**Zelia** *(Greek)* Zeal.

**Zelinda** *(Germanic)* Shield of victory.

**Zemirah** *(Hebrew)* Song of joy.

# Z

**Zena** *(Greek)* Alive.

**Zenani** *(Xhosa)* "What have you brought to the world?"
  *Variant:* Zeni.

**Zenda** *(Persian)* Sacred; womanly.
  *Variant:* Zendah.

**Zenia** *See* Xenia.

**Zenobia** *(Greek)* Father's ornament.

**Zera** *(Greek)* Seeds.

**Zerdali** *(Turkish)* Wild apricot.

**Zerlina** *(Latin)* Beautiful dawn.
  *Variant:* Zerlinda *(Hebrew)*.

**Zerrin** *(Turkish)* Golden.

**Zetta** *(Portuguese)* Rose.

**Zeva** *(Greek)* Sword.

**Zevida** *(Hebrew)* Gift.

**Zeynep** *(Turkish)* Daughter of the prophet Muhammad.

**Zhen** *(Chinese)* Chaste.

**Zia** *(Hebrew)* To tremble; *(Latin)* A kind of grain.

**Ziazan** *(Armenian)* Rainbow.

**Zigana** *(Hungarian)* Gypsy girl.
  *Variant:* Tzigana.

**Zila** *(Hebrew)* Shadow.
  *Variants:* Zilla, Zillah, Zilli.

**Zilya** *See* Theresa.

**Zimra** *(Hebrew)* Song of praise.

**Zina** *(African)* Name.

**Zinaida** *(Greek)* Of Zeus.

**Zindziswa** *(Xhosa)* "You are well established."
  *Variant:* Zindzi.

# Z

**Zinnia** *(English)* Flower name.

**Ziona** *(Hebrew)* A sign.

**Zipporah** *(Hebrew)* Bird; the wife of Moses.
*See also* Tzipporah.

**Zita** *(Hebrew)* The seeker; *(Persian)* Virgin.

**Ziva** *(Hebrew)* Bright; radiant.

**Zizi** *(Hungarian)* Dedicated to God.

**Zoe** *(Greek)* Life.
*Variants:* Zoë, Zoia.

**Zofia** *See* Sophia.

**Zoia** *See* Zoe.

**Zola** *(Italian)* Lump of earth.

**Zora** *(Greek)* Golden dawn.

**Zosa** *See* Susan.

**Zosia** *See* Sophia.

**Zosima** *(Greek)* Lively.

**Zotia** *(Polish)* Wise.

**Zsazsa, Zsuzsa, Zsuzsanna** *See* Susan.

**Zuleika** *(Arabic)* Fair-haired.

**Zulema** *(Arabic)* Peace.

**Zuza** *See* Susan.

# Names
*for*
# BOYS

**Aakarshan** *(Hindu)* Attraction.

**Aaron** *(Arabic)* High mountain; *(Hebrew)* Shining light.
Variants: Aharon, Aron, Haroun.

**Aasim** *(Arabic)* Protected.

**Aasivak** *(InupiaQ)* Spider.

**Abadi** *(Arabic)* Eternal.

**Abbot** *(English)* Abbey father.

**Abdel** *See* Abdul.

**Abdiel** *(Hebrew)* Servant of God.

**Abdul** *(Arabic)* Servant; son.
Variant: Abdel.

**Abdullah** *(Arabic)* Servant of Allah.

**Abejundio** *(Spanish)* Bee-like.

**Abel** *(Hebrew)* The breath; child.
Variants: Abell, Abelot, Able, Hebel.

**Abelard** *(Germanic)* Resolute.

**Abell, Abelot** *See* Abel.

**Abhay** *(Hindu)* A son of the god Dharma in Hindu
mythology.

**Abhijit** *(Hindu)* A constellation dear to the god Hari (Vishnu)
in Hindu mythology.

**Abie** *See* Abraham.

**Abijah** *(Hebrew)* The Lord is my father.

**Abira** *See* Abraham.

**Able** *See* Abel.

**Abner** *(Hebrew)* Father of light.

**Abou** *See* Abu.

**Abraham** *(Hebrew)* Father of many.
*Variants:* Abie, Abira, Abrahamo, Abram, Abramo, Arun, Ibrahim.

**Absalom** *(Hebrew)* Father of peace.

**Abu** *(Arabic)* Father.
*Variant:* Abou.

**Acario** *(Latin)* Ungrateful.

**Ace** *(Hebrew)* One who excels; unity.

**Achambault** *See* Archibald.

**Achilles** *(Greek)* Grief of the people; a hero in the Trojan war in Roman mythology.
*Variant:* Achille (French).

**Achimbald** *See* Archibald.

**Achyuta** *(Hindu)* One of the names of the god Vishnu in Hindu mythology.

**Acton** *(English)* Town with many oaks.

**Adair** *See* Edgar.

**Adal** *(Germanic)* Noble.
*Variants:* Adalardo, Adalgiso, Adalrico, Adelino.

**Adalbert** *See* Albert.

**Adam** *(Hebrew)* Of the red earth.
*Variants:* Adamo, Adan, Adao, Adhamh.

**Addai** *(Hebrew)* Man of God.

**Addison** *(English)* Adam's son.

**Adelbert, Adelberto** *See* Albert.

# A

**Adelino** *See* Adal.

**Adelphos** *(Greek)* Brother.

**Ademaro** *(Germanic)* Glorious in battle.

**Adin** *(Hebrew)* Beautiful; gentle; pleasant.

**Aditya** *(Hindu)* The Adityas are a group of solar deities in Hindu mythology.

**Adlai** *(Hebrew)* My witness; refuge of God.

**Adlbrecht** *See* Albert.

**Adler** *(Germanic)* Eagle.

**Adley** *(Hebrew)* Just and fair.

**Admon** *(Hebrew)* Red earth; a red peony flower.

**Adolf** *(Germanic)* Noble wolf; hero.
  *Variant:* Odolf.

**Adon** *(Hebrew)* Lord.

**Adonis** *(Greek)* Handsome; a hero in Greek mythology.

**Adrastos** *(Greek)* Undaunted.

**Adrian** *(Latin)* Of the Adriatic.
  *Variants:* Adriano, Adrien, Arne, Arrian, Hadrian.

**Adrien** *See* Adrian.

**Aeneas** *(Greek)* Praiseworthy; a hero in Roman mythology, the founder of Rome.

**Afniq** *(InupiaQ)* Blizzard.

**Afuyakti** *(InupiaQ)* Fighter; warrior.

**Agnolo** *See* Angel.

**Agostino, Agoston** *See* Augustus.

**Aharoun** *See* Aaron.

**Ahearn** *(Celtic)* Lord of the horses.

**Ahmed** *(Arabic)* Highly praised.

# A

**Ahren** *(Germanic)* Eagle.

**Aidan** *(Celtic)* Little fierce one; little fiery one.
*Variants:* Edan, Egan.

**Aiken** *(English)* Sturdy; made of oak.

**Ailean, Ailin** *See* Alan.

**Ailbert** *See* Albert.

**Aimery** *(Germanic)* Industrious ruler.

**Aindreas** *See* Andrew.

**Aineislis** *See* Stanislaus.

**Ainsley** *(English)* Ain's meadow.
*Variants:* Ainslee, Ainslie.

**Airlie** *See* Earl.

**Ajatashatru** *(Hindu)* One of the names of the god Vishnu in
Hindu mythology.

**Ajax** *(Greek)* Earthy; a hero in Greek mythology.

**Ajayi** *(African)* Born face down.

**Akaash** *(Hindu)* Sky.

**Akello** *(Ugandan)* I have bought.

**Akihiko** *(Japanese)* Bright.

**Akil** *(Arabic)* Intelligent; logical.

**Akim** *See* Joachim.

**Akira** *(Japanese)* Intelligent.

**Akiyama** *(Japanese)* Autumn.

**Akjaq** *(InupiaQ)* Grizzly bear.

**Akshay** *(Hindu)* Indestructible: a god in Hindu mythology.

**Akua** *(Arabic)* Sweet messenger.

**Aladdin** *(Arabic)* Servant of Allah.

**Alan** *(Celtic)* Handsome; harmonious one.
*Variants:* Ailean, Ailin, Alain, Aland, Alano, Alawn, Allan,
Allen, Allyn, Alun, Alunn, Aluon, Eilian.

# A

**Aland** *(English)* Bright as the sun.
  *See also* Alan.

**Alano** *See* Alan.

**Alard** *(Germanic)* Noble; hard.

**Alaric** *(Germanic)* To rule over all.

**Alasdair, Alastair** *See* Alexander.

**Alawn** *See* Alan.

**Alban** *(Latin)* White; *(Scotland)* from Alba.
  *Variants:* Alben, Albin.
  *See also* Aubin.

**Albert** *(Germanic)* Bright; noble.
  *Variants:* Adalbert, Adelbert, Adelberto, Adelbrecht,
  Ulbrecht; Bert, Elbert, Ethelbert *(English)*; Aubert *(French)*;
  Albrecht *(Germanic)*; Albertino, Alberto *(Italian)*; Ailbert
  *(Scottish)*.
  *See also* Bert.

**Albin** *See* Alban.

**Albion** *(Latin)* Blond; white; a medieval name for England.

**Albrecht** *See* Albert.

**Alcander** *(Greek)* Strong.

**Alcott** *(English)* Old cottage.

**Alden** *(English)* Wise protector; old friend.

**Alder** *(English)* Birch tree; revered one.

**Aldous** *(Germanic)* Old house.
  *Variants:* Aldis, Aldo, Aldus.

**Aldred** *See* Eldridge.

**Aldrich** *(English)* Old king.

**Aldus** *See* Aldous.

**Alec, Aleck, Alejandro, Aleksandr, Aleksandras**
  *See* Alexander.

**Aleron** *(French)* Knight's armour.

**Aleser** *(Arabic)* Lion.

**Alexander** *(Greek)* Protector of mankind.
*Variants:* Alex, Alexandros, Alexio, Alexis, Alysander, Xan, Xander; Alec, Aleck, Alick *(English)*; Alexandre, Sacha *(French)*; Alistair *(Gaelic)*; Sascha *(Germanic)*; Elek *(Hungarian)*; Alsandair *(Irish)*; Alessandro, Allesandro *(Italian)*; Aleksandras *(Lithuanian)*; Alexandru *(Romanian)*; Aleksandr, Sasha, Zander *(Russian)*; Alasdair, Alastair, Alister, Allister *(Scottish)*; Alejandro *(Spanish)*.

**Alfons, Alfonse, Alfonso** *See* Alphonso.

**Alfred** *(Germanic)* Elf counsel.
*Variants:* Aelfred, Alfrid, Avery, Fred *(English)*; Alfredo *(Italian, Spanish)*.

**Algernon** *(French)* With a moustache.

**Ali** *(Arabic)* Exalted one.

**Alick** *See* Alexander.

**Alim** *(Arabic)* Wise; learned.

**Alistair, Alister** *See* Alexander.

**Allan** *See* Alan.

**Allard** *(English)* Noble and brave.

**Allen** *See* Alan.

**Allesandro, Allister** *See* Alexander.

**Allyn** *See* Alan.

**Almeric** *(Germanic)* Work to rule.
*Variants:* Americ, Emeric.
*See also* Eric.

**Aloin** *See* Alvin.

**Alois** *See* Lewis.

**Alonso, Alonzo** *See* Alphonso.

# A

**Aloys, Aloysius** *See* Lewis.

**Alphonso** *(Germanic)* Noble; ready for battle.
*Variants:* Alfons, Alfonse; Alphonsus *(Irish)*; Alfonso *(Italian)*; Alonso, Alonzo *(Spanish)*.

**Alsandair** *See* Alexander.

**Alston** *(Anglo-Saxon)* Old manor.

**Altair** *(Arabic)* Bird; *(Greek)* Star.

**Alton** *See* Elton.

**Alun, Alunn, Aluon** *See* Alan.

**Alvan** *See* Alvin.

**Alvin** *(Germanic)* Friend of all; noble friend.
*Variants:* Aloin, Alvan, Alvino, Alwin, Alwyn, Elvin.

**Alvis** *See* Elvis.

**Alwin, Alwyn** *See* Alvin.

**Alysander** *See* Alexander.

**Amadeus** *(Latin)* Beloved of God.
*Variant:* Amédée *(French)*.

**Amadi** *(Nigerian)* General rejoicing.

**Amado** *(Latin)* Loving deity.

**Amador** *(Spanish)* Lover.

**Amal** *(Hindu)* Bright and pure; hope; wish.

**Amar** *(Hindu)* Forever.

**Amato** *(Spanish)* Beloved.

**Ambrose** *(Greek)* Immortal one.
*Variants:* Ambroise *(French)*; Ambros *(Irish)*; Ambrogio, Ambrosi *(Italian)*; Ambrosius *(Latin)*; Ambroz *(Polish)*; Ambrosio *(Spanish)*.

**Amédée** *See* Amadeus.

**Americ** *See* Almeric.

# A

**Amerigo** *See* Emery.

**Amery** *(French)* Divine.
Variants: Amory, Emery.
*See also* Emery.

**Amherst** *(English)* A place name.

**Amiel** *(Hebrew)* God of my people.

**Amik** *(Algonquin)* Beaver.

**Amir** *(Arabic)* Prince.

**Amistad** *(Spanish)* Friendship.

**Amit** *(Hindu)* Endless.

**Amo** *(Algonquin)* Bee.

**Amon** *(Egyptian)* The hidden one; a deity in Egyptian mythology.
*Variant:* Amun.

**Amory** *(Latin)* Loving.
*See also* Amery.

**Amos** *(Hebrew)* Courageous and strong.

**Amrit** *(Hindu)* Nectar.

**Amulya** *(Hindu)* Priceless.

**Amun** *See* Amon.

**Anand** *(Hindu)* Bliss; happiness.

**Ananda** *(Sanskrit)* A blessing.

**Anatole** *(Greek)* From the east.

**Andrew** *(Greek)* Strong; manly.
Variants: Andreadis, Drew; Ondre, Ondro *(Czech)*; André *(French)*; Andreas *(Germanic)*; Aindreas *(Irish)*; Andrzej *(Polish)*; Andrei, Andrey *(Russian)*; Anders *(Scandinavian)*; Andres *(Spanish)*.

**Angel** *(Greek)* Heavenly messenger.
Variants: Agnolo, Angelo *(Italian)*.

**Angus** *(Scottish)* Unique choice.
Variants: Aenas, Aenghus, Aonghus.

# A

**Anicet** *(French)* Invincible; a French saint.

**Annson** *See* Anson.

**Anntoin** *See* Anthony.

**Ansley** *(English)* Pastureland of the noble.

**Anson** *(Anglo-Saxon)* Son of a nobleman; son of Andrew or Hans.

*Variants:* Annson, Ansson, Hansen, Hanson, Hanssen, Hansson.

**Antal** *(Latin)* Prince.

**Anthony** *(Latin)* Inestimable.

*Variants:* Atoan *(Abenaki)*; Antony; Antonin *(Czech)*; Tony *(English)*; Antoine, Anton *(French)*; Anntoin *(Irish)*; Antonio, Antonius, Tonio *(Italian)*.

**Anwatin** *(Algonquin)* Calm weather.

**Aodh, Aoidh** *See* Hugh.

**Aonghus** *See* Angus.

**Apollo** *(Greek)* The god of music, light, and learning in Greek and Roman mythology.

**Aquila** *(Latin)* Eagle.

**Aralt** *See* Harold.

**Aram** *(Assyrian)* High place.

**Archibald** *(Germanic)* Noble and bold.

*Variants:* Archie, Achimbald; Archambault *(French)*; Gilleasbuig *(Gaelic)*; Arcibaldo *(Portuguese)*.

**Arden** *(English)* Dwelling place.

**Ardon** *(Hebrew)* Bronze.

**Aren** *(Nigerian)* Eagle.

**Arend** *See* Arnold.

**Ares** *(Greek)* The god of war in Greek mythology.

*Variant:* Arian, Aries.

**Argan** *(French)* A fruitful North African tree.

**Aricin** *(Norwegian)* The eternal king's son.
*Variant:* Arkin.

**Ariel** *(Hebrew)* Lion of God.
*Variant:* Ari.

**Aries** *See* Ares.

**Aristotle** *(Greek)* An ancient Greek philosopher.

**Arjun** *(Hindu)* Bright; shining; silver; a hero in the epic Hindu poem *Mahabharata*.

**Arkin** *See* Aricin.

**Arland** *(Celtic)* Pledge.
*Variant:* Arlen.

**Arley** *(Latin)* The bowman.

**Armand, Armando, Armant, Armin** *See* Herman.

**Armstrong** *(English)* Of the strong arm.

**Arnaldo, Arnaud** *See* Arnold.

**Arne** *See* Adrian, Arnold.

**Arnold** *(Germanic)* Powerful eagle.
*Variants:* Arend, Arno, Arnoud; Arne *(Dutch)*; Arnie *(English)*; Arnaud *(French)*; Arnaldo, Arnoldo *(Italian, Spanish)*; Arnulfo *(Spanish)*.

**Arnon** *(Hebrew)* Rushing stream.

**Aron** *See* Aaron.

**Arpiar** *(Armenian)* Sunny.

**Arrian** *See* Adrian.

**Arthur** *(Celtic)* Strong as a bear; a mythical English king.
*Variants:* Artair, Artor, Artur, Arturo, Artus.

**Arun** *See* Abraham.

**Arvel** *(Welsh)* Wept over.

**Asa** *(Hebrew)* The healer.

# A

**Asbjorn** *(Norse)* Divine bear.

**Ascott** *(English)* Eastern cottage.

**Asher** *(Hebrew)* Happy; blessed; laughing one.

**Ashley** *(English)* Meadow of ash trees.
Variants: Ashlee.

**Asija** *(Hindu)* A great sage, brother of Brihaspati, in Hindu mythology.

**Aston** *(English)* Eastern place.

**Atai** *(InupiaQ)* Cute; sweet.

**Atalik** *(Hungarian)* Like his father.

**Atanbirrun** *(InupiaQ)* Liberty.

**Athan** *(Greek)* Immortal.

**Atharvan** *(Hindu)* A legendary sage in Hindu mythology.

**Athelstan** *(Norse)* Noble stone.

**Athol** *(Scottish)* A place name.
Variant: Athole.

**Atik** *(Innu)* Caribou.

**Atilla** *(Hungarian)* Beloved father.
Variant: Atila.

**Attis** *(Greek)* Handsome boy.

**Auberon** *See* Aubrey.

**Aubert** *See* Albert.

**Aubrey** *(Germanic)* Elf; power; the king of the elves in German mythology.
Variants: Auberon, Oberon.

**Augustus** *(Latin)* High; mighty; honoured.
Variants: Agostino, Agosto, Agoston, August, Auguste, Augustin, Augustine, Augusto, Austen, Austin.

**Aulay** *See* Olaf.

**Aurek** *(Polish)* Golden-haired.

**Austen, Austin** *See* Augustus.

**Avery** *See* Alfred.

**Axel** *(Norse)* Divine peace.

**Axseenayi** *(Tlingit)* My light.

**Axyeet** *(Tlingit)* My son.

**Aylmer** *(English)* Famous; noble.
*Variant:* Elmer.

**Aymeric** *(French)* King of the house.

**Azadi** *(Algonquin)* Poplar tree.

**Baden** *(Germanic)* Bath.

**Bailey** *(French)* Baliff.
*Variant:* Baily.

**Baird** *See* Bard.

**Baldovino** *See* Baldwin.

**Baldric** *(Germanic)* Bold ruler.

**Baldwin** *(Germanic)* Bold protector.
*Variants:* Baudoin, Boden; Baudouin *(French)*; Bowden *(Gaelic)*; Baldovino *(Italian)*; Maldwyn *(Welsh)*.

**Banan** *See* Banquo.

**Banquo** *(Celtic)* White.
*Variant:* Banan.

# B

**Baptist** *(Greek)* One who baptizes.
*Variants:* Baptiste, Battiste.

**Bard** *(Gaelic)* Minstrel; poet singer.
*Variant:* Baird.

**Barnaby** *(Aramaic)* Son of consolation.
*Variants:* Barna, Barnaba, Barnabas, Barnabe, Barnabus,
Barnebas, Barney, Bernabe.

**Barnard** *See* Bernard.

**Barnebas** *See* Barnaby.

**Barnett** *See* Bernard.

**Barney** *See* Barnaby.

**Barret** *(Germanic)* Strength of a bear.
*Variant:* Barrett.

**Barry** *(Celtic)* Fine marksman.
*Variant:* Barrie.

**Bartholomew** *(Hebrew)* War-like son; one of the twelve
apostles in the Bible.
*Variants:* Bartholomeus *(Dutch)*; Bart, Barton *(English)*;
Barthel, Barthélémy, Bartholomé *(French)*; Parlan *(Gaelic)*;
Bartholomaus *(Germanic)*; Bartolomeo *(Italian)*; Bartek
*(Polish)*.

**Bartok, Bartram** *See* Bertram.

**Basil** *(Greek)* Royal; kingly.
*Variants:* Basileos, Bazel, Vasilos; Basile *(French)*; Basilius
*(Italian)*; Vassily *(Russian)*; Basilio *(Spanish)*.

**Bastian, Bastien** *See* Sebastian.

**Battiste** *See* Baptist.

**Baudoin, Baudouin** *See* Baldwin.

**Baxter** *(English)* Baker.

**Bazel** *See* Basil.

**Bearnard** *See* Bernard.

# B

**Beathan** *See* Benjamin.

**Beau** *(French)* Handsome.

**Beaumont** *(French)* Beautiful mountain.

**Beauregard** *(French)* Handsome face.

**Beavan, Beaven** *See* Bevan.

**Bede** *(Germanic)* Prayer.

**Beltran** *See* Bertram.

**Ben** *See* Benedict, Benjamin.

**Benedict** *(Latin)* The blessed.
*Variants:* Benedictus; Ben, Bennett *(English)*; Benoit *(French)*; Benedick *(Germanic)*; Benedetto *(Italian)*; Benedicto, Benito *(Spanish)*.

**Benjamin** *(Hebrew)* Son of my right hand.
*Variants:* Ben; Beniamino *(Italian)*; Beathan *(Scottish)*.

**Bennett, Benoit** *See* Benedict.

**Benson** *(Hebrew)* Son of Benjamin.

**Benvenuto** *(Italian)* The right way.

**Berenger** *(Germanic)* A bear spear.

**Bernabe** *See* Barnaby.

**Bernard** *(Germanic)* Brave as a bear; strong.
*Variants:* Pelnal *(Abenaki)*; Barnard, Berngard, Bernhard, Burnard; Bernhart *(Dutch)*; Barnett *(English)*; Bearnard *(Gaelic)*; Bernardo *(Italian, Spanish)*; Bernat, Nardo *(Spanish)*.

**Bert** *(English)* Illustrious.
*See also* Albert, Berthold, Bertram, Hubert, Robert.

**Berthold** *(Germanic)* Bright ruler.
*Variants:* Berthoud, Bertolde, Bertoldi, Bertolt; Bert *(English)*.
*See also* Bert.

**Bertram** *(Germanic)* Bright raven.

# B

*Variants:* Bartok, Beltran, Bertrand; Bartram, Bert *(English)*;
Bertrando, Bertuccio *(Italian)*.
*See also* Bert.

**Bevan** *(Celtic)* Young archer.
*Variants:* Beavan, Beaven, Beven, Bevin.

**Bjorn** *(Scandinavian)* Bear.

**Blain** *(Celtic)* Slim; lean; *(Gaelic)* Yellow.
*Variants:* Blaine, Blane, Blayne.

**Blair** *(Celtic)* Field; plain.

**Blaise** *(Latin)* Stammerer.
*Variants:* Blayse, Blaze; Blasé *(French)*; Blasien,
Blasius *(Germanic)*; Biagio, Blasio *(Italian)*;
Blas *(Spanish)*.

**Blake** *(English)* Dark; black.

**Bland** *(Latin)* Mild; gentle.

**Blane, Blayne** *See* Blain.

**Bob** *See* Robert.

**Boden** *See* Baldwin.

**Bonar** *(French)* Courteous.

**Boris** *(Russian)* A fighter.

**Bowden** *See* Baldwin.

**Bowen** *(Celtic)* Son of Owen.

**Boyce** *(French)* Of the woods.

**Boyd** *(Celtic)* Fair-haired.

**Braden** *(English)* Wide valley.

**Bradey** *(English)* Broad meadow.

**Bradford** *(English)* Broad river crossing.

**Brand** *(English)* Firebrand.

**Brandan** *See* Brendan.

# B

**Brandon** *(English)* Gorse hill.
*Variants:* Branton.
*See also* Brendan.

**Branko** *See* Brian.

**Bray** *(English)* Brow of the hill.

**Breandan** *See* Brendan.

**Brecon** *(Welsh)* Mountains in Wales
(the Brecon Beacons).

**Breese** *(English)* Son of Rhees.

**Brendan** *(Celtic)* Prince.
*Variant:* Brandan, Brandon, Breandan, Brenden,
Brendin, Brendon.
*See also* Brandon.

**Brenton** *(English)* Tall and erect.
*Variant:* Brent.

**Brett** *(Celtic)* From Brittany.

**Brewster** *(Germanic)* A brewer.

**Brian** *(Celtic)* Strong; powerful.
*Variants:* Branko, Briano, Briant, Brien, Brion, Bryan,
Bryant, Bryon.

**Brice** *(Celtic)* Swift; ambitious.
*Variants:* Brisson, Bryce, Bryson.

**Brinsley** *(English)* Brin's meadow.
*Variant:* Brinsleigh.

**Brisson** *See* Brice.

**Brock** *(English)* A badger.

**Broderick** *(English)* Broad ridge.

**Brodie** *(Irish)* A ditch.
*Variant:* Brody.

# C

**Bruce** *(Scottish)* From the woods.

**Bruno** *(Germanic)* Brown.

**Bryan, Bryant** *See* Brian.

**Bryce** *See* Brice.

**Bryon** *See* Brian.

**Bryson** *See* Brice.

**Buadhach** *See* Victor.

**Burleigh** *(English)* Fort in a clearing.
  *Variants:* Burl, Burley, Burly.

**Burnard** *See* Bernard.

**Burton** *(English)* Dweller in the fortified town.

**Byron** *(English)* At the cow shed.

**Cadell** *See* Cadman.

**Cadman** *(Celtic)* Warrior.
  *Variants:* Cadmon, Caedmon; Cadell *(Welsh)*.

**Cadmus** *(Greek)* To the east.

**Cadwal** *(Gaelic)* Battle.

*Variant:* Cadwallader.

**Caesar** *(Latin)* Long hair; an ancient Roman emperor.
  *Variants:* Casar, Caesario, Caesarius; Cesar *(French, Spanish)*;
  Cesare *(Italian)*.

# C

**Caffar** *(Celtic)* Helmet.

**Cahil** *See* Kahil.

**Cailean** *See* Columba.

**Cain** *(Hebrew)* Possessed.
  *Variant:* Caine.

**Caine** *See* Cain, Kane.

**Caleb** *(Hebrew)* Bold and impetuous.
  *Variant:* Kaleb.

**Callaghan** *(Irish)* Strife.
  *Variant:* Callahan.

**Callum** *See* Columba, Malcolm.

**Calum** *See* Malcolm.

**Calvin** *(Latin)* Little bald one.

**Cameron** *(Gaelic)* Crooked nose.

**Camillus** *(Etruscan)* Religious attendant.
  *Variants:* Camille, Camillo.

**Campbell** *(Gaelic)* Crooked mouth.

**Caradoc** *(Welsh)* Affection; amiable.
  *Variants:* Caradog; Caradec *(French)*.

**Carey** *See* Cary, Charles.

**Carl** *See* Charles.

**Carleton** *See* Charlton.

**Carlos** *See* Charles.

**Carlton** *See* Charlton.

**Carney, Carny** *See* Karney.

**Carolus** *See* Charles.

**Carrick** *(Irish)* Rocky headland.

**Carroll** *(Celtic)* Warrior; champion fighter.

**Carter** *(English)* Maker of carts.

# C

**Cary** *(Celtic)* A place name.
*Variant:* Carey.
*See also* Charles.

**Casey** *(Irish)* Brave.

**Casimir** *(Slavic)* Destroyer of peace; a Polish duke who brought peace to the nation.

**Caspar** *(Persian)* Treasure keeper.
*Variants:* Casper; Jasper *(English)*; Gaspar, Gaspard *(French)*; Kaspar *(Germanic)*; Gasparo *(Italian)*; Kasper *(Polish)*; Gasper *(Slovenian)*.

**Cassidy** *(Irish)* Clever.

**Cassius** *(Latin)* Vain.

**Cecil** *(Latin)* Blind.
*Variants:* Cecile, Ceilius.

**Cedric** *(English)* Bounteous; friendly.
*Variant:* Cédric *(French)*.

**Cenhelm** *See* Kenelm.

**Cerdic** (Welsh) Beloved.

**Ceri** *See* Kerry.

**Cesar, Cesare** *See* Caesar.

**Chad** *(English)* Warrior.

**Chaim** *(Hebrew)* Life.
*Variant:* Hyram.

**Chandler** *(French)* Candle maker.

**Chandra** *(Sanskrit)* Moon.

**Charles** *(Germanic)* Virile; strong.
*Variants:* Carl, Karl; Carey *(Celtic)*; Karel *(Dutch, Swedish)*; Tearlach *(Gaelic)*; Cary *(Irish)*; Carlo *(Italian)*; Carolus *(Latin)*; Karoly *(Hungarian)*; Carlos *(Spanish)*.

**Charlton** *(English)* Free men's settlement.
*Variants:* Carleton, Carlton.

# C

**Chaske** *(Sioux)* Nickname for a first son.

**Chauncy** *(French)* Chancellor; church official.

**Cheng** *(Chinese)* Accomplished; successful.

**Chester** *(Latin)* Of the fortified camp.

**Chetan** *(Sioux)* Hawk.

**Chilton** *(English)* Of the children's farm.

**Christian** *(Latin)* A Christian.
*Variants:* Chrestien, Christen, Karstin, Kit, Krispin, Kristian, Kruschen; Christien, Chretien *(French)*.

**Christopher** *(Greek)* Bearer of Christ.
*Variants:* Christof, Christofer; Kit, Kristopher *(English)*; Christoph, Christophe *(French)*; Christophorus *(Germanic)*; Kristof *(Hungarian, Slovenian)*; Cristoforo *(Italian)*; Christoffer, Kris, Kristofor *(Scandinavian)*; Gillecriosd *(Scottish)*; Cristobal, Christoval *(Spanish)*.

**Ciaran** *(Gaelic)* Dark-haired one.
*Variants:* Cairan, Keir, Keiran, Kieran, Kieren, Kieron, Kyrin, Piran.

**Cirillo** *See* Cyril.

**Clarence** *(Latin)* Bright; illustrious.

**Clark** *(English)* An educated man or cleric.

**Claudius** *(Latin)* The lame.
*Variants:* Claud, Claudius, Klaud; Claudio *(Italian, Spanish)*.

**Claude** *See* Claudius.

**Claus, Clause** *See* Nicholas.

**Clayton** *(English)* Clay town.
*Variant:* Clay.

**Clement** *(Latin)* Merciful and kind.
*Variants:* Clemens, Clementius; Klement, Kliment *(Czech)*; Klemens *(Germanic)*; Keleman *(Hungarian)*; Clemente *(Italian)*; Clemento *(Spanish)*.

# C

**Clifford** *(English)* Cliff-side ford.
  *Variant:* Cliff.

**Clinton** *(English)* Hilltop town.
  *Variant:* Clint.

**Clive** *(English)* Cliff; slope.

**Clovis** *See* Lewis.

**Clunies** *(Gaelic)* Resting place.

**Cohen** *(Hebrew)* Priest.

**Coireall** *See* Kerry.

**Coisomo** *See* Cosmo.

**Colan** *See* Columba.

**Colby** *(English)* Of Cole's farm.

**Cole** *(Celtic)* Pledge.
  *See also* Nicholas.

**Colin** *See* Columba, Nicholas.

**Colm** *See* Malcolm.

**Columba** *(Latin)* Dove.
  *Variants:* Colan; Cailean, Callum, Colin, Collin, Colum
  *(Gaelic)*.
  *See also* Malcolm.

**Conal** *See* Conan.

**Conan** *(Celtic)* High and mighty.
  *Variants:* Conal, Connell, Konan, Kynan.

**Connor** *(Irish)* Lofty aims or desires.
  *Variant:* Conor.

**Conrad** *(Germanic)* Wise; bold.
  *Variants:* Conrade, Cort, Konrad, Konradin; Koenraad
  *(Dutch)*; Kurt *(English)*; Kort *(Scandinavian)*; Conrado
  *(Spanish)*.
  *See also* Curtis.

# C

**Conroy** *(Irish)* Wise man.

**Constantine** *(Latin)* Firm in faith.
Variants: Constantin *(French)*; Constantinos, Kostas *(Greek)*;
Konstantin *(Russian)*; Constantino *(Spanish)*.

**Corbin** *(French)* Raven.

**Corentin** *(French)* Friend.

**Corin** *(Latin)* Spear; several Christian saints.
Variants: Coren, Corrin, Korin, Korrin.

**Cormac** *(Gaelic)* Son of the charioteer; ancient high king of
Ireland.
Variants: Cormack, Cormick.

**Cornelius** *(Latin)* A horn.
Variants: Kornelius; Cornelis *(Dutch)*; Corneille *(French)*;
Cornelio *(Spanish)*.

**Cort** *See* Conrad.

**Cosmo** *(Greek)* Harmony and order.
Variants: Coisomo, Cosme.

**Courtney** *(French)* A place name.

**Craig** *(Celtic)* Stony hill; crag.

**Crichton** *(Gaelic)* Boundary.
Variants: Creighton.

**Crispin** *(Latin)* Curly-haired.
Variants: Crispianus, Crispo, Crispus, Krispin; Crispino
*(Italian)*.

**Cristobal, Cristoforo** *See* Christopher.

**Curtis** *(French)* Courteous.
Variants: Curt, Kurt.
See also Conrad.

**Cuthbert** *(English)* Famous; bright.

# D

**Cyrano** *(Greek)* Of Cyrene.
*Variant:* Cyran.

**Cyriack** *(Greek)* Lordly.
*Variant:* Syriack.

**Cyril** *(Greek)* Lord and master.
*Variants:* Cyrill, Cyrillus; Cyrille *(French)*; Cirillo *(Italian)*.

**Cyrus** *(Greek)* Throne.

**Dag** *(Norwegian)* Day.

**Dafod** *See* David.

**Dahana** *(Hindu)* A god in Hindu mythology.

**Daibidh** *See* David.

**Daichi** *(Japanese)* Great land.

**Daisuke** *(Japanese)* Great help.

**Dakarai** *(African)* Happiness.

**Dale** *(English, Norse)* Valley; dale dweller.

**Daley** *(Gaelic)* Assembly; descendant of Dalach.

**Dallas** *(Scottish)* A place name; wise.

**Dallin** *(English)* Pride's people.

**Dalton** *(English)* Valley farm.

**Daly** *(Gaelic)* Advisor.

**Damek** *(Czech)* Earth.

# D

**Damon** *(Greek)* One who tames.
  *Variants:* Damian, Damien; Damir *(Croatian)*; Damiano *(Italian)*; Damiao *(Portuguese)*.

**Dane** *(English)* From Denmark.
  *Variant:* Dana.

**Daniel** *(Hebrew)* God is my judge.
  *Variants:* Tanial *(Abenaki)*; Taniel *(Armenian)*; Daniele *(Italian)*; Danilo *(Spanish)*; Dannel *(Swiss)*.

**Danior** *(English)* Born with teeth.

**Dannel** *See* Daniel.

**Dante** *(Italian)* Long-lasting.
  *Variants:* Duran, Durand.

**Daran** *See* Darren.

**Darcy** *(Gaelic)* Dark-haired; from the castle.
  *Variants:* D'Arcey, Darcey, Darci, Darcie.

**Daren** *(Nigerian)* Born at night.

**Darius** *(Persian)* Possessing wealth.
  *Variants:* Darian, Darien.

**Darnell** *(English)* Hidden nook.

**Darrell** *(English)* Darling; beloved one.
  *Variants:* Darrel, Daryl, Derrell.

**Darren** *(Gaelic)* Little one.
  *Variants:* Daran, Darrin, Dorian.

**Darshan** *(Hindu)* A god in Hindu mythology.

**Darwin** *(English)* Beloved friend.

**Daryl** *See* Darrell.

**Dattatreya** *(Hindu)* A god, the son of Atri, in Hindu mythology.

**David** *(Hebrew)* Beloved; loved by God.
  *Variants:* Tabid *(Abenaki)*; Dafod, Davidas; Dawud *(Arabic)*; Taniel *(Armenian)*; Taavi *(Finnish)*; Davidde, Davide, Davin *(French)*; Daibhidh, Davis *(Gaelic)*; Tavi, Tavid *(Hebrew)*; Dafydd, Davyn, Dewi, Taffy *(Welsh)*.

# D

**Davin** *(Scandinavian)* Bright fin.
   *See also* David.

**Davis, Dawfydd, Dawud, Davyn** *See* David.

**Deacon** *(Greek)* Servant; messenger.

**Dean** *(English)* From the valley.
   *Variants:* Deane, Dene.

**Decimus** *(Latin)* Tenth child.

**Decker** *(Belgian)* Roofer.

**Declan** *(Gaelic)* Goodness.

**Delano** *(French)* Of the night.

**Deli** *(Hungarian)* Warrior.

**Delmar** *(French)* Mariner.

**Delmore** *(Latin)* Sea.

**Delsin** *(Native American)* He is so.

**Deman** *(Dutch)* Man.

**Demetrios** *(Greek)* Sacred.
   *Variants:* Demetri, Dimitri, Dimitry.

**Dempsey** *(Gaelic)* Proud.

**Dempster** *(English)* Judge.

**Denholm** *(Swedish)* Home of the Danes.

**Denis** *See* Dennis.

**Denley** *(English)* Valley meadow.

**Dennis** *(Greek)* Follower of Dionysos, the god of wine in
   Greek mythology.
   *Variants:* Denys, Dionysius; Denis *(French)*; Dionysus
   *(Germanic)*; Denes *(Hungarian)*; Dion, Dionigio, Dionisio
   *(Italian)*; Dionysos *(Latin)*.

**Dennison** *See* Tennyson.

**Denver** *(French)* Green valley.

**Denys** *See* Dennis.

# D

**Denzil** *(Cornish)* High.
*Variant:* Denzell.

**Deodatus** *(Latin)* Given to God.
*Variants:* Deodonatus; Deo *(Greek)*.

**Derek** *(Germanic)* Ruler of the people.
*Variants:* Derk, Derrick, Deryk, Diederich, Dirck, Dirk;
Diederik *(Danish)*; Ric, Rick, Ricky, Rickie *(English)*.

**Dermot** *(Gaelic)* Free man.
*Variants:* Dermott, Diarmid, Diarmit, Diarmuid, Duibhne.
*See also* Jeremiah.

**Derrell** *See* Darrell.

**Derrick** *See* Derek.

**Derry** *(Celtic)* Oak grove; a place name.
*Variant:* Derrie.

**Derwin** *(English)* Beloved friend.
*Variants:* Derryn, Derwyn.

**Deryk** *See* Derek.

**Desmond** *(Irish)* Man of South Munster.

**Devante** *(Spanish)* Fighter of wrong.

**Devarsi** *(Hindu)* The sage of the Gods in
Hindu mythology.

**Deverell** *(Welsh)* Riverbank.

**Devin** *(Gaelic)* Poet.

**Devlin** *(Gaelic)* Brave.

**Dewi** *See* David.

**Dewitt** *(Welsh)* Blond.

**Dexter** *(Latin)* Right-handed; skilful.

**Dhatri** *(Hindu)* A solar deity in Hindu mythology.

**Diarmaid** *See* Dermot, Jeremiah.

**Diarmid, Diarmit, Diarmuid** *See* Dermot.

# D

**Dick** *See* Richard.

**Dickinson** *(English)* Powerful, wealthy ruler.

**Diederich, Diederik** *See* Derek.

**Diego** *See* Jacob.

**Dieter** *(Germanic)* The people's ruler.

**Digby** *(English)* Settlement near a ditch; a place name.

**Dilip** *(Hindu)* A king who was an ancestor of King Rama in the epic Hindu poem *Ramayana*.

**Dillon** *(Gaelic)* Faithful.
*See also* Dylan.

**Dion, Dionigio, Dionisio, Dionysius, Dionysos, Dionysus** *See* Dennis.

**Dirck, Dirk** *See* Derek.

**Dixon** *(Germanic)* Powerful ruler.

**Dobry** *(Polish)* Good.

**Dobroslav** *(Slavic)* Glorious.

**Dolf** *See* Rudolph.

**Dominic** *(Latin)* Belonging to the Lord.
*Variants:* Dominichino, Dominick, Domenech; Dominik *(Czech, Polish)*; Dominique *(French)*; Domingo *(Italian, Spanish)*.

**Donald** *(Gaelic)* Prince of the universe; ruler of the world.
*Variants:* Donley; Tauno *(Finnish)*; Donal, Donnal, Donnell *(Gaelic)*.

**Donatien** *(French)* Gift.
*Variants:* Donat, Donatus, Donnet.

**Donley, Donnal, Donnell** *See* Donald.

**Donnelly** *(Celtic)* Brave black man.

**Donnet** *See* Donatien.

**Donovan** *(Irish)* Dark warrior.

# D

**Dorian** *See* Darren.

**Doron** *(Hebrew)* Gift.

**Dorset** *(English)* Tribe near the sea.

**Dougal** *See* Dugald.

**Douglas** *(Celtic)* Dark blue water.
*Variant:* Douglass.

**Doyle** *(Irish)* Dark foreigner.

**Drake** *(English)* Dragon; sign of the dragon.

**Drew** *(Welsh)* Wise.
*Variants:* Dru, Drue.
*See also* Andrew.

**Driscoll** *(Celtic)* Interpreter.

**Drostan** *See* Tristram.

**Dru, Drue** *See* Andrew, Drew.

**Duane** *See* Dwayne.

**Duarte** *See* Edward.

**Dudley** *(English)* From the meadow.

**Dugald** *(Irish)* Dark stranger.
*Variant:* Dougal.

**Duibhne** *See* Dermot.

**Duke** *See* Marmaduke.

**Duncan** *(Celtic)* Brown warrior.

**Dwayne** *(Gaelic)* Little dark one.
*Variant:* Duane, Dwane.

**Dwight** *(English)* Blond; white one.

**Dylan** *(Welsh)* Man of the sea.
*See also* Dillon.

# E

**Eadgar** *See* Edgar.

**Eadmund, Eamon, Eamonn** *See* Edmund.

**Eanruig** *See* Henry.

**Earl** *(English)* Nobleman; chief.
*Variants:* Airlie, Earle, Erle, Errol.

**Eaton** *(English)* Riverside village; a place name.

**Eban** *(Hebrew)* Stone.

**Ebenezer** *(Hebrew)* Stone of help; a battle site
in the Bible.

**Eberhard, Eberhart** *See* Everard.

**Eberto** *See* Herbert.

**Edan** *See* Aidan.

**Eden** *(Hebrew)* Delightful; adornment; paradise.

**Edgar** *(English)* Lucky spear.
*Variants:* Eadgar; Edgard *(French)*; Edgardo *(Italian,
Spanish)*; Adair *(Scottish)*.

**Edison** *(English)* Son of Edward.

**Edmund** *(English)* Wealthy protector.
*Variants:* Eadmund, Emmon, Ned, Ted, Teddy; Edmond
*(Dutch, French)*; Eamon *(Irish)*; Edmondo *(Italian)*.

**Edouard** *See* Edward.

**Edric** *(Anglo-Saxon)* Prosperous ruler.

**Edsel** *(English)* Wealthy man's house.

# E

**Edward** *(English)* Prosperous friend or guardian.
*Variants:* Edoal *(Abenaki)*; Edwardus, Edwin, Edwyn, Ned;
Eduart *(Albanian)*; Ted, Teddy *(English)*; Edouard *(French)*;
Eduard *(Germanic)*; Eduino *(Italian)*; Edvard *(Scandinavian)*;
Duarte, Eduardo *(Spanish)*.

**Egan** *See* Aidan.

**Egbert** *(English)* Bright sword.

**Egerton** *(English)* Edge.

**Egil** *(Scandinavian)* Edge or point of a weapon.

**Egmont** *(Germanic)* Weapon; defender.

**Egor** *See* George.

**Egyed** *(Hungarian)* Shield bearer.

**Eilian** *See* Alan.

**Einar** *(Norwegian)* Warrior; leader.

**Eirik** *See* Eric.

**Eisig** *(Hebrew)* He who laughs.

**Ekachakra** *(Hindu)* The son of Kashyapa, the father of the
gods and all of humanity in Hindu mythology; a place name.

**Eknath** *(Hindu)* Poet; a saint.

**Elbert** *See* Albert.

**Elden** *(English)* Older.

**Eldon** *(English)* Ella's mound.

**Eldridge** *(Germanic)* Venerable counsel.
*Variant:* Aldred, Eldred *(English)*.

**Eldwin** *(Germanic)* Old friend.

**Elek** *See* Alexander.

**Elgan** *(Welsh)* Bright circle.

**Elias** *(Hebrew)* Jehovah is God.
*Variants:* Eli, Elia, Elijah, Elijas, Eliott, Elisha, Elliot, Ely;
Ellis *(English)*.

# E

**Elkan** *(Hebrew)* He belongs to God.

**Ellery** *(English)* Elder tree.

**Elliot, Ellis** *See* Elias.

**Elmer** *See* Aylmer.

**Elroy** *(French)* The king.

**Elton** *(English)* Old town.
Variant: Alton.

**Elvin** *See* Alvin.

**Elvis** *(Norse)* All wise.
Variant: Alvis.

**Ely** *See* Elias.

**Emanuel, Emanuele** *See* Emmanuel.

**Emeri** *See* Emery.

**Emeric** *See* Almeric, Emery, Eric.

**Emerson** *(English)* Emery's son.

**Emery** *(Germanic)* To work and rule; strong home.
Variants: Amerigo, Amery, Emeri, Emeric, Emmery, Emory.
See also Amery.

**Emil** *(Germanic)* Hard working.
Variants: Emile, Emilio.

**Emir** *(Arabic)* Charming prince.

**Emmanuel** *(Hebrew)* God is with us.
Variants: Emanuel, Emanuele, Immanuel; Manny *(French, Spanish)*; Manovello, Manuel *(Spanish)*.
See also Manuel.

**Emmery** *See* Emery.

**Emmett** *(English)* Universal; all-embracing. Masculine form of Emma.
Variants: Emmet, Emmit, Emmott.

# E

**Emmon** *See* Edmund.

**Emmott** *See* Emmett.

**Emory** *See* Emery.

**Emrick** *(Welsh)* Immortal.

**Enrico, Enrique, Enzio** *See* Henry.

**Eoghan** *See* John.

**Eoin** *See* Owen.

**Ephraim** *(Hebrew)* Doubly fruitful.
  *Variants:* Ephram, Ephrem.

**Erasmus** *(Greek)* Desired; friendly.

**Erastus** *(Greek)* Loving.
  *Variant:* Rastus.

**Ercole** *See* Hercules.

**Erek** *(Polish)* Lovable.

**Erhard** *(Germanic)* Strong and determined.

**Eric** *(Norse)* Powerful ruler.
  *Variants:* Erick; Ric, Rick, Rickie, Ricky *(English)*;
  Emeric, Erich *(Germanic)*; Eirik *(Norwegian)*;
  Erik *(Swedish)*.

**Erle** *See* Earl.

**Ermanno, Ermin** *See* Herman.

**Ernest** *(Germanic)* Earnest.
  *Variants:* Ernst; Ernesto *(Italian)*; Ernestus *(Spanish)*.

**Errol** *See* Earl.

**Erskine** *(Gaelic)* High cliff; a place name.

**Erwin** *See* Irving.

**Eryx** *(Greek)* The son of Aphrodite and King Butes in Greek
  mythology.

**Esau** *(Hebrew)* Hairy.

# E

**Esdras** *See* Ezra.

**Esiban** *(Algonquin)* Raccoon.

**Esmond** *(English)* Beauty and grace.

**Esra** *See* Ezra.

**Essien** *(African)* Sixth-born son.

**Esteban, Estevan** *See* Stephen.

**Ethan** *(Hebrew)* Steadfast and strong.

**Ethelbert** *See* Albert.

**Etienne** *See* Stephen.

**Ettore** *See* Hector.

**Euan** *See* Evan.

**Eubule** *(Greek)* Good counsel.

**Eudo** *(Norse)* Child.

**Eudor** *(Greek)* Good gift.

**Eugene** *(Greek)* Well-born, noble.
*Variants:* Gene; Eugenius *(Celtic)*; Eugen *(Germanic)*;
Yevgenij *(Russian)*; Eugenio *(Spanish)*.

**Eustace** *(Greek)* Fruitful.
*Variants:* Eustas; Eustache *(French)*; Eustachio *(Italian)*;
Eustaquio *(Spanish)*.

**Evan** *(Welsh)* The young.
*Variants:* Euan, Ewan, Jevon, Owen.
*See also* John.

**Evander** *(Greek)* Benevolent ruler; a cultural hero in Greek
mythology.

**Everard** *(English)* Strong as a bear.
*Variants:* Eberhart, Everado, Evered, Everett, Everhart,
Evraud; Eberhard *(Germanic)*.

**Everett** *(Norse)* Wild boar.
*See also* Everard.

**Everhart, Evraud** *See* Everard.

**Ewan, Ewen** *See* Evan.

**Ezekiel** *(Hebrew)* God will strengthen.
*Variant:* Zeke.

**Ezio** *(Hebrew)* Friend; lover.

**Ezra** *(Hebrew)* Helper.
*Variants:* Esdras, Esra.

**Fabian** *(Latin)* Bean grower.
*Variants:* Fabien, Fabio, Fabius, Faliano.

**Fabrice** *(French)* Mechanic.
*Variants:* Fabrician, Fabricus, Fabron.

**Fagan** *(Gaelic)* Fiery one.
*Variant:* Fagin.

**Fairfax** *(English)* Blond-haired.

**Falgun** *(Hindu)* A month in the Hindu calendar.

**Faliano** *See* Fabian.

**Falkner** *(English)* Falcon trainer.

**Faraji** *(African)* Consolation.

**Faramond** *(Germanic)* Traveller's protection.

**Farkas** *(Hungarian)* Wolf.

**Farley** *(English)* Distant meadow.

**Farman** *(Anglo-Saxon)* Traveller.

**Farouk** *(Arabic)* To know right from wrong.

# F

**Farrar** *(Latin)* Blacksmith.

**Farrell** *(Celtic)* Courageous; man of valour.

**Farruco** *See* Frederick.

**Farquhar** *(Gaelic)* Brave; manly.

**Faustas** *(Latin)* Happy.

**Faxon** *(Germanic)* Long hair.

**Fearghas, Feargus** *See* Fergus.

**Felipe, Felipino** *See* Philip.

**Felix** *(Latin)* Happy.

**Fenton** *(English)* Marshland dweller.

**Feodore** *See* Theodore.

**Ferdinand** *(Germanic)* Adventurer.
Variants: Ferrand *(French)*; Ferdinando, Ferrante *(Italian)*; Fernando, Hernando *(Spanish)*.

**Ferenc** *(Latin)* Independent; free.
*See also* Francis.

**Fergus** *(Celtic)* The best choice.
Variants: Fearghas, Feargus.

**Ferguson** *(Celtic)* Son of Fergus.

**Ferran** *(Arabic)* Baker.

**Ferrand, Ferrante** *See* Ferdinand.

**Ferris** *See* Peter.

**Fidel** *(Latin)* Faithful and sincere.
Variant: Fidèle *(French)*.

**Fielding** *(English)* Field.

**Filib, Filip, Filippo** *See* Philip.

**Findlay** *(Gaelic)* Fair hero.
Variants: Finlay, Finn.

**Fineas** *See* Phineas.

# F

**Finlan** *(Gaelic)* Fair child.

**Finlay** *See* Findlay.

**Finn** *(Gaelic)* Fair; white; *(Norwegian)* Laplander.
*See also* Findlay.

**Fisk** *(Swedish)* Fisherman.

**Fitz** *(Latin)* Son.

**Fitzgerald** *(Germanic)* Son of Gerald.

**Flannan** *(Celtic)* Blood-red.

**Fleming** *(English)* A native of Flanders.

**Fletcher** *(French)* Arrow maker and seller.

**Floke** *(Germanic, Norse)* Guardian of the people.

**Florian** *(Latin)* Flourishing.

**Floyd** *See* Lloyd.

**Flynn** *(Irish)* Son of the red-haired one.

**Fodor** *(Hungarian)* Curly-haired.

**Fonda** *(Spanish)* Profound.

**Forbes** *(Scottish)* Man of prosperity.

**Ford** *(English)* River crossing.

**Forrest** *(Latin)* Woodsman; protector of the forest.
*Variants:* Forrester, Foster.

**Francis** *(Latin)* Frenchman.
*Variants:* Plasoa *(Abenaki)*; Franciscus, Frane, Frants;
François *(French)*; Frank, Franz, Franzisk *(Germanic)*;
Ferenc *(Hungarian)*; Francesco, Franco *(Italian)*;
Franciszek *(Polish)*; Frans *(Scandinavian)*; Francisco, Paco,
Pancho *(Spanish)*.

**François** *(French)* Frenchman; free.
*See also* Francis.

**Frank** *See* Franklin.

**Franklin** *(English)* Free man; freeholder.
*Variant:* Frank.

# G

**Frans, Frants, Franz, Franzisk** *See* Francis.

**Fraser** *(French)* Strawberry.
Variants: Frasier, Frazer.

**Fred** *See* Alfred, Frederick, Manfred.

**Frederick** *(Germanic)* Peaceful ruler.
Variants: Fredric, Friedrich, Fritz; Frederik *(Danish)*; Fred,
Fridrick, Ric, Rick, Rickie, Ricky *(English)*; Frederic
*(French)*; Federigo *(Italian)*; Fredericus *(Latin)*; Farruco,
Frederico *(Spanish)*; Fredrik *(Swedish)*.

**Fremont** *(Germanic)* Guardian of freedom.

**Fridrick, Friedrich, Fritz** *See* Frederick.

**Fujita** *(Japanese)* Field.

**Fulbert** *(French)* Abundance; brilliance.

**Fuller** *(English)* One who presses cloth for a living.

**Fulton** *(English)* Town near the field.

**Fu** *(Chinese)* Man.

**Fu-Hai** *(Chinese)* Man of the lake.

**Fyodor** *See* Theodore.

**Gabai** *(Hebrew)* Delight, adornment.

**Gabin** *(French)* Force of God.

**Gabriel** *(Hebrew)* Messenger of God; the archangel in the Bible.
Variants: Gabe, Gabel; Jibril *(Arabic)*; Gabor *(Hungarian)*;

Gabriele, Gabriello *(Italian)*; Gavriel *(Russian)*; Gabela *(Spanish)*.

**Gadil** *(Arabic)* God is my wealth.

**Gage** *(French)* Pledge; oath.

**Galen** *(Gaelic)* Calm.

**Galeno** *(Spanish)* Little bright one.

**Galéran** *(French)* Strange raven.

**Galip** *(Turkish)* Winner.

**Gallagher** *(Celtic)* Eager aide.

**Galloway** *(Latin)* From Gaul.

**Galterius** *See* Walter.

**Galvin** *(Irish)* Sparrow.

**Gamal** *(Arabic)* Camel.

**Gamba** *(African)* Warrior.

**Gamel** *(Norse)* Old.
  *Variant:* Gamble.

**Gannon** *(Irish)* Fair-skinned.

**Garcia** *See* Gerald.

**Gardner** *(Anglo-Saxon)* Gardener.
  *Variant:* Gardiner.

**Gareth** *(Welsh)* Gentle.
  *Variant:* Gary.

**Garett, Garret, Garrett, Garrick** *See* Gerard.

**Garfield** *(English)* Field of spears.
  *Variant:* Gary.

**Garin** *(Germanic)* Warrior.

**Garnet** *(English)* Dark red stone.

**Garth** *(Norse)* Keeper of the garden.

**Gary** *See* Gareth, Garfield, Gerald.

# G

**Gaspar, Gaspard, Gasparo, Gasper** *See* Caspar.

**Gaston** *(French)* Native of Gascony.

**Gates** *See* Yates.

**Gauthier, Gautier, Gualterior, Gualtiero** *See* Walter.

**Gavin** *(Scottish)* White hawk.
Variants: Gavan, Gaven, Gawayne, Gawen, Gawin; Gauvain *(French)*; Gawain *(Welsh)*.

**Gavrie** *(Russian)* Man of God.

**Gavriel** *See* Gabriel.

**Gawayne, Gawen, Gawin** *See* Gavin.

**Gaylord** *(French)* Brave strength.

**Gaynor** *(Gaelic)* Son of the fair-haired one.

**Gearalt** *See* Gerald.

**Geb** *See* Keb.

**Gebhard** *See* Gerard.

**Gedeon** *(Hungarian)* Warrior; destroyer.

**Geert** *(Germanic)* Brave strength.

**Geir** *(Norse)* Spear.

**Gene** *See* Eugene.

**Genkichi** *(Japanese)* Fortunate source.

**Geoffrey** *(Germanic)* Divine peace.
Variants: Geoff; Godfrey, Jeff, Jeffery, Jeffrey *(English)*; Geoffroi *(French)*; Gotfryd, Gottfried *(German)*; Goffredo *(Italian)*; Gotfryd *(Polish)*; Godfredo, Godofredo *(Spanish)*.

**George** *(Greek)* Tiller of the soil; farmer.
Variants: Georas, Georgious, Yiorgos; Jory *(Cornish)*; Jiri *(Czech)*; Jorgen *(Danish)*; Yorick *(English)*; Yrjo *(Finnish)*; Georges *(French)*; Georg *(Germanic)*; Gyorgy *(Hungarian)*; Giorgio *(Italian)*; Jerzy *(Polish)*; Egor, Igor, Yura, Yuri *(Russian)*; Jorge *(Spanish)*.

**Gerald** *(Germanic)* Ruler with a spear.
 *Variants:* Geralde, Gerold; Gerrit *(Dutch)*; Gary, Gerry, Jerry, Jervis *(English)*; Geraud, Giraud *(French)*; Jerald *(Germanic)*; Gearalt *(Irish)*; Giraldo *(Italian)*; Garcia *(Spanish)*.

**Gerard** *(Germanic)* Spear warrior.
 *Variants:* Gebhard, Gerhard, Gerhart; Garett, Garret, Garrett, Garrick, Gerry *(English)*; Geraud *(French)*; Gheradino *(Italian)*; Gerardo *(Spanish)*.

**Geraud** *See* Gerald, Gerard.

**Geremia** *See* Jeremiah.

**Gerhart** *See* Gerard.

**Germain** *See* Jermaine.

**Gerold** *See* Gerald.

**Gerome, Geronimo** *See* Jerome.

**Gerrit** *See* Gerald.

**Gerry** *See* Gerald, Gerard.

**Gersham** *(Hebrew)* Exiled.

**Gervaise** *See* Jarvis.

**Gerzson** *(Hungarian)* Stranger; banished.

**Gherardino** *See* Gerard.

**Giacobbe, Giacobo, Giacomo, Giacopo** *See* Jacob.

**Gian** *See* John.

**Gideon** *(Hebrew)* Feller of trees.

**Gifford** *(Germanic)* Bold gift.

**Gil** *(Hebrew)* Joy.
 *See also* Gilbert, Giles.

**Gilbert** *(Germanic)* Pledge.
 *Variant:* Gil.

**Gilchrist** *(Gaelic)* Servant of Christ.

# G

**Giles** *(Greek)* Wearer of the shield.
*Variant:* Gil.

**Gilleasbuig** *See* Archibald.

**Gillecriosd** *See* Christopher.

**Gilmer** *(Scottish)* Servant of the Virgin Mary.

**Gilroy** *(Latin)* Servant of the king.

**Ginton** *(Arabic)* Garden.

**Gioidano** *See* Jordan.

**Giorgio** *See* George.

**Giovanni** *See* John.

**Giraldo, Giraud** *See* Gerald.

**Giulio** *See* Julian.

**Givon** *(Arabic)* Hill; high.

**Glen** *(Celtic)* Of the glen.
*Variants:* Glenn, Glyn, Glynn, Glynne.

**Goddard** *(English)* Brave; firm.

**Godfrey, Godofredo** *See* Geoffrey.

**Godwin** *(English)* God's friend.

**Gofredo** *See* Geoffrey.

**Goldwin** *(English)* Golden friend.

**Gonzales** *(Spanish)* Wolf of war.
*Variant:* Gonzalo.

**Gordon** *(English, Gaelic)* Strong fortification.
*Variants:* Gordan, Gorden.

**Gotfryd** *See* Geoffrey.

**Gough** *(Welsh)* Red-haired.

**Grady** *(Gaelic)* Noble; illustrious.

**Graham** *(English)* Grey home.
*Variants:* Graeme, Grahame, Grame.

**Gram** *(Latin)* Grain.

**Grame** *See* Graham.

**Granger** *(English)* Farmer.

**Grant** *(French)* Big; tall.

**Grantham** *(English)* Big field.
Variants: Grantland, Grantley.

**Granville** *(French)* Big town.

**Grayson** *(English)* Son of Gray.

**Gregory** *(Greek)* Watchful.
Variants: Klegual *(Abenaki)*; Gregorie; Gregos *(Danish)*;
Greg, Gregg *(English)*; Gregoire *(French)*; Greagoir,
Griogair *(Gaelic)*; Grioghar *(Irish)*; Gregorio *(Italian)*;
Gregorius *(Latin)*; Grigori, Grigory *(Russian)*; Gregor,
Greig *(Scottish)*; Grigor *(Welsh)*.

**Gresham** *(English)* Grasslands.

**Griffith** *(Welsh)* Fierce chief.

**Grigor, Grigori, Grigory, Griogair, Grioghar** *See* Gregory.

**Griswold** *(Germanic)* A place name.

**Grosvenor** *(Latin)* Mighty hunter.

**Grover** *(English)* Grove of trees.

**Guénolé** *(French)* White; fair.

**Guglielmo** *See* William.

**Guido** *See* Guy.

**Guilhermo** *See* William.

**Guillaume, Guillermo** *See* William.

**Guiseppe** *See* Jonah, Joseph.

**Guistino** *See* Justin.

**Gunther** *(Germanic)* Warrior.
Variants: Gunnar, Gunthar.

# H

**Gustavus** *(Germanic)* Staff of God.
*Variant:* Gustav.

**Guy** *(French)* Guide.
*Variant:* Guido.

**Gwilym** *See* William.

**Gyorgy** *See* George.

**Gyula** *See* Julian.

**Haakon** *See* Hakon.

**Habib** *(Arabic)* Beloved.

**Hackett** *(Germanic)* Little woodsman.

**Hacon** *(Norse)* Useful; handy.
*Variant:* Haakon.

**Hadden** *(English)* Heather-covered moors.
*Variant:* Haden.

**Hadi** *(Arabic)* Guiding to the light.

**Hadrian** *See* Adrian.

**Hadwin** *(Germanic)* Friend in war.

**Hagan** *(Germanic)* Strong defence.

**Hagain** *(Gaelic)* The young one.

**Hahn** *(Germanic)* Rooster.

**Hai** *(Chinese)* Sea.

**Hakan** (*Norse*) Noble; highborn; exalted son; royal.
   *Variant:* Haakon.

**Halbert** (*Germanic*) Bright stone; shining hero.

**Halden** (*Scandinavian*) Half Danish.
   *Variant:* Halfdan.

**Hale** (*English*) Hero; army ruler.

**Hall** (*English*) From the hall or manor.
   *Variant:* Halen (*Swedish*).

**Halsey** (*English*) Hal's island.

**Hamal** (*Arabic*) Lamb.

**Hamilton** (*Scottish*) Flat-topped hill; a place name.

**Hamish** *See* Jacob.

**Hamlin** (*French*) Home lover.

**Hamlyn** *See* Henry.

**Hamon** (*Germanic*) House or home.

**HaNeul** (*Korean*) Sky.

**Hanley** (*English*) High meadow.

**Hannibal** (*Phoenician*) By the grace of God.

**Hannu** *See* John.

**Hanraoi** *See* Henry.

**Hans** *See* John.

**Hansen, Hanson, Hanssen** *See* Anson.

**Harailt, Harald** *See* Harold.

**Harbert** *See* Herbert.

**Harcourt** (*French*) A place name.

**Harden** (*English*) Hare valley.
   *Variant:* Hareton.

**Hardy** (*Germanic*) Robust; enduring.

**Harith** (*North African*) Cultivator.

**Harley** (*English*) The meadow where hares live.

# H

See also Harden.

**Harman, Harmann, Harmon** *See* Herman.

**Harold** *(English)* Ruler of the army.

> *Variants:* Harris, Harry; Harailt *(Gaelic)*; Aralt *(Irish)*; Harald *(Scandinavian)*.

**Haroun** *See* Aaron.

**Harper** *(English)* Harp player.

**Harris** *See* Harold.

**Harrison** *(English)* Son of Harry.

**Harry** *See* Harold, Henry.

**Harsh** *(Hindu)* Joy.

**Hartley** *(English)* Deer pasture.

**Haru** *(Japanese)* Born in the spring.

**Harvey** *(Breton)* Battle worthy.

> *Variant:* Hervey.

**Hassan** *(Arabic)* Handsome.

**Hastin** *(Hindu)* Elephant.

**Hastings** *(Germanic)* Swift one.

**Hauk** *(Norwegian)* Wild hawk.

**Havelock** *See* Oliver.

**Hayden** *(English)* Hedged valley.

> *Variants:* Haydon, Haydn, Hayes.

**Heath** *(English)* Heath.

**Heathcliff** *(English)* Cliff near heath.

**Heathcote** *(English)* Cottage among the heath.

**Hebel** *See* Abel.

**Hebert** *See* Herbert.

**Hector** *(Greek)* Steadfast.

> *Variant:* Ettore.

**Heikki, Heine, Heinrich, Heinz** *See* Henry.

# H

**Helmut** *(Germanic)* Courage and fame.
*Variant:* Helmuth.

**Henry** *(Germanic)* Home ruler; noble.
*Variants:* Heine, Heinrich, Heinz; Henk, Hendrik *(Dutch)*;
Hamlyn, Harry *(English)*; Heikki *(Finnish)*; Henri *(French)*;
Henrik *(Hungarian)*; Hanraoi *(Irish)*; Enrico, Enzio *(Italian)*;
Henricus *(Latin)*; Henrikas *(Lithuanian)*; Hendrick
*(Scandinavian)*; Eanruig *(Scottish)*; Enrique, Henrique
*(Spanish)*; Henrici *(Swedish)*.

**Heracles** *See* Hercules.

**Herbert** *(Germanic)* Outstanding warrior.
*Variants:* Hebert; Harbert *(Dutch)*; Hoireabard *(Irish)*;
Eberto, Heriberto *(Spanish)*.

**Hercules** *(Greek)* Lordly fame.
*Variants:* Heracles, Hercule; Ercole *(Italian)*.

**Heriberto** *See* Herbert.

**Herman** *(Germanic)* Warrior.
*Variants:* Armin, Harmon, Hermann, Hermon; Harman
*(English)*; Armand *(French)*; Ermin *(Greek)*; Armando,
Armant, Ermanno *(Italian)*.

**Hermes** *(Greek)* Noble.

**Hermon** *See* Herman.

**Hernando** *See* Ferdinand.

**Hervé** *(French)* Strong and brave.
*See also* Harvey.

**Hervey** *See* Harvey.

**Hideaki** *(Japanese)* Wisdom; cleverness.

**Hieronymus** *See* Jerome.

**Hilary** *(Latin)* Cheerful; merry.
*Variants:* Hillary, Hillery; Hilaire *(French)*; Ilario *(Italian)*;
Hilario *(Spanish)*.

**Hilliard** *(Germanic)* Guardian in war.

# H

**Hilton** *(English)* Manor on the hill.

**Hiram** *(Hebrew)* God is high.

**Hiroshi** *(Japanese)* Generous.

**Hisahito** *(Japanese)* Serene; virtuous.

**Hoa** *(Vietnamese)* Peace-loving.

**Hobart** *See* Hubert.

**Hoireabard** *See* Herbert.

**Holbrook** *(English)* Stream near a hollow; a place name.

**Holden** *(Germanic)* Kind; gracious.

**Holt** *(English)* Forest.

**Homer** *(Greek)* Pledge; security.
Variants: Homere, Homerus, Omero.

**Hongvi** *(Hopi)* Strong.

**Hont** *(Hungarian)* Breeder or friend of dogs.

**Horace** *(Latin)* From the ancient Roman surname Horatius.
*Variants:* Horacio, Horatio, Horatius, Horats, Orazio.

**Hoshi** *(Japanese)* Star.

**Houston** *(English)* Hill town.

**Howard** *(English)* Brave heart and mind.

**Hrodebert** *See* Robert.

**Hu** *(Chinese)* Brave as a tiger.

**Hubert** *(Germanic)* Bright-minded.
*Variants:* Bert, Hobart *(English)*; Uberto *(Italian)*;
Huberto *(Spanish)*.

**Hugh** *(Germanic)* Thoughtful mind.
Variants: Aodh, Aoidh *(Celtic)*; Hugo, Hugues *(French)*;
Ugo *(Italian)*; Hugo *(Latin)*.

**Hugo** *See* Hugh.

**Humphrey** *(Germanic)* Protector of peace.
*Variants:* Humfried; Humfry *(English)*; Humfrey *(French)*;
Onofrio *(Italian)*; Humfrid *(Scandinavian)*; Onofre *(Spanish)*.

**Hung** *(Vietnamese)* Powerful one.

**Hunter** *(English)* Hunter.

**Huntley** *(English)* Hunter's meadow.

**Hwang Fu** *(Chinese)* Rich future.

**Hyram** *See* Chaim.

**Iachimo, Iacovo, Iago** *See* Jacob.

**Iain, Ian, Iannis** *See* John.

**Ibrahim** *See* Abraham.

**Ichabod** *(Hebrew)* Glory has departed.

**Iestin** *See* Justin.

**Iggabri** *(InupiaQ)* Black bear.

**Ignatius** *(Latin)* Ardent; fiery.
*Variants:* Ignace *(French)*; Ignaz *(Germanic)*; Ignazio
*(Italian)*; Ignacio, Inigo *(Spanish)*.

**Igor** *See* George.

**Ikniq** *(InupiaQ)* Fire.

**Ilario** *See* Hilary.

**Ilias** *(Latin)* Jehovah is my God.

**Immanuel** *See* Emmanuel.

# I

**Imre** *(Germanic)* Great king.

**Incencio** *See* Kenneth.

**Indra** *(Hindu)* God of rain and thunder.

**Ingemar** *(Norse)* Famous son.
*Variant:* Ingmar.

**Inigo** *See* Ignatius.

**Inocente** *See* Kenneth.

**Ioan, Ioannes, Ion** *See* John.

**Ira** *(Hebrew)* A watcher.

**Irving** *(English)* Friend of the sea.
*Variants:* Erwin, Irvin, Irvine, Irwin.

**Isaac** *(Hebrew)* Laughter.
*Variants:* Itzhak, Yitzhak; Isaak, Izaak *(Germanic)*;
Isacco *(Italian)*.

**Isabulik** *(InupiaQ)* Angel.
*Variant:* Israbulik.

**Isaiah** *(Hebrew)* God's helper.

**Isas** *(Japanese)* Deserving.

**Irael** *(Hebrew)* Ruling with the Lord.

**Isha** *(Hindu)* Protector.

**Ishkode** *(Algonquin)* Fire.

**Istvan** *See* Stephen.

**Itzhak** *See* Isaac.

**Ivan** *See* John.

**Ivar, Iver** *See* Ivor.

**Ives, Ivo** *See* Yves.

**Ivor** *(Norse)* Archer.
*Variants:* Ifor, Ivar, Iver.

**Izaak** *See* Isaac.

**Jabari** *(African)* Brave; fearless.
  *Variant:* Jabbar.

**Jabez** *(Hebrew)* Born in pain or sorrow.

**Jabir** *(Arabic)* Comforter.

**Jabulani** *(Zulu)* Be happy.

**Jacabo** *See* Jacob.

**Jacek** *(Polish)* Hyacinth flower.
  *Variant:* Jacinto *(Spanish)*.

**Jack** *See* Jacob, John.

**Jackson** *(English)* Son of Jack.

**Jacob** *(Hebrew)* Supplanter; one who takes over.
  *Variants:* Jan *(Belgian, Scandinavian, Slavic)*; Jago *(Cornish)*;
  Jakov *(Croatian)*; Janco, Janek *(Czech)*; Jens *(Danish)*; Jack,
  Jake, James, Jamie, Jay, Jem, Jim, Jimmy *(English)*; Jacques
  *(French)*; Jakob *(Germanic)*; Jakab, Janos *(Hungarian)*;
  Giacobbe, Giacobo, Giacomo, Giacopo, Iachimo, Iacovo
  *(Italian)*; Jacobus *(Latin)*; Jakub, Jas, Kobi, Koby, Kuba
  *(Polish)*; Jascha, Yakov *(Russian)*; Diego, Iago, Jacobo,
  Jaime, Jaimie, Jayme, Jaymie *(Spanish)*.

**Jael** *(Hebrew)* To ascend.

**Jafar** *(Hindu)* Little stream.

**Jagdish** *(Sanskrit)* World leader.

**Jagger** *(English)* Carrier; carter.

**Jago** *See* Jacob.

# J

**Jai** *See* Jay.

**Jaime, Jaimie** See Jacob.

**Jairo** *(Spanish)* God sheds light.

**Jakab** *See* Jacob.

**Jake** *See* Jacob, John.

**Jakeem** *(Arabic)* Noble.

**Jakob, Jakov, Jakub** See Jacob.

**Jalil** *(Arabic)* Majestic; great.
 *Variant:* Jaleel.

**Jamal** *(Arabic)* Handsome.

**James** *(English/Hebrew)* Supplanter; one who takes over.
 Originally a form of Jacob but now used as a distinct name
 on its own.
 *Variants:* Jamie, Jem, Jim, Jimmy; Seamus, Shamus *(Irish)*;
 Hamish *(Scottish)*.
 *See also* Jacob.

**Jamieson** *(English)* Son of James.
 *Variants:* Jameson, Jamison.

**Jan, Janco, Janos, Janek** See Jacob, John.

**Janson** *(Scandinavian)* Son of Jan.
 *Variants:* Jansen, Jantzen, Janzen.

**Jared** *See* Jordan.

**Jarek** *(Polish)* Month of the year.

**Jaret, Jareth** *See* Jordan.

**Jaron** *(Hebrew)* A cry or song of rejoicing.

**Jarratt** *(Germanic)* Spearman.
 *Variant:* Jarrett.
 *See also* Jordan.

**Jarred** *See* Jordan.

**Jarrett** *See* Jarratt, Jordan.

# J

**Jarrod** *See* Jordan.

**Jarvis** *(Germanic)* Sharp spear.

  *Variants:* Jervis *(English)*; Gervaise *(French)*.

**Jas** *See* Jacob, John.

**Jascha** *See* Jacob.

**Jason** *(Greek)* Healer.

**Jasper** *See* Caspar.

**Javan** *(Latin)* Angel of Greece.

**Javier** *See* Salvador, Xavier.

**Jay** *(Latin)* Jaybird.

  *Variant:* Jai.

  *See also* Jacob.

**Jayant** *(Hindu)* Victorious.

**Jayme, Jaymie** *See* Jacob.

**Jayvyn** *(African)* Light spirit.

**Jean** *See* John.

**Jean-Baptiste** *(French)* John the Baptist.

**Jedidiah** *(Hebrew)* Loved by God.

  *Variants:* Jed, Jedediah.

**Jedrek** *(Polish)* Strong; manly.

**Jeevan** *(Hindu)* Life.

**Jeff** *See* Geoffrey.

**Jefferson** *(English)* Son of Jeffrey.

  *See also* Geoffrey.

**Jeffery, Jeffrey** *See* Geoffrey.

**Jelani** *(African)* Mighty; strong.

**Jem** *See* Jacob, Jeremiah.

**Jenci** *See* Jensi.

**Jenda** *(Czech)* God is good.

**Jens** *See* Jacob.

# J

**Jensen** *(Nordic)* God is gracious

**Jensi** *(Hungarian)* Well-born.
  *Variant:* Jenci.

**Jerald** *See* Gerald.

**Jeremiah** *(Hebrew)* Exalted by the Lord.
  *Variants:* Jeremias; Jem, Jeremy, Jerry *(English)*; Jorma
  *(Finnish)*; Diarmaid, Diarmuid *(Irish)*; Geremia *(Italian)*.

**Jericho** *(Arabic)* City of the moon.

**Jermaine** *(French)* German.
  *Variants:* Germain, Jermain.

**Jermyn** *(Cornish)* The name of a saint.

**Jerome** *(Greek)* Holy name.
  *Variants:* Hieronymus; Jeroen *(Dutch)*; Jerry *(English)*;
  Jérôme *(French)*; Jeronimus *(Germanic)*; Jerolin *(Latin)*;
  Gerome, Geronimo *(Spanish)*.

**Jerrod** *See* Jordan.

**Jerry** *See* Gerald, Jeremiah, Jerome.

**Jervis** *See* Gerald, Jarvis.

**Jerzy** *See* George.

**Jesse** *(Hebrew)* God's grace; he beholds.

**Jesus** *(Hebrew)* Saviour; God is salvation.
  *Variant:* Yeshua.

**Jet** *(Latin)* Black; stone.
  *Variant:* Jett.

**Jethro** *(Hebrew)* Abundance; excellence.

**Jett** *See* Jet.

**Jevon** *See* Evan.

**Jiang** *(Chinese)* River.

**Jibril** *See* Gabriel.

**Jie** *(Chinese)* Wonderful boy.

**Jim, Jimmy** *See* Jacob.

**Jimuta** *(Hindu)* A name for the sun god in Hindu mythology.
*Variant:* Jivana.

**Jin** *(Chinese)* Gold; *(Korean)* Truth.

**Jindra** *(Czech)* Leader.

**Jing** *(Chinese)* Pure.

**Jiro** *(Japanese)* Second son.

**Jitendra** *(Hindu)* Conqueror of the god Indra.
*Variant:* Jitender.

**Jiri** *See* George.

**Jivana** *See* Jimuta.

**Jivanta** *(Sanskrit)* Long-lived.

**Jo** *See* Joseph.

**Joachim** *(Hebrew)* God will establish.
*Variants:* Jochim *(Germanic)*; Akim, Yakim *(Russian)*;
Joaquim, Joaquin *(Spanish)*.

**Joao** *See* John.

**Job** *(Hebrew)* The persecuted one.

**Jochim** *See* Joachim.

**Jock** *See* John.

**Joe** *See* Joseph.

**Joel** *(Hebrew)* The Lord is God.
*Variant:* Yoel.

**Joey** *See* Joseph.

**John** *(Hebrew)* God is gracious.
*Variants:* Jon; Yahya *(Arabic)*; Jan *(Belgian, Scandinavian, Slavic)*; Eoghan, Eoin *(Celtic)*; Janco, Janek *(Czech)*; Evan, Jack, Jake, Johnny, Zane *(English)*; Hannu, Juhani, Jussi *(Finnish)*; Jean, Jonn, Yann, Yannick, Yannis *(French)*; Hans, Johann, Yohann *(Germanic)*; Iannis, Ioannes, Yiannis *(Greek)*; Janos *(Hungarian)*; Sean,

# J

Shane, Shaun, Shawn *(Irish)*; Gian, Giovanni *(Italian)*; Johannes *(Latin)*; Jas *(Polish)*; Joao *(Portuguese)*; Ioan, Ion *(Romanian)*; Ivan, Vanya *(Russian)*; Iain, Ian, Jock *(Scottish)*; Juan *(Spanish)*.

**Johnathan** *See* Jonathan.

**Johnny** *See* John.

**Johnson** *(English)* Son of John.
*Variants:* Johnston, Jonson.

**Jojo** *(African)* Born on Monday.

**Jon** *See* John.

**Jonah** *(Hebrew)* The dove.
*Variants:* Jonas *(Germanic)*; Giuseppe *(Italian)*.

**Jonathan** *(Hebrew)* Gift of the Lord.
*Variants:* Johnathan, Jon, Jonathen, Jonathon, Jonothon.

**Jonn** *See* John.

**Jordan** *(Hebrew)* To descend.
*Variants:* Jared, Jaret, Jareth, Jarred, Jarrett, Jarrod, Jerrod; Jourdain, Jourdan *(French)*; Gioidano *(Italian)*.

**Jorge, Jorgen** *See* George.

**Jorma** *See* Jeremiah.

**Jory** *See* George.

**Joseph** *(Hebrew)* God will increase.
*Variants:* Sozap *(Abenaki)*; Yosef; Yusuf *(Arabic)*; Josip *(Croatian)*; Jozef *(Czech, Polish)*; Jo, Joe, Joey *(English)*; Giuseppe, Peppe, Pino *(Italian)*; Jose, Pepe *(Spanish)*.

**Joshua** *(Hebrew)* God is generous.
*Variants:* Josh; Yusha *(Arabic)*; Giosa *(Italian)*; Joaquin *(Spanish)*; Yehosha *(Yiddish)*.
*See also* Joachim.

**Josiah** *(Hebrew)* Healed by the Lord.
*Variants:* Josias.

**Josip** *See* Joseph.

**Jourdain, Jourdan** *See* Jordan.

**Joza** *(Czech)* God will give.
Variants: Jozanek, Jozka.

**Jozef** *See* Joseph.

**Juan** *See* John.

**Jude** *(Hebrew)* Praised; Judas was the name of one of the
twelve apostles in the Bible, the one who betrayed Jesus.
*Variants:* Judah, Judas, Yehudi.

**Juhani** *See* John.

**Julian** *(Greek)* Youthful one.
*Variants:* Juliao, Julion, Julius, Julot; Jules, Julien *(French)*;
Gyula *(Hungarian)*; Giulio *(Italian)*; Julio *(Spanish)*.

**Juma** *(Swahili)* Born on Friday.

**Jun** *(Chinese)* Truth; *(Japanese)* Swift steed.

**Junior** *(English)* Young.

**Junius** *(Latin)* Born in June.

**Jupiter** *(Latin)* The supreme god in Roman mythology;
a planet.

**Jur** *(Czech)* Farmer.

**Juri** *See* George.

**Jussi** *See* John.

**Justin** *(Latin)* Just; justice.
*Variants:* Justis; Justyn *(Czech, Polish)*; Justus *(Germanic)*;
Guistino *(Italian)*; Justino *(Spanish)*; Iestin, Yestin *(Welsh)*.

# K

**Kacey** *See* Kasey.

**Kadar** *(Arabic)* Powerful; talented.
  *Variants:* Kadir, Kedar, Qadir.

**Kadin** *(Arabic)* Friend.
  *Variant:* Kadeen.

**Kadir** *See* Kadar.

**Kado** *(Japanese)* To enter.

**Kaelan** *(Gaelic)* Strong soldier.
  *Variants:* Kalan, Kalen, Kalin.

**Kafir** *(Arabic)* Infidel.

**Kahil** *(Greek)* Beautiful; *(Hebrew)* Perfect one.
  *Variants:* Cahil, Kaleel, Kahlil.
  *See also* Kalil.

**Kai** *(Hawaiian)* Sea; *(Persian)* King.
  *See also* Kay.

**Kaii** *(Gwich'in)* Willow.

**Kain** *See* Kane.

**Kaiser** *(Germanic)* Hairy one; ruler.

**Kaj** *(Greek)* From the earth.

**Kala** *(Sanskrit)* Black.

**Kalan** *See* Kaelan.

**Kale** *(Hawaiian)* Man.

**Kaleb** *See* Caleb.

**Kaleel** *See* Kahil.

# K

**Kalen** *See* Kaelan.

**Kalil** *(Arabic)* Friend.
*Variants:* Kahlil, Khalil.

**Kalin** *See* Kaelan.

**Kaliq** *(Arabic)* Artistic one.

**Kalkin** *(Hindu)* Eternity; time; the final incarnation of the god Vishnu in Hindu mythology.

**Kalmin** *(Scandinavian)* Man.

**Kamau** *(Kenyan)* Warrior.

**Kanai** *(Hawaiian)* Winner.

**Kane** *(Celtic)* Bright; radiant; warrior.
*Variants:* Caine, Kain, Kayne.

**Kang** *(Chinese)* Healthy.

**Kaniq** *(InupiaQ)* Frost.

**Kano** *(Japanese)* Lord of the water.

**Kantu** *(Hindu)* Happy.

**Kanu** *(Hindu)* Beautiful.

**Kapildev** *(Hindu)* A god in Hindu mythology.

**Karam** *(Arabic)* Generous; charitable.

**Kare** *(Norwegian)* Large one.

**Karel** *See* Charles.

**Kari** *(Norse)* Breeze; curly hair.

**Karim** *(Arabic)* Generous; *(Sanskrit)* Valuable.

**Karl** *See* Charles.

**Karney** *(Irish)* Winner.
*Variants:* Carney, Carny, Karny, Kearney.

**Karoly** *See* Charles.

**Karstin** *See* Christian.

**Kaseeb** *See* Kasib.

# K

**Kaseko** *(African)* One who teases.

**Kasey** *(English)* Man who speaks of peace.
*Variant:* Kacey.

**Kasi** *(Hindu)* Clever one.

**Kasib** *(Arabic)* Fertile one.
*Variant:* Kaseeb.

**Kasim** *See* Qasim.

**Kaspar, Kasper** *See* Caspar.

**Katsutoshi** *(Japanese)* To win cleverly.

**Kaul** *(Arabic)* Trustworthy.

**Kay** *(Welsh)* Joy.
*Variant:* Kai.
*See also* Kai.

**Kayin** *(Nigerian)* Famous.

**Kayne** *See* Kane.

**Kazuki** *(Japanese)* Shining one.

**Kazuo** *(Japanese)* Man of peace; first son.

**Kazuya** *(Japanese)* To be harmonious.

**Keane** *(English)* Bold; intelligent; sharp.
*Variants:* Kean, Keen, Keene.

**Keanu** *(Hawaiian)* Breeze across the mountains.

**Kearn** *(Irish)* Dark.
*Variant:* Kern.

**Kearney** *See* Karney.

**Keaton** *(English)* From the place where hawks fly.
*Variants:* Keeton, Keyton.

**Keb** *(Egyptian)* Earth; the God of the earth in Egyptian mythology.
*Variant:* Geb, Seb.

**Kedar** *See* Kadar.

**Keef, Keefer** *See* Keifer.

**Keegan** *(Irish)* Little high-spirited one.

**Keelan** *(Irish)* Small one.

**Keen** *See* Keane.

**Keenan** *(Irish)* Little wise one.
   *Variants:* Kienan, Kienen, Kynan.

**Keene** *See* Keane.

**Keeton** *See* Keaton.

**Kefir** *(Hebrew)* Lion cub.

**Keifer** *(Irish)* Beautiful; beloved.
   *Variants:* Keefe, Keefer.

**Keiran** *See* Ciaran.

**Keitaro** *(Japanese)* Blessed one.

**Keith** *(Gaelic)* Woods; forest.

**Kel** *See* Kelvin.

**Kelby** *(Germanic)* Farm near the spring.

**Kele** *(Native American)* Hawk.

**Keleman** *See* Clement.

**Kell** *(Norse)* Well; spring.

**Kelly** *(Irish)* Warrior.
   *Variants:* Kelle, Kellen, Kelley.

**Kelsey** *(Norse)* Island.
   *Variants:* Kelsie, Kelsy.

**Kelvin** *(English)* Sailor's friend.
   *Variants:* Kel, Kelvan, Kelven, Kelvyn, Kelwin, Kelwyn.

**Kemal** *(Turkish)* Honourable one.

**Keme** *(Algonquin)* Secret.

**Kemp** *(English)* Warrior; champion.

**Kempton** *(English)* Town of warriors.

# K

**Ken** *See* Kennedy, Kenneth.

**Kendall** *(Celtic)* Chief of the valley.
*Variant:* Kendal.
*See also* Kenneth.

**Kendrick** *(English)* Royal ruler.
*Variants:* Kendrik, Kendryck.

**Kenelm** *(English)* Brave protector.
*Variant:* Cenhelm.

**Kenji** *(Japanese)* Second son.

**Kennard** *(English)* Powerful; brave.
*Variant:* Kennerd.

**Kennedy** *(Gaelic)* Ugly head; helmet head.
*Variant:* Ken.

**Kenneth** *(Gaelic)* Handsome.
*Variants:* Ken, Kennett, Kenney, Kenny; Kendall, Kennith
*(English)*; Kesha *(Russian)*; Incencio, Inocente *(Spanish)*.

**Kent** *(Welsh)* Bright one.

**Kenton** *(English)* Royal town.

**Kenward** *(English)* Brave guard.
*Variant:* Kenway.

**Kenwyn** *(Welsh)* Splendid leader.

**Kenyon** *(Irish)* Blond boy.

**Keon** *(Irish)* Well-born.
*Variant:* Kion.

**Kerel** *(African)* Young man.

**Kermit** *(Irish)* Without jealousy.

**Kern** *See* Kearn.

**Kerr** *(Irish)* Sword; spear; *(Scandinavian)* Swampland.

**Kerry** *(Irish)* Dark one.
*Variants:* Ceri, Coireall, Kerrill.

**Kesha** *See* Kenneth.

# K

**Kevin** *(Irish)* Handsome; kind.
  *Variants:* Kevan, Keven.

**Keyton** *See* Keaton.

**Khaii** *(Gwich'in)* Winter.

**Khalil** *See* Kalil.

**Kienan, Kienen** *See* Keenan.

**Kieran, Kieren, Kieron** *See* Keiran.

**Kiet** *(Thai)* Honour.

**Kilian** *(Celtic)* Warrior.
  *Variants:* Keelan, Killian, Killin.

**Killian, Killin** *See* Kilian.

**Kim** *(Vietnamese)* Gold.
  *See also* Kimball, Kimberly.

**Kimball** *(English)* Brave warrior; leader.
  *Variants:* Kembell, Kim, Kimbal, Kimbell, Kimble.

**Kimberley** *(English)* Ruler.
  *Variant:* Kim.

**Kin** *(Japanese)* Golden.

**Kingsley** *(English)* Of the king's meadow.

**Kingston** *(English)* The king's town.
  *Variant:* Kinston.

**Kinnard** *(Irish)* Tall hill.

**Kinston** *See* Kingston.

**Kion** *See* Keon.

**Kipp** *(English)* Peaked hill.
  *Variant:* Kip.

**Kir** *(Bulgarian)* Sun.

**Kiran** *(Sanskrit)* Ray of light.

**Kirby** *(Norse)* Village church.

**Kirgavik** *(InupiaQ)* Peregrine falcon.

# K

**Kirill** *(Russian)* Ruler.

**Kirk** *(Norse)* Place by the church.
  *Variants:* Kirke, Kirkland.

**Kishi** *(Japanese)* Long and happy life.

**Kit** *See* Christian, Christopher.

**Kito** *(Swahili)* Jewel.

**Kiyoshi** *(Japanese)* Quiet one.

**Klaud** *See* Claude.

**Klaus** *See* Nicholas.

**Klemens** *See* Clement.

**Knox** *(Irish)* Boy from the hill.

**Knut** *(Norse)* Knot.
  *Variant:* Knute.

**Koby** *See* Jacob.

**Koenraad** *See* Conrad.

**Kofi** *(Ghanaian)* Born on Friday.

**Koji** *(Japanese)* Child.

**Kojo** *(Ghanaian)* Born on Monday.

**Konan** *See* Conan.

**Konrad, Konradin** *See* Conrad.

**Konstantin** *See* Constantine.

**Koren** *(Hebrew)* Shining one.

**Kornelius** *See* Cornelius.

**Kort** *See* Conrad.

**Kosma** *(Ukrainian)* Peace and order.

**Kostas** *See* Constantine.

**Kouhei** *(Japanese)* Calm peace.

**Kris** *See* Christopher.

**Krishna** *(Sanskrit)* Black.

**Krispin** *See* Christian, Crispin.

**Kristian** *See* Christian.

**Kristof, Kristofer, Kristopher, Kristova** *See* Christopher.

**Kruschen** *See* Christian.

**Kuba** *See* Jacob.

**Kuma** *(Japanese)* Bear.

**Kumar** *(Sanskrit)* Son; prince.

**Kunik** *(InupiaQ)* Kiss.

**Kurt** *See* Conrad, Curtis.

**Kuwakei** *(Tlingit)* Good weather.

**Kwame** *(Ghanaian)* Born on Saturday.

**Kwan** *(Korean)* Powerful.

**Kwas** *(Ghanaian)* Born on Sunday.

**Kyle** *(Gaelic)* Fair and handsome; from the channel.

**Kynan** *See* Conan, Keenan.

**Kyne** *(English)* Royal.

**Kyrin** *See* Keiran.

**Kyros** *(Greek)* Master.

**Kyubok** *(Korean)* Blessed.

**Labhrainn, Labhras** *See* Laurence.

**Lacey** *(French)* Lace.
   *Variant:* Lacy.

# L

**Lachlan** *(Scottish)* War-like.
  *Variant:* Laughlan.

**Lacy** *See* Lacey.

**Ladan** *(Hebrew)* Witness.

**Ladd** *(English)* Young man.

**Ladislav** *(Slavic)* Glory; power; leadership.
  *Variants:* Vladislav *(Czech)*; Laszlo *(Hungarian)*; Ladislo
  *(Italian)*; Ladislaus *(Latin)*.

**Lael** *(Hebrew)* Belonging to God.

**Laine** *See* Lane.

**Laird** *(Scottish)* Lord of the manor.

**Lajos** *See* Lewis.

**Lamar** *(Germanic)* Famous.
  *Variant:* Lemar *(French)*.

**Lambert** *(Germanic)* Bright land.
  *Variants:* Lambard; Lammert *(Dutch)*; Lamberto *(Italian)*.

**Lamont** *(Norse)* Lawman.
  *Variant:* Lamond.

**Lance** *(French)* Land.
  *Variants:* Lancelin, Lancelot, Launcelot; Launce *(English)*;
  Lanzo *(Germanic)*.

**Landon** *(English)* Grassy meadow.
  *Variants:* Landen, Landin.

**Lane** *(English)* Narrow road.
  *Variant:* Laine.

**Lang** *(Germanic)* Long; tall.

**Langdon** *(English)* Long hill.

**Langley** *(English)* Long meadow.

**Lanzo** *See* Lance.

**Lap** *(Vietnamese)* Independent.

**Larkin** *(Irish)* Cruel.

**Laron** *(French)* Thief.

**Larrance, Larry, Lars, Lasse** *See* Laurence.

**Laszlo** *See* Ladislav.

**Lateef** *(Arabic)* Gentle and pleasant.
*Variant:* Latif.

**Latimer** *(French)* Teacher of Latin.

**Laughlan** *See* Lachlan.

**Launce, Launcelot** *See* Lance.

**Laurence** *(Latin)* Crowned with laurel.
*Variants:* Larrance, Laurans; Lauritz *(Danish)*; Lorenz
*(Danish, Germanic, Polish)*; Laurens *(Dutch)*; Larry, Laurie,
Lawrance, Lawrence *(English)*; Lasse *(Finnish)*; Lauren,
Laurent *(French)*; Laurenz *(Germanic)*; Labhras *(Irish)*;
Lorenzo *(Italian, Spanish)*; Lourenco *(Portuguese)*; Lars,
Loren *(Scandinavian)*; Labhrainn *(Scottish)*.

**Lawson** *(English)* Son of Lawrence.

**Layland** *See* Leland.

**Lazarus** *(Hebrew)* He whom God helps.
*Variants:* Lazare *(French)*; Lazaro, Lazzaro *(Italian)*.

**Lazare** *See* Lazarus.

**Leander** *(Greek)* Lion man.
*Variants:* Leandre *(French)*; Leandros *(Greek)*; Leandro
*(Italian, Spanish)*.

**Lear** *(Germanic)* From the sea.

**Lee** *(English)* Meadow; clearing.
*Variant:* Leigh.

**Lei** *(Chinese)* Thunder.

**Leibel** *(Hebrew)* Lion.
*Variant:* Leib.

**Leicester** *See* Lester.

# L

**Leif** *(Scandinavian)* Love.
*Variants:* Leiv, Lief.

**Leigh** *See* Lee.

**Leith** *(Celtic)* Wide river.

**Leiv** *See* Leif.

**Leland** *(English)* Meadowland.
*Variants:* Layland, Leyland.

**Lemar** *See* Lamar.

**Len, Lenny, Lennard** *See* Leonard.

**Leo** *(Latin)* Lion; an astrological sign.
*Variants:* Lyle *(English)*; Leon, Lionel *(French)*; Lionello *(Italian)*; Levin *(Russian)*.

**Leoline** *See* Llewellyn.

**Leon** *See* Napoleon.

**Leonard** *(Germanic)* As strong as a lion.
*Variants:* Leonhard; Len, Lennard, Lenny *(English)*; Leonardo, Lionardo *(Italian, Spanish)*; Leonid *(Russian)*.

**Leopold** *(Germanic)* Brave people.
*Variants:* Leupold, Luitpoid; Leopoldo *(Italian, Spanish)*.

**Leron** *(Hebrew)* Song.

**Leroy** *(French)* King.

**Leslie** *(Scottish)* Grey castle.

**Lester** *(English)* From the city of Leicester.
*Variant:* Leicester.

**Leupold** *See* Leopold.

**Levi** *(Hebrew)* Promise; united.

**Levin** *See* Leo.

**Lewin** *(English)* Beloved friend.

**Lewis** *(Germanic)* Famous fighter.
*Variants:* Alois, Ludwig; Lodewijk *(Dutch)*; Ludovic *(English)*; Lajos *(Hungarian)*; Lugaidh *(Irish)*; Lodovico,

Luigi *(Italian)*; Aloys, Aloysius, Ludovicus *(Latin)*; Clovis, Louis *(French)*; Luiz *(Portuguese)*; Ludvig *(Scandinavian)*; Luthais *(Scottish)*; Luis *(Spanish)*.

**Leyland** *See* Leland.

**Leyton** *(English)* Town by the meadow.
*Variants:* Layton, Leighton.

**Li** *(Chinese)* Strength.

**Liam** *See* William.

**Liang** *(Chinese)* Good.

**Libor** *(Czech)* Freedom.
*Variants:* Liborek; Liberio *(Portuguese)*.

**Lief** *See* Leif.

**Liem** *(Vietnamese)* Honest.

**Lin** *(Chinese)* Forest.

**Lincoln** *(Celtic)* Lake town.

**Lindell** *(English)* Valley of lime trees.
*Variants:* Lindall, Lyndall, Lyndell.

**Lindsay** *(English)* Of the lime tree.
*Variants:* Linden, Lindley, Lindon, Linsay, Linsey, Lyndon; Lysander *(Scottish)*.

**Linford** *(English)* Ford of lime trees.
*Variant:* Lynford.

**Linsay, Linsey** *See* Lindsay.

**Linton** *See* Lynton.

**Lintu** *(Maliseet)* To sing.

**Linus** *(Greek)* Flax-coloured hair.

**Lionardo** *See* Leonard.

**Lionel, Lionello** *See* Leo.

**Lisandro** *See* Lysander.

**Lisimba** *(Kenyan)* Lion.

**Lister** *(English)* Cloth dyer.

# L

**Llewellyn** *(Welsh)* Lion-like leader.
  *Variants:* Leoline, Llewllyn.

**Lloyd** *(Welsh)* The grey.
  *Variant:* Floyd.

**Loch** *(Scottish)* Lake.
  *Variant:* Lochie.

**Lodewijk, Lodovico** *See* Lewis.

**Logan** *(Irish)* Hollow in a meadow.

**Lok** *(Chinese)* Happiness.

**Loman** *(Irish)* Little naked one; delicate.

**Long** *(Vietnamese)* Dragon.

**Loren, Lorenz, Lorenzo** *See* Laurence.

**Lorne** *(Scottish)* A place name.

**Lothar** *(Germanic)* Famous warrior.
  *Variants:* Luther *(English)*; Lothaire *(French)*; Lotario *(Italian)*.

**Louis** *See* Lewis.

**Loukas** *See* Lucas.

**Lourenco** *See* Laurence.

**Lovell** *(French)* Wolf cub; dearly beloved.
  *Variants:* Lowe, Lowel, Lowell.

**Lowe, Lowel, Lowell** *See* Lovell.

**Loy** *(Chinese)* Open.

**Lucas** *(Latin)* Light.
  *Variants:* Lucan, Lucas, Lucian, Luke *(English)*; Luc, Lucien, Lucius *(French)*; Lukas *(Germanic)*; Loukas *(Greek)*; Luca, Luciano, Luzio *(Italian)*; Lucio *(Spanish)*.

**Ludoslav** *(Czech)* Great people.

**Ludovic, Ludovicus, Ludvig, Ludwig** *See* Lewis.

**Lugaidh, Luigi, Luis** *See* Lewis.

# M

**Luitpold** *See* Leopold.

**Luiz** *See* Lewis.

**Lukas, Luke** *See* Lucas.

**Luong** *(Vietnamese)* Bamboo.

**Luthais** *See* Lewis.

**Luther** *See* Lothar.

**Luzio** *See* Lucas.

**Lyle** *(French)* From the island.
  *See also* Leo.

**Lyndall, Lyndell** *See* Lindell.

**Lyndon** *See* Lindsay.

**Lynford** *See* Linford.

**Lynton** *(English)* Town of lime trees.
  *Variant:* Linton.

**Lysander** *(Greek)* Liberator.
  *Variants:* Lisandro, Sandy.
  *See also* Lindsay.

**Mabon** *(Welsh)* Son.

**Mac** *(Scottish)* Son; heir.
  *Variant:* Mack.
  *See also* Maximilian.

**cauley** *(Scottish)* Righteous son; son of the moral one.

**Maccoy** *(Scottish)* Son of Hugh.
  *Variants:* MacCoy, McCoy.

# M

**Macdonald** *(Scottish)* Son of Donald.
*Variant:* MacDonald.

**Macdougal** *(Scottish)* Son of the dark one.
*Variant:* MacDougal.

**Mace** *(French)* Club; weapon.

**MacGee** *See* Magee.

**Mack** *See* Mac, Maximilian.

**Mackenzie** *(Scottish)* Son of the wise leader.
*Variants:* MacKenzie, McKenzie.

**Macmahon** *(Irish)* Son of the bear.
*Variants:* MacMahon, McMahon.

**Macmurray** *(Irish)* Son of the mariner.
*Variants:* MacMurray, McMurray.

**Macy** *See* Matthew.

**Maddox** *(Welsh)* Fortunate; generous.
*Variants:* Maddock, Madoc, Madog, Madox.

**Madison** *(English)* Son of a soldier.

**Madron** *(Latin)* Noble.

**Mael** *(Welsh)* Prince.

**Magee** *(Irish)* Son of Hugh.
*Variant:* MacGee.

**Magnus** *(Latin)* The great.
*Variant:* Manus.

**Magus** *(Greek)* Priest; magician.

**Mahendra** *(Sanskrit)* Great Indra (God).

**Mahesh** *(Sanskrit)* Great leader.

**Mahir** *(Hebrew)* Hard working; capable.

**Mahmood, Mahmoud, Mahmud** *See* Mohammed.

**Mahon** *(Celtic)* Bear.

# M

**Maikan** *(Innu)* Wolf.

**Maimun** *(Arabic)* Lucky.

**Makarios** *(Greek)* Blessed.
*Variants:* Macario *(Italian, Spanish)*; Makar *(Russian)*.

**Makoto** *(Japanese)* Honest.

**Makram** *(Arabic)* Noble.

**Makwa** *(Algonquin)* Bear.

**Mal** *See* Malcolm.

**Malachi** *(Hebrew)* Messenger of God.
*Variants:* Malachie, Malachy, Malechy.

**Malcolm** *(Gaelic)* Servant of St. Columbus.
*Variants:* Callum, Calum, Colm, Mal.

**Maldwyn** *See* Baldwin.

**Maleaume** *(French)* Luminous pledge.

**Malechy** *See* Malachi.

**Malibuaqti** *(InupiaQ)* Disciple; learner.

**Malik** *(Arabic)* Master; king.
*Variant:* Maliq.

**Malin** *(English)* Small fighter.
*Variant:* Mallin.

**Maliq** *See* Malik.

**Malise** *(Gaelic)* Servant of Jesus.

**Mallery, Mallorie, Mallory** *See* Malory.

**Malo** *(Polynesian)* Winner.

**Malory** *(French)* Luckless.
*Variants:* Mallery, Mallorie, Mallory.

**Malsom** *(Maliseet)* Wolf.

**Malvern** *(Welsh)* Bare hill.

# M

**Malvin** *See* Melvin.

**Man** *(Vietnamese)* Clever.

**Manar** *(Arabic)* Inspirational.

**Mandla** *(Zulu)* Strength; power.

**Manfred** *(Germanic)* Peaceful man.
  *Variants:* Manfried; Fred *(English)*; Manfredo *(Italian)*.

**Mani** *(Hindu)* The jewel; *(Indigenous Australian)* Equal.

**Manning** *(English)* Son of a good man.

**Manny** *See* Emmanuel.

**Mano** *(Hawaiian)* Shark.

**Manovello** *See* Emmanuel.

**Mansa** *(African)* King.

**Mansfield** *(English)* Field by a river.

**Mansur** *(Arabic)* Helped by God; victorious.

**Manuel** *See* Emmanuel.

**Manus** *See* Magnus.

**Maolmuire** *See* Maurice.

**Marc, Marcel, Marcellus, Marcello, Marcelo, Marco,
  Marcos** *See* Marcus.

**Marcus** *(Latin)* Dedicated to Mars, the god of war in Roman
  mythology.
  *Variants:* Marcellus; Marten, Martijn *(Dutch)*; Mark, Marko,
  Mart, Martin *(English)*; Marc, Marcel *(French)*; Markus
  *(Germanic)*; Markos *(Greek)*; Marton *(Hungarian)*; Marcello,
  Marco, Mario, Marius, Martino *(Italian)*; Martynas
  *(Lithuanian)*; Marcelo, Marco, Marcos, Marti *(Spanish)*.

**Marion** *(French)* Defiant.

**Marius, Mark, Marko, Markos, Markus** *See* Marcus.

**Marley** *(English)* Meadow near a lake.
  *Variants:* Marleigh, Marly.

# M

**Marlin** *(English)* Small hawk.
*Variant:* Marlon *(French)*.
*See also* Merlin.

**Marlon** *See* Marlin, Merlin.

**Marly** *See* Marley.

**Marmaduke** *(Celtic)* Servant of Saint Madoc.
*Variant:* Duke.

**Maro** *(Japanese)* Myself.

**Marron** *(French)* Chestnut; *(Indigenous Australian)* Leaf.

**Marshall** *(French)* Steward.

**Mart, Martainn, Marten, Marti, Martijn, Martin, Martino, Marton, Martynas** *See* Marcus.

**Marvin** *(English)* Sea friend; famous friend.
*Variants:* Mervin, Mervyn, Merwin; Merfyn *(Welsh)*.

**Masajun** *(Japanese)* Good and obedient.

**Mason** *(French)* Worker in stone.

**Massimiliano** *See* Maximilian.

**Mata** *See* Matthew.

**Mateo, Mateusz, Mathaeus, Mathew, Mathhaus, Mathias, Mathieu** *See* Matthew.

**Matok** *(Hebrew)* Sweet one.

**Matthew** *(Hebrew)* Gift of the Lord.
*Variants:* Mata, Matthaus, Matthias, Mattheus; Matt, Matthew *(English)*; Macy, Mathieu, Mayhew *(French)*; Matthaeus, Matthias *(Germanic)*; Matyas *(Hungarian)*; Matteo *(Italian)*; Mateusz *(Polish)*; Mattias *(Scandinavian)*; Mateo *(Spanish)*.

**Maurice** *(Latin)* Dark-skinned.
*Variants:* Mauritius; Maurits *(Dutch)*; Morris *(English)*; Moritz *(French)*; Moss *(Hebrew)*; Maurizio *(Italian)*; Maolmuire *(Scottish)*; Mauricio *(Spanish)*.

# M

**Maximilian** *(Latin)* The greatest.
*Variants:* Mac, Mack, Max, Maxim; Maximilien *(French)*;
Massimiliano *(Italian)*; Maksimilian *(Russian)*; Maximiliano,
Maximo *(Spanish)*.

**Maxwell** *(Scottish)* A place name; old family name.

**Mayhew** *See* Matthew.

**Maynard** *(Germanic)* Strong and hardy.
*Variants:* Mayne.

**McAdam** *See* Macadam.

**McAllister** *See* Macallister.

**Melbourne** *(English)* Mill stream; a place name.

**Melville** *(French)* Bad town.

**Melvin** *(Irish)* Chief.
*Variants:* Malvin, Mel, Melvyn, Melwyn.

**Meredith** *(Welsh)* Leader.

**Merivale** *(English)* Pleasant valley.

**Merle** *(French)* Blackbird.

**Merlin** *(Welsh)* Falcon.
*Variants:* Marlin, Marlon, Merle, Merlyn.

**Merrick** *(Welsh)* Ruler of the seas.
*Variant:* Merryck.

**Mervin, Mervyn, Merwin** *See* Marvin.

**Meyer** *(Germanic)* Farmer.

**Michael** *(Hebrew)* Like God.
*Variants:* Missal *(Abenaki)*; Micah; Mitch, Mitchell *(English)*;
Michel *(French)*; Micheil *(Gaelic)*; Mihaly *(Hungarian)*;
Michan *(Irish)*; Michele *(Italian)*; Mikhail, Misha *(Russian)*;
Mihael *(Slovenian)*; Miguel *(Spanish)*; Mikael *(Swedish)*.

**Mihku** *(Maliseet)* Squirrel.

**Mika** *(Japanese)* New moon; *(Omaha, Osage)* Raccoon;
*(Russian)* God's child.

# M

**Miklos** *See* Nicholas.

**Mikolas** *(Czech)* From the victorious people.

**Milan** *(Latin)* Loveable.

**Miles** *(Germanic)* Merciful; *(Latin)* Soldier; eager to please.
*Variants:* Milo, Myles.

**Milton** *(English)* Mill town.

**Ming** *(Chinese)* Brilliant; bright.

**Mingus** *See* Angus.

**Minh** *(Vietnamese)* Clear; brilliant.

**Minush** *(Innu)* Cat.

**Miron** *See* Myron.

**Miroslav** *(Czech)* Glory.

**Misha, Mitch, Mitchell** *See* Michael.

**Mitiq** *(InupiaQ)* Duck.

**Moesen** *See* Moses.

**Mohammed** *(Arabic)* Praiseworthy; the prophet and founder
of Islam.
*Variants:* Mahmood, Mahmoud, Mahmud, Mohamad,
Mohamed, Mohammad, Muhammad.

**Mohan** *(Sanskrit)* Enchanting.

**Moise, Moises** *See* Moses.

**Mongo** *See* Mungo.

**Monro** *(Scottish)* Near the Roe River, Ireland.
*Variants:* Monroe, Munro, Munroe.

**Montague** *(French)* Pointed hill.

**Montgomery** *(French)* The wealthy one's hill.

**Morcant** *(Welsh)* Brilliant.
*See also* Morgan.

**Morcum** *(Cornish)* Valley by the sea.

# M

**Mordecai** *(Hebrew)* Little man; follower of the god Marduk in Babylonian mythology; a character in the Bible.
*Variants:* Mord, Mort.

**Morgan** *(Celtic)* From the sea; great; bright.
*Variants:* Morcant, Morien.
*See also* Morcant.

**Moritz, Morris** *See* Maurice.

**Mortimer** *(French)* Dead sea.
*Variant:* Mort.

**Moses** *(Egyptian, Hebrew)* Gave birth to him; saved from the water; the prophet and leader of the Israelites in the Bible.
*Variants:* Moshe; Mozes *(Dutch)*; Moe *(English)*; Moise *(French)*; Moises *(Spanish)*; Moesen *(Welsh)*; Moyse *(Yiddish)*.

**Mosi** *(Swahili)* First born son.

**Moss** *See* Maurice.

**Moyse, Mozes** *See* Moses.

**Muhammad** *See* Mohammed.

**Mungo** *(Scottish)* Beloved; dear friend.
*Variant:* Mongo.

**Munro, Munroe** *See* Monro.

**Murdoch** *(Scottish)* Mariner.
*Variant:* Murtagh *(Irish)*.

**Murphy** *(Irish)* Fighter at sea.

**Murray** *(Gaelic)* Lord and master; from the sea.

**Musa** *(Zulu)* Kindness; mercy.

**Mustafa** *(Arabic)* Chosen; one of the names of Mohammed.

**Murtagh** *See* Murdoch.

**Muwin** *(Maliseet)* Bear.

**Myles** *See* Miles.

**Mynor** *See* Minor.

**Myron** *(Greek)* Perfumed; a saint.
  *Variant:* Miron.

**Nabil** *(Arabic)* Noble one.

**Nadim** *(Arabic)* Friend.
  *Variant:* Nadeem.

**Nadir** *(Arabic)* Precious one.

**Nagataka** *(Japanese)* Everlasting filial duty.

**Nagi** *See* Naj.

**Nagib** *See* Najib.

**Nahmana** *(Dakota)* Secretive; sly.

**Nahum** *(Hebrew)* Comforter.

**Nairn** *(Scottish)* River with alder trees.

**Naj** *(Arabic)* To save.
  *Variants:* Nagi, Naji.

**Najib** *(Arabic)* Smart one; of noble parentage.
  *Variants:* Nagib, Najeeb.

**Nakal** *(Gwich'in)* Cloudberry.

# N

**Naldo** *(Spanish)* Wise advisor.
  *See also* Reginald.

**Namir** *(Hebrew)* Leopard.

**Nanda** *(Sanskrit)* Joy.

**Nansen** *(Swedish)* Son of Nancy.

**Nanuk** *(InupiaQ)* Polar bear.
  *Variants:* Nanook, Nanuq.

**Naoto** *(Japanese)* Honest person.

**Napoleon** *(French, Italian)* From Naples; lion.
  *Variant:* Leon.

**Narayan** *(Sanskrit)* Son of man.

**Narcissus** *(Greek)* Daffodil.
  *Variant:* Narcisse *(French)*.

**Nardo** *(Spanish)* Strong.
  *See also* Bernard.

**Narendra** *(Sanskrit)* Mighty one.

**Naresh** *(Sanskrit)* Ruler.

**Naseem** *See* Nasim.

**Nash** *(English)* From the cliff.
  *Variant:* Nashe.

**Nasim** *(Arabic)* Fresh air.
  *Variant:* Naseem.

**Nat** *See* Nathan.

**Natal, Natale** *See* Noel.

**Natan** *See* Nathan.

**Natanael, Nataniel** *See* Nathaniel.

**Nate** *See* Nathan, Nathaniel.

**Natesh** *(Sanskrit)* The destroyer.

**Nathan** *(Hebrew)* Gift.
Variants: Nat, Natan, Nathen, Nathon; Nate *(English)*.

**Nathaniel** *(Hebrew)* Gift of God.
Variants: Natanael, Nataniel, Nathanael; Nate *(English)*.

**Nathen, Nathon** *See* Nathan.

**Navarro** *(Spanish)* Plains.
Variant: Navarre.

**Navroz** *(Persian)* New day.

**Ndumiso** *(Zulu)* Praise.

**Neal, Neale, Neall** *See* Neil.

**Nealson** *See* Nelson.

**Nectarios** *(Greek)* Saintly.

**Ned** *See* Edward, Edmund.

**Neil** *(Gaelic)* Champion.
Variants: Nial; Neal, Neale, Neall, Neel, Neill, Niel, Nigel, Niles *(English)*; Nels, Niels, Nils, Njal *(Scandinavian)*; Niall *(Scottish)*.

**Nelek** *(Polish)* Like a horn.

**Nels** *See* Neil.

**Nelson** *(English)* Son of the champion; son of Neil.
Variants: Nealson, Niles, Nilson, Nilsson.

**Nemesio** *(Spanish)* Just.

**Neptune** *(Latin)* A planet; the god of the sea in Roman mythology.

**Nero** *(Latin)* Dark-haired.

**Nesbit** *(English)* Nose-shaped bend; curve in the river or road.
Variants: Nesbitt, Nisbet, Nisbett.

**Nestor** *(Greek)* Wise one; traveller.
Variant: Nester.

# N

**Nevada** *(Spanish)* Snow.

**Neville** *(French)* New town.
*Variants:* Nevil, Nevile.

**Nevin** *(Irish)* Servant of the saints.
*Variants:* Nevan, Neven.

**Newell** *(English)* New hall.
*See also* Noel.

**Newland** *(English)* New land.

**Newman** *(English)* Newcomer.

**Newton** *(English)* New town.

**Ngai** *(Vietnamese)* Herb.

**Ngozi** *(Nigerian)* Good luck.

**Nial, Niall** *See* Neil.

**Nicholas** *(Greek)* Victory of the people.
*Variants:* Nikpla *(Abenaki)*; Nikolos, Nikos; Nikolay
*(Bulgarian)*; Nicolaas *(Dutch)*; Cole, Colin, Nic, Nick
*(English)*; Nicolas *(French)*; Claus, Clause, Klaus, Nickel,
Nickolaus *(Germanic)*; Miklos *(Hungarian)*; Niccolo,
Nicolo *(Italian)*; Nikita, Nikolai *(Russian)*; Nicol *(Scottish)*.
*See also* Nikita.

**Nicodemus** *(Greek)* Conqueror.
*Variants:* Nicodeme, Nikodemos.

**Nicol, Nicolaas, Nicolas** *See* Nicholas.

**Niel, Niels** *See* Neil.

**Nigel** *(Latin)* Dark-haired; of the night.
*Variant:* Nygell.
*See also* Neil.

**Nika** *(Algonquin)* Goose.

**Nikita** *(Russian)* Cannot be conquered.
*See also* Nicholas.

# N

**Nikolai, Nikolay** *See* Nicholas.

**Nikolos, Nikos** *See* Nicholas.

**Niles** *See* Neil, Nelson.

**Nils** *See* Neil.

**Nilson, Nilsson** *See* Nelson.

**Nimrod** *(Hebrew)* Valiant hunter; rebel.

**Ninian** *(Scottish)* The name of a saint.
See also Vivian.

**Nipi** *(InupiaQ)* Voice; sound.

**Niran** *(Thai)* Eternal.

**Nissan** *(Hebrew)* Omen.
*Variant:* Nisan.

**Nixon** *(English)* Son of Nicholas.

**Njal** *See* Neil.

**Noah** *(Hebrew)* Comforter; long-lived; the character in the
Bible who survived the Great Flood.
*Variants:* Noach, Noak, Noe.

**Noam** *(Hebrew)* Delightful.

**Noble** *(Latin)* Noble; high born.
*Variant:* Nobel.

**Noel** *(French)* Christmas.
*Variants:* Newell, Nowell; Nollaig *(Gaelic)*; Natale *(Italian)*;
Natal *(Spanish)*.

**Nolan** *(Irish)* Noble.
*Variant:* Noland.

**Norbert** *(French)* Light from the north; *(Germanic)* Famous
man from the north.

**Noris** *See* Norris.

# N

**Norman** *(English)* Northern man.

**Norris** *(English, French)* From the north.
  *Variants:* Noris, Norriss.

**Northcliff** *(English)* North cliff.
  *Variants:* Northcliffe, Northclyffe.

**Northrop** *(English)* Northern farm.
  *Variant:* Northrup.

**Norton** *(English)* Northern town.

**Norville** *(English)* Northern town.

**Norvin** *(English)* Friend from the north.
  *Variants:* Norvyn, Norwin.

**Norwood** *(English)* North wood.

**Nowell** *See* Noel.

**Ntuthuko** *(Zulu)* Development.

**Numa** *(Arabic)* Kindness.

**Nuna** *(InupiaQ)* Land; earth.

**Nuncio** *(Italian)* Messenger.
  *Variant:* Nunzio.

**Nur** *(Hebrew)* Fire; light.

**Nuren** *(Arabic)* Bright light.

**Nutabaq** *(InupiaQ)* Fresh snow.

**Nye** *(Welsh)* Honour.

# O

**Oakley** *(English)* Meadow of oaks.
  *Variant:* Oakes.

**Oalo** *See* Paul.

**Oba** *(Nigerian)* King.
  Obadiah (Hebrew) Servant of Jehovah.
  *Variants:* Obe, Obediah.

**Oberon** *See* Aubrey.

**Obert** *(Germanic)* Wealthy one.

**Obi** *(Nigerian)* Heart.

**Octavius** *(Latin)* Eighth child.
  *Variants:* Octavian; Octave *(French)*; Ottavio *(Italian)*;
  Octavio *(Spanish)*.

**Oddo, Odo** *See* Otto.

**Odell** *(Norse)* Wealthy one.

**Odilo** *(French)* The name of a saint.

**Odin** *(Norse)* Ruler; the god of creation and wisdom in Norse
  mythology.

**Odo** *(Germanic)* Wealthy.

**Odolf** *See* Adolf.

**Odysseus** *(Greek)* The wily hero in Homer's *Odyssey*.

**Ogden** *(English)* Valley of oak trees.

**Ogier** *(French)* "Riches by the spear."

**Ogilvie** *(Scottish)* From the hill.

**Ogun** *(African)* God of war.

# O

**Okpara** *(Nigerian)* First son.

**Olaf** *(Norse)* Ancestor.
 *Variants:* Olav *(Danish)*; Aulay *(Gaelic)*.

**Oldrich** *(Czech)* Noble king.

**Oleg** *(Russian)* Holy one.

**Oliver** *(French)* Olive tree; peacemaker.
 *Variants:* Olivier; Olivero *(Portuguese)*; Oliverio, Oliveros
 *(Spanish)*; Havelock *(Welsh)*.

**Olivier** *See* Oliver.

**Omar** *(Arabic)* Highest; first son.

**Omero** *See* Homer.

**Onan** *(Turkish)* Wealthy one.

**Ondre, Ondro** *See* Andrew.

**Onofre, Onofrio** *See* Humphrey.

**Ophir** *(Hebrew)* Faithful.

**Oran** *(Irish)* Pale.

**Orazio** *See* Horace.

**Orbon** *(Hungarian)* Born in the city.

**Ordell** *(Latin)* Beginning.

**Oren** *(Hebrew)* Tree.

**Orestes** *(Greek)* From the mountains.
 *Variant:* Oreste.

**Orfeo** *See* Orpheus.

**Orion** *(Greek)* Son of fire or light.

**Orlan** *(English)* Sharp land.

**Orland, Orlando, Orlondo** *See* Roland.

**Orman** *(Germanic)* Mariner

**Ormond** *(English)* Spear carrier.
 *Variants:* Ormand, Ormonde.

**Oro** *(Spanish)* Golden-haired.

# O

**Orpheus** *(Greek)* The god of song in Greek mythology.
*Variant:* Orfeo (Italian).

**Orson** *(Latin)* Courage of a bear.
*Variant:* Orsino (Italian).

**Orton** *(English)* Town by the river.

**Ortzi** *(Basque)* Sky.

**Orville** *(French)* Golden town.
*Variants:* Orvell; Orval *(English)*.

**Osagie** *(African)* Sent by God.

**Osbert** *(English)* Divine one.

**Osborne** *(English)* Divine bear.
*Variants:* Osborn, Osbourne, Osburne, Oz, Ozzie.

**Oscar** *(English)* Sacred spearman.
*Variants:* Osgar, Oskar, Oz, Ozzie.

**Osgood** *(English)* Divinely good.

**Oskar** *See* Oscar.

**Osman** *(Turkish)* Ruler.
*Variant:* Ottmar.

**Osmond** *(English)* God's protection.
*Variant:* Osmund.

**Osten** *(Latin)* Revered and respected.
*Variant:* Ostin.

**Oswald** *(English)* God's power.
*Variants:* Oz, Ozzie.

**Oswin** *(English)* Divine friend.
*Variants:* Oswinn, Oswyn, Oswynn.

**Ota** *(Czech)* Wealthy.
*Variant:* Otik.

**Otes** *See* Otis.

**Othello, Othol** *See* Otto.

**Otik** *See* Ota.

**P**

**Otis** *(Greek)* Keen hearing; son of Otto.
  *Variants:* Otes, Otys.

**Ottar** *(Norwegian)* Warrior.

**Ottavio** *See* Octavius.

**Ottmar** *See* Osman.

**Otto** *(Germanic)* Wealthy.
  *Variants:* Oddo, Odo, Othol; Othello *(Italian)*.

**Otys** *See* Otis.

**Ovid** *(Hebrew)* Worker.

**Owen** *(Welsh)* Well-born.
  *Variants:* Eoin *(Gaelic)*; Owain, Owayne, Ywain.
  *See also* Evan.

**Owethu** *(Zulu)* He is ours.

**Oxford** *(English)* Place where oxen cross a river.

**Oz** *(Hebrew)* Power.
  *See also* Osborn, Oscar, Oswald.

**Ozzie** *See* Osborn, Oscar, Oswald.

**Paavali, Paavo** *See* Paul.

**Pablan** *(InupiaQ)* Welcome; greeting.

**Pablo** *See* Paul.

**Paco** *See* Francis.

**Paddy, Padraic, Padraig, Padric, Padrig, Padruig**
  *See* Patrick.

# P

**Paget** *(French)* Young attendant.
  *Variants:* Padget, Page, Pagett, Paige.

**Paikea** *(Maori)* Whale.
  *Variant:* Pai.

**Paine** *(French)* Countryman.
  *Variant:* Payne.

**Pakma** *(InupiaQ)* Heaven.

**Pal** *See* Paul.

**Palben** *(Basque)* Fair-haired.

**Palmer** *(English)* Peacemaker.

**Pan** *(Greek)* Music lover; the god of fields and flocks in Greek
  mythology.

**Panas** *(Russian)* Immortal.

**Pancho** *See* Francis.

**Panos** *(Greek)* Rock.

**Paolo** *See* Paul.

**Paris** *(Greek)* The lover of Helen of Troy and son of Priam,
  king of Troy, in Greek mythology.

**Parker** *(English)* Park keeper.

**Parkin** *(English)* Rock.

**Parlan** *See* Bartholomew.

**Parnell** *(Latin)* Stone.
  *Variant:* Parnel.

**Parry** *(Welsh)* Son of Harry.

**Parsafal, Parsefal, Parsifal** *See* Percival.

**Parson** *(Latin)* From the church.

**Pascal** *(Latin)* Born at Easter.
  *Variants:* Paschal; Pascoe *(English)*; Pascal, Pascale *(French)*;
  Pasquale *(Italian)*; Pasqual *(Spanish)*.

**Paton** *See* Payton.

# P

**Patrick** *(Latin)* Noble.
*Variants:* Paddy, Padraic, Padraig, Padric *(Celtic)*; Pat, Patten, Ric, Rick, Ricky, Rickie *(English)*; Patrice *(French)*; Patrizius *(Germanic)*; Padruig *(Scottish)*; Patricio *(Portuguese, Spanish)*; Padrig *(Welsh)*.

**Paul** *(Latin)* Small.
*Variants:* Paulin; Poul *(Danish)*; Paavali, Paavo *(Finnish)*; Paulot *(French)*; Pavlos *(Greek)*; Pol *(Hungarian)*; Paolo *(Italian)*; Paulo *(Portuguese)*; Pavel *(Russian)*; Oalo, Pablo *(Spanish)*; Pal *(Swedish)*.

**Pax** *(Latin)* Peace.
*Variant:* Paz *(Spanish)*.

**Paxton** *(English)* Town of peace.
*Variants:* Paxon, Paxten.

**Payne** *See* Paine.

**Payton** *(English)* Town of warriors.
*Variants:* Paton, Peyton.

**Paz** *See* Pax.

**Peadair, Peadar, Peder, Pedro, Peer, Pekka** *See* Peter.

**Peleke** *(Hawaiian)* Wise.

**Peli** *(Basque)* Happy.

**Pemba** *(Tibetan)* Born on Saturday.

**Penn** *(English)* Enclosure.

**Penwyn** *(Welsh)* Fair-haired.

**Pepe** *See* Joseph.

**Pepin** *(Germanic)* One who perseveres.

**Peppe** *See* Joseph.

**Per** *See* Peter.

**Perben** *(Greek)* Stone.

# P

**Percival** *(French)* To cut through a valley.
Variants: Parsafal, Parsefal, Perseval, Persifal; Percy *(English)*; Parsifal *(Germanic)*.

**Peregrine** *(Latin)* Wanderer.
Variants: Peregrin, Perry.

**Perseval, Persifal** *See* Percival.

**Peter** *(Greek)* Stone; rock; one of the twelve apostles in the Bible.
Variants: Pial *(Abenaki)*; Petros, Takis, Takius; Piotr *(Bulgarian, Polish)*; Pero *(Croatian)*; Petr *(Czech)*; Peder *(Danish)*; Pieter *(Dutch)*; Perry, Pete, Pierce, Piers *(English)*; Pekka *(Finnish)*; Perrin, Pierre, Pierrot *(French)*; Peer *(Germanic)*; Ferris, Peadair, Peadar *(Irish)*; Piero, Pietro *(Italian)*; Petru *(Romanian)*; Pyotr *(Russian)*; Pedro *(Spanish)*; Per, Petrus *(Swedish)*.

**Peyton** *See* Payton.

**Phelan** *(Celtic)* Wolf.

**Phelim** *(Irish)* Always good.

**Philemon** *(Greek)* Loving.
Variant: Philo.

**Philip** *(Greek)* Lover of horses.
Variants: Phil, Phillip, Phillipp; Phelps *(English)*; Philippe *(French)*; Filib, Philp *(Gaelic)*, Filippo, Pino *(Italian)*; Filip *(Russian)*; Felipe, Felipino *(Spanish)*.

**Philo** *See* Philemon.

**Philp** *See* Philip.

**Phineas** *(Hebrew)* Oracle.
Variants: Fineas, Phineus, Pinchas.

**Phirun** *(Cambodian)* Rain.

**Phoenix** *(Greek)* Immortal.

**Phurba** *(Tibetan)* Born on Thursday.

**Piao** *(Chinese)* Handsome.

# P

**Pierce, Piero, Pierre, Pierrot, Piers** *See* Peter.

**Pierson** *(English, French)* Son of Peter or Piers.

**Pieter, Pietro** *See* Peter.

**Pilar** *(Spanish)* Pillar.

**Pin** *(Vietnamese)* Faithful.

**Pinchas** *See* Phineas.

**Pino** *See* Joseph, Philip.

**Pio** *(Italian)* Reverent.

**Piotr** *See* Peter.

**Piran** *See* Keiran.

**Pixiun** *(InupiaQ)* Blessing; passing of power from a shaman.

**Placido** *(Spanish)* Placid; calm.

**Pluto** *(Latin)* The god of the underworld in Roman mythology; a planet.

**Pol** *See* Paul.

**Polo** *See* Apollo.

**Pomeroy** *(French)* Apple orchard.

**Porter** *(Latin)* Guardian of the door.

**Poul** *See* Paul.

**Prasad** *(Hindu)* Brilliant.

**Pravin** *(Hindu)* Clever.

**Prem** *(Hindu)* Love.

**Premo** *See* Primo.

**Prentice** *(French)* Apprentice.
  *Variant:* Prentiss.

**Prescott** *(English)* Priest's cottage.
  *Variant:* Prescot.

**Presley** *(English)* Priest's meadow.
  *Variants:* Presleigh, Presly.

**Preston** *(English)* Priest's place.

**Prewitt** *(French)* Small brave one.
  *Variants:* Prewett, Pruitt.

**Price** *(Welsh)* Child with a loving father.
  *Variant:* Pryce.

**Primo** *(Latin)* First-born son.
  *Variant:* Premo.

**Prince** *(Latin)* Prince.
  *Variants:* Prinz, Prinze.

**Prior** *See* Pryor.

**Priya** *(Hindu)* Beloved.

**Probert** *(Welsh)* Son of Robert.

**Prospero** *(Italian, Spanish)* Prosperous.
  *Variant:* Prosper *(French)*.

**Pruitt** *See* Prewitt.

**Pryce** *See* Price.

**Pryor** *(Latin)* Head of the monastery.
  *Variant:* Prior.

**Purvis** *(French)* Provider.
  *Variant:* Purves.

**Pyotr** *See* Peter.

**Qabim** *(Arabic)* Ancient.

**Qadir** *See* Kadar.

**Qamar** *(Arabic)* Moon.

**Qannik** *(InupiaQ)* Snowflake.

# Q

**Qapvik** *(InupiaQ)* Wolverine.
  *Variant:* Qavvik.

**Qasim** *(Arabic)* Provider; one who shares.
  *Variant:* Kasim.

**Qayyim** *(Arabic)* Right and generous one.

**Quade** *(Scottish)* From McQuade, a Scottish clan name.

**Quemby, Quenby** *See* Quimby.

**Quennell** *(French)* Oak tree.
  *Variants:* Quennel, Quinnell.

**Quentin** *(Latin)* Fifth child.
  *Variants:* Quenton, Quinn, Quintin; Quinton *(English)*;
  Quito *(Spanish)*.

**Quigley** *(Irish)* Messy-haired one.

**Quillan** *(Irish)* Cub.
  *Variant:* Quillen.

**Quilliam** *See* William.

**Quillon** *(Latin)* Sword hilt.
  *Variant:* Quillian.

**Quimby** *(Norse)* A woman's house.
  *Variants:* Quemby, Quenby, Quinby.

**Quincy** *(French)* Home of the fifth son; a place name.

**Quinian** *(Irish)* Strong.

**Quinn** *(Irish)* Wise; chief; counsel; descendant of Conn.
  *See also* Quentin.

**Quinnell** *See* Quennell.

**Quintin, Quinton, Quito** *See* Quentin.

**Quong** *(Chinese)* Bright.
  *Variant:* Quon.

**Qusay** *(Arabic)* Far; distant.

# R

**Rabi** *(Arabic)* Breeze.

**Rachim** *(Hebrew)* Compassionate.
  *Variants:* Racham, Rahim.

**Rad** *(English)* Advisor.
  *Variant:* Radd.

**Radcliffe** *(English)* Red cliff.

**Radd** *See* Rad.

**Radek** *(Czech)* Leader; ruler; glad one.
  *Variant:* Radik.

**Radford** *(English)* Red ford.

**Radick** *See* Radek.

**Radimir** *See* Radomar.

**Radman** *(Slavic)* Joyful.

**Radmund** *See* Raymond.

**Radnor** *(English)* Red beach.

**Radomar** *(Czech)* Happy; famous.
  *Variant:* Radimir.

**Radwan** *(Arabic)* Delight.

**Rafa** *(Hebrew)* Cure.

**Rafael, Rafaelle, Raffaello** *See* Raphael.

**Rafat** *(Arabic)* Merciful.

**Rafe, Raff** *See* Ralph.

**Rafferty** *(Irish)* Wealthy.

# R

**Raghnall** *See* Reginald.

**Rahim** *See* Rachim.

**Raiden** *(Japanese)* The thunder god in Japanese mythology.

**Raimond, Raimondo, Raimund, Raimundo**
*See* Raymond.

**Rainart** *(Germanic)* Wise advisor.
*Variants:* Rainhard, Rainhardt, Reinart, Reinhard,
Reinhardt, Reinhart.
*See also* Reynard.

**Rainer** *See* Raynor.

**Rainhard, Rainhardt** *See* Rainart.

**Rainier** *See* Raynor.

**Raj** *(Sanskrit)* King.

**Raleigh** *(English)* Red clearing.
*Variant:* Rawley.

**Ralph** *(Norse)* Wolf counsel; brave adviser.
*Variants:* Ral, Rolph; Ralf, Rafe, Raff, Rolfe *(English)*; Raoul
*(French)*; Raul *(Italian, Spanish)*; Rolf *(Scandinavian)*.
*See also* Rudolph.

**Rama** *(Hindu)* One who pleases.
*Variant:* Ram.

**Rambert** *(Germanic)* Strong; clever.

**Rameses, Ramesses** *See* Ramses.

**Ramon** *See* Raymond.

**Ramsay** *See* Ramsey.

**Ramses** *(Egyptian)* Born of the sun god; name of eleven
Egyptian pharaohs.
*Variants:* Rameses, Ramesses.

**Ramsey** *(Germanic)* Strong.
*Variant:* Ramsay.

**Ranald** *See* Reginald.

# R

**Randolph** *(English)* Wolf's shield.
  *Variants:* Randal, Randall, Randell, Randi, Randolf, Randy;
  Randolphus *(Latin)*.

**Ranger** *(French)* Protector of the forest.

**Rangi** *(Polynesian)* Heaven.

**Ranjit** *(Hindu)* Delight.

**Raoul** *See* Ralph.

**Raphael** *(Hebrew)* God has healed.
  *Variants:* Rafaelle, Raffaello *(Italian)*; Rafael *(Spanish)*.

**Rasmus** *(Greek)* Beloved.

**Rastus** *See* Erastus.

**Ratan** *(Hindu)* Gem.

**Raven** *(English)* Black; black bird.
  *Variants:* Ravenel, Ravin, Ravon.

**Raymond** *(Germanic)* Wise and mighty protector.
  *Variants:* Ray, Reymond *(English)*; Raimund *(French)*;
  Radmund, Redmond, Redmund *(Irish)*; Raimond,
  Raimondo, Ramone *(Italian)*; Reamonn *(Scottish)*;
  Raimundo, Ramon *(Spanish)*.

**Raynard** *See* Reynard.

**Raynor** *(Germanic)* Protecting warrior.
  *Variants:* Rayner; Rainer, Rainier *(French)*.

**Read** *See* Reid.

**Readen** *See* Riordan.

**Reagan, Reagen** *See* Regan.

**Reamonn** *See* Raymond.

**Reardon** *See* Riordan.

**Redman** *(English)* Rider.

**Redmond, Redmund** *See* Raymond.

**Reece** *(Welsh)* Ardent; passionate.
  *Variants:* Rees, Reese, Rhett, Rhys.

# R

**Reed** *See* Reid.

**Regan** *(Irish)* Little king.
Variants: Reagan, Reagen, Regen.

**Regin** *(Scandinavian)* One with good judgment.

**Reginald** *(Latin)* Mighty; powerful.
Variants: Reinhold, Reinold, Reinwald; Reynold *(English)*;
Regnaud, Regnault, Renault *(French)*; Raghnall *(Gaelic)*;
Reinald, Reinaldos *(Germanic)*; Naldo, Rinaldo *(Italian)*;
Roald *(Norwegian)*; Ranald, Ronald *(Scottish)*; Renato
*(Spanish)*.
See also Naldo, Reynold.

**Regis** *(French)* Leader; king.

**Regnaud, Regnault** *See* Reginald.

**Rei** *(Japanese)* Rule; law.

**Reid** *(English)* Red-haired.
Variants: Read, Reed, Reide.

**Reilly** *See* Riley.

**Reinald** *See* Reginald.

**Reinaldo** *See* Reginald, Reynold.

**Reinaldos** *See* Reginald.

**Reinart** *See* Rainart.

**Reinhard, Reinhardt** *See* Rainart, Reynard.

**Reinhart** *See* Rainart.

**Reinhold, Reinold, Reinwald** *See* Reginald.

**Remington** *(English)* Home of the ravens.

**Remus** *(Latin)* Fast; swift; one of the original founders of
Rome (with twin brother Romulus) in Roman mythology.

**Renaldo** *See* Reynold.

**Renato** *See* Reginald, Rene.

**Renard, Renaud** *See* Reynard.

# R

**Renauld** *See* Reynold.

**Renault** *See* Reginald, Reynold.

**Rendor** *(Hungarian)* Policeman.

**René** *(French)* Reborn.
*Variants:* Rene; Renato *(Italian, Spanish)*.

**Renfred** *(English)* Good peace.

**Renjiro** *(Japanese)* Pure; virtuous.

**Rennard** *See* Reynard.

**Renton** *(English)* Home of the deer.

**Reuben** *(Hebrew)* Behold a son.
*Variants:* Rube, Ruben.

**Rex** *(Latin)* King.

**Rey** *See* Roy.

**Reymond** *See* Raymond.

**Reynaldo** *See* Reynold.

**Reynard** *(Germanic)* Fox.
*Variants:* Raynard, Reinhard, Reinhardt, Renard, Rennard;
Renaud *(French)*.
*See also* Rainart.

**Reynold** *(English)* Mighty.
*Variants:* Renauld, Renault *(French)*; Reinaldo *(Germanic)*;
Rinaldo *(Italian)*; Renaldo, Reynaldo *(Spanish)*.
*See also* Reginald.

**Rhett** *(Welsh)* Fiery one.
*See also* Reece.

**Rhien** *See* Ryan.

**Rhisart** *See* Richard.

**Rhodri** *(Welsh)* Ruler.

**Rhun** *(Welsh)* Grand.

**Rhys** *See* Reece.

# R

**Rian** *See* Ryan.

**Ric** *See* Derek, Eric, Frederick, Patrick, Richard.

**Richard** *(Germanic)* Strong ruler.
*Variants:* Dick, Ric, Rick, Rickie, Ricky *(English)*; Ricard *(French)*; Riccardo *(Italian)*; Richardus *(Latin)*; Ryszard *(Polish)*; Ricardo *(Spanish)*; Rhisiart *(Welsh)*.

**Rick, Rickie, Ricky** *See* Derek, Eric, Frederick, Patrick, Richard.

**Riddley** *See* Ridley.

**Rider** *(English)* Horse rider.
*Variant:* Ryder.

**Ridley** *(English)* Red meadow.
*Variants:* Riddley, Ridleigh, Ridly.

**Rigby** *(English)* The ruler's valley.

**Riley** *(Irish)* Descendant of the valiant one.
*Variant:* Reilly.

**Rinaldo** *See* Reynold.

**Rinchen** *See* Rinzen.

**Ringo** *(English)* Bell ringer.

**Rinzen** *(Tibetan)* Clever; wise.
*Variant:* Rinchen.

**Rio** *(Spanish)* River.

**Riobard** *See* Robert.

**Riordan** *(Irish)* Minstrel; poet.
*Variants:* Readen, Reardon.

**Rip** *(Dutch)* Ripe.

**Ripley** *(English)* Shouting man's meadow.
*Variants:* Ripleigh, Riply.

**Ritter** *(Germanic)* Knight.

**Rive** *(French)* River.

**Roald** *See* Reginald.

# R

**Roan** *See* Rohan.

**Roark** *(Irish)* Mighty.
*Variant:* Rourke.

**Robert** *(Germanic)* Bright; shining; famous.
*Variants:* Lobal *(Abenaki)*; Hrodebert, Rudbert, Ruprecht;
Rubert *(Czech)*; Bert, Bob, Rob, Robbie, Robby, Rupert
*(English)*; Robin *(French)*; Riobard *(Irish)*; Roberto *(Italian)*;
Robertus *(Latin)*; Ruperto *(Spanish)*.
*See also* Bert, Robertson, Robinson.

**Robertson** *(English)* Son of Robert.

**Robeson** *See* Robinson.

**Robin** *See* Robert.

**Robinson** *(English)* Son of Robert or Robin.
*Variants:* Robeson, Robson.

**Roch** *(French)* An ancient garment.
*See also* Rocco.

**Rocco** *(Italian)* To rest.
*Variants:* Rock, Rocky *(English)*; Roch, Roche *(French)*.

**Rochester** *(English)* Stone fort.
*Variants:* Chester, Chet, Rock, Rocky.

**Rock, Rocky** *See* Rocco, Rochester.

**Rod** *See* Roderick, Rodney.

**Roderick** *(Germanic)* Famous ruler.
*Variants:* Roderich; Rod, Roddy *(English)*; Rodrigue *(French)*;
Ruaidhri *(Gaelic)*; Roderigo, Rodrigo *(Italian, Spanish)*.
*See also* Rodney.

**Rodger** *See* Roger.

**Rodney** *(English)* Island clearing.
*Variants:* Rod, Roddy.
*See also* Roderick.

**Rodolf, Rodolfo, Rodolph, Rodolphe** *See* Rudolph.

# R

**Rodrigue** *See* Roderick.

**Roe** *(English)* Deer.

**Roeland** *See* Roland.

**Rogan** *(Irish)* Red-haired.

**Roger** *(English)* Famous spear.
  *Variants:* Rodger; Rogier *(Dutch)*; Rudiger, Rutger
  *(Germanic)*; Rogero, Ruggiero *(Italian)*; Rogerio *(Spanish)*.

**Rohan** *(Irish)* Red-haired.
  *Variants:* Roan, Rowan, Rowen.

**Roi** *See* Roy.

**Roka** *(Japanese)* Wave.

**Roland** *(Germanic)* Fame of the land.
  *Variants:* Rollan; Roeland *(Dutch)*; Rolland, Rollin, Rowland
  *(English)*; Orland, Orlando, Orlondo, Rolando *(Italian)*;
  Roldan *(Spanish)*.

**Rolf, Rolfe, Rolph** *See* Ralph, Rudolph.

**Rolihlahla** *(Xhosa)* Troublemaker.

**Roman** *(Latin)* From Rome.
  *Variants:* Romain *(French)*; Romano, Romeo *(Italian)*.

**Ronald** *See* Reginald.

**Ronan** *(Irish)* Small seal.

**Ronel** *(Hebrew)* God's song.

**Roper** *(English)* Rope maker.

**Rorek** *See* Rurik.

**Rory** *(Irish)* Red.
  *Variants:* Rorie, Ruairi, Ruari.

**Rosario** *(Portuguese)* Rosary.

**Roscoe** *(Norse)* Deer forest.
  *Variant:* Rosco.

**Ross** *(Gaelic)* Peninsula.

# R

**Roth** *(Germanic)* Red.

**Rourke** *See* Roark.

**Rousse** *(French)* Red-haired.

**Rowan** *(Scandinavian)* Mountain ash tree.
*See also* Rohan.

**Rowen** *See* Rohan.

**Rowland** *See* Roland.

**Roy** *(French)* King.
*Variants:* Rey, Roi, Ruy.

**Royd** *(Scandinavian)* Clearing.

**Royden** *(English)* Hill growing rye.
*Variant:* Roydon.

**Ruaidhri** *See* Roderick.

**Ruairi, Ruari** *See* Rory.

**Rube, Ruben** *See* Reuben.

**Rubert, Rudbert** *See* Robert.

**Rudek, Rudi** *See* Rudolph.

**Rudiger** *See* Roger.

**Rudolph** *(Germanic)* Famous wolf.
*Variants:* Dolf, Rudolf, Rudolfe; Rodolf *(Dutch)*; Rolfe,
Rolph, Rudy *(English)*; Rodolph, Rodolphe *(French)*; Rudi
*(Hungarian)*; Rodolfo *(Italian)*; Rudek *(Polish)*; Rolf
*(Scandinavian)*; Rufo *(Spanish)*.

**Rudyard** *(English)* Red field.

**Rufo** *See* Rudolph.

**Ruford** *(English)* Red ford.

**Rufus** *(Latin)* Red-haired.

**Ruggiero** *See* Roger.

**Rupert, Ruperto, Ruprect** *See* Robert.

# S

**Rurik** *(Scandinavian)* King.
   *Variants:* Rorek, Ruric.

**Russell** *(Latin)* Red; ruddy.

**Rutger** *See* Roger.

**Rutherford** *(English)* Cattle crossing.

**Ruy** *See* Roy.

**Ryan** *(Irish)* Little king.
   *Variants:* Rhien, Rian, Ryen.

**Ryder** *See* Rider.

**Ryen** *See* Ryan.

**Ryszard** *See* Richard.

**Ryuu** *(Japanese)* Dragon.

**Saben** *See* Sabin.

**Saber** *(French)* Sword.
   *Variants:* Sabir, Sabre.

**Sabin** *(Latin)* An ancient Roman family name; the name of
   a saint.
   *Variants:* Saben, Sabian.

**Sabir** *(Arabic)* Patient.

**Saburo** *(Japanese)* Third son.

**Sacha** *See* Alexander.

**Sacheverell** *(French)* Kid gloves.

**Sachiel** *(Hebrew)* Angel of water.

**Sachio** *(Japanese)* Fortunate.

**Saddam** *(Arabic)* Tough.

**Sadler** *(English)* Saddle maker.

**Saeed** *See* Said.

**Safa** *(Arabic)* Pure.

**Sagar** *(Sanskrit)* Ocean.

**Sage** *(French)* Wise; a herb.

**Sahen** *(Sanskrit)* Falcon.

**Sahn** *(Vietnamese)* Comparable.

**Said** *(Arabic)* Cheerful; lucky.
    *Variants:* Saeed, Saiyid, Sayeed, Sayid.

**Sajan** *(Sanskrit)* Beloved one.

**Sakari, Sakaria, Sakarios, Sakia** *See* Zachary.

**Salah** *(Arabic)* Virtuous.

**Salam** *(Arabic)* Lamb.

**Salim** *(Arabic)* Peaceful.

**Salman** *(Arabic)* High.

**Salomo, Salomon** *See* Solomon.

**Salvador** *(Spanish)* The saviour.
    *Variants:* Javier, Salvadore, Xavier; Sauveur *(French)*;
    Salvatore *(Italian)*.
    *See also* Xavier.

**Sam** *See* Samson, Samuel.

**Samai** *(Hebrew)* Symbol.

**Samaru** *(Japanese)* Sun.

**Sameer** *(Arabic)* Little breeze.

**Samie** *See* Samuel.

**Samir** *(Arabic)* Evening entertainer.

# S

**Sammel, Sammy** *See* Samuel.

**Samson** *(Hebrew)* Of the sun; a hero with superhuman strength in the Bible.
*Variants:* Sampson, Sansom, Sanson; Sam *(English)*; Sansone *(Italian)*.

**Samuel** *(Hebrew)* Heard by God.
*Variants:* Sam, Sammy *(English)*; Zamiel *(Germanic)*; Samie *(Hungarian)*; Samuele *(Italian)*; Sammel *(Swedish)*.

**Sancho** *(Spanish)* Holy; sanctified.
*Variant:* Santo.

**Sanders** *(English)* Son of Alexander.
*Variants:* Sanderson, Saunders, Saunderson.

**Sandford** *(English)* Sandy crossing.
*Variant:* Sanford.

**Sandy** *See* Alexander, Lysander.

**Sanford** *See* Sandford.

**Sanjay** *(Sanskrit)* Winner; conqueror.

**Sansom, Sanson, Sansone** *See* Samson.

**Santo** *See* Sancho.

**Sargent** *(French)* officer.
*Variants:* Sergeant, Sergent.

**Sarkara** *(Sanskrit)* Sugar; sweetness.

**Sascha, Sasha** *See* Alexander.

**Saul** *(Hebrew)* Asked for; long awaited.

**Saunders, Saunderson** *See* Sanders.

**Sauveur** *See* Salvador.

**Sawyer** *(English)* Woodsman.
*Variant:* Sayer.

**Saxon** *(English)* Dagger; sword.
*Variants:* Saxen, Saxton.

# S

**Sayeed** *See* Said.

**Sayer** *See* Sawyer.

**Sayid** *See* Said.

**Schmidt** *See* Smith.

**Scipio** *(Latin)* Walking stick.
  *Variants:* Scipion, Scipione.

**Scott** *(English)* Scotsman.
  *Variant:* Scotty.

**Scout** *(French)* Scotsman.

**Scully** *(Irish)* With the peace of God.
  *Variants:* Seafraid, Seathra.

**Seager** *See* Seger.

**Seamus** *See* James.

**Sean** *See* John.

**Searle** *(English)* Shield; armour.
  *Variant:* Serle.

**Seathra** *See* Scully.

**Seb** *See* Keb, Sebastian.

**Sebastian** *(Latin)* Revered one.
  *Variants:* Bastian, Bastien, Seb, Sebastiano, Sebastien.

**Sef** *(Egyptian)* Yesterday.

**Seger** *(English)* Sea warrior.
  *Variants:* Seager, Seeger.

**Segev** *(Hebrew)* Majestic.

**Seiorse** *See* George.

**Seldon** *(English)* Valley of willows.
  *Variant:* Selden.

**Selig** *See* Zelig.

**Semyon** *See* Simon.

# S

**Sen** *(Japanese)* Wood sprite.

**Senior** *(French)* Lord.

**Sennett** *(French)* Venerable.
*Variant:* Sennet.

**Septimus** *(Latin)* Seventh child.

**Serge, Sergei** *See* Sergius.

**Sergent** *See* Sargent.

**Sergius** *(Latin)* Servant; attendant; the name of a saint.
*Variants:* Serge *(French)*; Sergio *(Italian)*; Sergei *(Russian)*.

**Serle** *See* Searle.

**Seth** *(Hebrew)* Appointed one; one of Adam and Eve's sons
in the Bible.

**Seward** *(English)* Sea guard.

**Sexton** *(French)* Church official.

**Sextus** *(Latin)* Sixth child.

**Seve** *(Spanish)* Severe.
*Variants:* Severin *(French)*; Severiano *(Italian)*.

**Seymour** *(English)* Derived from a place name (Saint Maur).

**Shah** *(Persian)* King.

**Shakir** *(Arabic)* Grateful.

**Shamus** *See* James.

**Shandy** *(English)* Lively; boisterous.

**Shane** *See* John.

**Shannon** *(Irish)* Old wise one; an Irish river.

**Shaquille** *(Arabic)* Handsome.

**Sharif** *(Arabic)* Honest; honourable.
*Variant:* Shareef.

**Shaun** *See* John.

**Shaw** *(English)* Woodland.

**Shawn** *See* John.

**Shea** *(Irish)* Stately.
  *Variant:* Shay.

**Shelby** *(English)* From the estate.

**Sheldon** *(English)* Steep valley.

**Shelley** *(English)* Meadow near the hill.

**Shem** *(Hebrew)* Famous.

**Shepherd** *(English)* Shepherd.
  *Variant:* Shepard.

**Sher** *(Persian)* Lion.

**Sheridan** *(Irish)* Seeker.

**Sherlock** *(English)* Fair-haired.

**Sherman** *(English)* Cutter of cloth.

**Sherwood** *(English)* Bright woods.

**Shimon** *(Hebrew)* Amazed.

**Shin** *(Gwich'in)* Summer; *(Japanese)* Faithful.

**Shinakio** *(Japanese)* Faithful and bright.

**Shiva** *(Sanskrit)* The pure one; the supreme god in Hindu
  mythology.

**Shiro** *(Japanese)* Fourth son.

**Shoh** *(Gwich'in)* Bear.

**Shu-sai-chong** *(Chinese)* Happy all his life long.

**Sidney** *(English)* From the city of Saint Denis.
  *Variants:* Sid, Sydney.

**Siegfried** *(Germanic)* Peaceful victory.
  *Variants:* Siegfrid, Siffre, Sigfrid, Sigvard; Zygfryd *(Polish)*;
  Sigfredo *(Spanish)*; Zigfrid *(Russian)*.

**Siemen** *See* Simon.

**Sigmund** *(Germanic)* Protecting conqueror.

# S

*Variants:* Sigismund; Sigismond *(Hungarian)*; Sigismundo *(Italian)*; Sigismundus *(Latin)*; Zygmunt *(Polish)*.

**Sigvard** *See* Siegfried.

**Siku** *(InupiaQ)* Ice.

**Silvanus** *(Latin)* Forest; the god of trees in Roman mythology.
*Variants:* Silas; Silvain *(French)*; Silvano *(Italian, Spanish)*.

**Silvère** *(French)* Forest; name of a French Saint.

**Silvester** *(Latin)* Forested area.
*Variants:* Sylvester *(English)*; Silvestro *(Italian)*; Silvestre *(Spanish)*.

**Sim** *See* Simon.

**Simba** *(African)* Lion.

**Simon** *(Hebrew)* One who listens; two of the apostles in the Bible.
*Variants:* Simo *(Abenaki)*; Siemen *(Dutch)*; Simeon *(French)*; Sim *(Gaelic)*; Siomonn *(Irish)*; Simion *(Romanian)*; Semyon *(Russian)*; Ximen, Ximenes, Ximun *(Spanish)*.

**Sinclair** *(French)* Shining light.

**Sion** *See* Zion.

**Sithembiso** *(Zulu)* Promise.

**Skyler** *(Dutch)* Shelter; schoolmaster.
*Variants:* Skye, Skylar, Skylor.

**Sloan** *(Irish)* Warrior.
*Variant:* Sloane.

**Smil** *(Slavic)* Beloved.

**Smith** *(English)* Blacksmith.
*Variants:* Schmidt, Smyth, Smythe.

**Sol** *(Latin)* Sun.
*See also* Solomon.

**Solomon** *(Hebrew)* Peace.

*Variants:* Solamon, Soloman, Solomone; Sol, Sulaiman, Suleiman *(Arabic)*; Salomo *(Germanic)*; Solamh *(Irish)*; Salomon *(Spanish)*; Zalman, Zelman *(Yiddish)*.

**Somerset** *(English)* Summer place.

**Sonam** *(Tibetan)* Fortunate.

**Sonny** *(English)* Son; dear one.

**Soren** *(Danish)* Stern.
*Variant:* Sorin.

**Spencer** *(French)* Storekeeper; provider.
*Variants:* Spence, Spenser.

**Spike** *(English)* Spiky-haired (usually an acquired name, not given at birth).

**Spiro** *(Greek)* Breath of the gods.
*Variants:* Spiridion, Spyros; Spiridione *(Italian)*.

**Stacy** *(Latin)* Prosperous.
*Variant:* Stacey.
*See also* Eustace.

**Stafford** *(English)* Landing place; a place name.
*Variants:* Stafforde, Staford.

**Stanford** *(English)* Stony ford.

**Stanislaus** *(Slavic)* Glorious leader; a Polish saint.
*Variants:* Aineislis, Stanislas, Stanislav.

**Stanley** *(English)* Stony meadow.
*Variants:* Stanleigh, Stanly.

**Starling** *(English)* A bird.

**Steadman** *(English)* Farmer.
*Variant:* Stedman.

**Steaphan** *See* Stephen.

**Stephen** *(Greek)* Crown; garland.
*Variants:* Atian *(Abenaki)*; Steven *(English)*; Etienne *(French)*; Istvan *(Hungarian)*; Stefano *(Italian)*; Stephanos *(Latin)*;

# S

Stefan *(Scandinavian)*; Steaphan *(Scottish)*; Esteban, Estevan *(Spanish)*; Steffan *(Welsh)*.

**Sterling** *See* Stirling.

**Sterne** *(English)* Austere; stern.
*Variant:* Stearne.

**Steven** *See* Stephen.

**Stewart** *(English)* Steward or caretaker of the estate.
*Variant:* Stuart.

**Stig** *(Scandinavian)* Wanderer.

**Stirling** *(English)* Genuine; valuable.
*Variant:* Sterling.

**Stuart** *See* Stewart.

**Sulaiman, Suleiman** *See* Solomon.

**Suluk** *(InupiaQ)* Wing feather.

**Suman** *(Sanskrit)* Happy; wise.

**Sumner** *(English)* One who summons by authority.

**Sun** *(Chinese)* Descending.

**Sundar** *(Sanskrit)* Handsome.

**Sutton** *(English)* Southern town.

**Sven** *(Swedish)* Young boy.
*Variants:* Svend, Swain; Swen *(Danish)*; Svein *(Norwegian)*.

**Swain** *(Germanic)* Pig herder.

**Sweeney** *(Irish)* Little hero.

**Swen** *See* Sven.

**Sydney** *See* Sidney.

**Sylvester** *See* Silvester.

**Syriack** *See* Cyriack.

**Taavi** *See* David.

**Taber** *(Gaelic)* Spring; well.

**Tabor** *(Persian)* Drummer; *(Turkish)* Fortified encampment.

**Tad** *(Irish)* Poet; philosopher.
*See also* Thaddeus.

**Tadaes** *See* Thaddeus.

**Tadashi** *(Japanese)* Honest.

**Tadd, Taddeo, Tadeo, Tadhg** *See* Thaddeus.

**Tadhaa** *(Gwich'in)* Golden eagle.

**Tage** *(Danish)* Day.

**Taffy** *See* David.

**Taggart** *(Irish, Scottish)* Son of the priest.

**Tai** *(Vietnamese)* Talented; prosperous.

**Tailer, Tailor** *See* Taylor.

**Taimufa** *(InupiaQ)* Forever.

**Tait** *See* Tate.

**Takahiro** *(Japanese)* Great and valuable.

**Takeshi** *(Japanese)* Unbending like a bamboo tree.
*Variant:* Takashi.

**Takis, Takius** *See* Peter.

**Takumi** *(Japanese)* Artisan.

**Talbot** *(English)* Woodcutter.
*Variant:* Talbott.

# T

**Taliesin** *(Welsh)* Radiant brow.

**Tallis** *(Persian)* Wise.

**Talman** *(Hebrew)* Injured; to oppress.
  *Variant:* Talmon.

**Talor** *See* Taylor.

**Tamas** *See* Thomas.

**Tancred** *(Germanic)* Considered counsel.

**Tane** *(Maori)* The god of forests and birds in Maori
  mythology.

**Tanguy** *(French)* Warrior.

**Tangwyn** *(Welsh)* Peace.

**Tani** *(Japanese)* From the valley.

**Taniel** *See* Daniel.

**Tao** *(Chinese)* Peach (the symbol of longevity in
  Chinese culture).

**Taro** *(Japanese)* First-born son; big boy.

**Tarquin** *(Latin)* Two kings of ancient Rome.

**Tarrant** *(Welsh)* Thunder.

**Tashi** *(Tibetan)* Prosperous.

**Tasiq** *(InupiaQ)* Lake; lagoon.

**Tate** *(English)* Cheerful one.
  *Variant:* Tait. ———

**Tauno** *See* Donald.

**Tavi** *(Aramaic)* Good.
  *See also* David.

**Tavid** *See* David.

**Tavish** *See* Thomas.

**Taylor** *(English)* Tailor.
  *Variants:* Tailer, Tailor, Talor, Tayler.

# T

**Teague** *(Irish)* Poet; philosopher.
*Variants:* Teagan, Tegan.

**Teal** *(English)* A water bird.
*Variant:* Teale.

**Tearlach** *See* Charles.

**Ted, Teddy** *See* Edmund, Edward, Theodore.

**Tegan** *See* Teague.

**Templar** *(French)* Knight.

**Tennyson** *(English)* Son of Dennis.
*Variants:* Dennison, Tennison.

**Teodoro, Teodus** *See* Theodore.

**Terence** *(Latin)* Smooth; polished.
*Variants:* Terry *(English)*; Thierry *(French)*; Terenz
*(Germanic)*; Terencio *(Spanish)*.

**Terry** *(Germanic)* Powerful tribe.
*Variants:* Theodoric; Thierry *(French)*.

**Teruyuki** *(Japanese)* Light from heaven.

**Tetsuo** *(Japanese)* Iron husband; philosophical man.

**Tex** *(North American)* After the American state of Texas.

**Thaddeus** *(Aramaic)* Praiser; *(Greek)* Courageous;
stout-hearted.
*Variants:* Thaddaeus; Tadaes *(Czech)*; Tad, Tadd *(English)*;
Tadhg *(Gaelic)*; Taddeo *(Italian)*; Tadeo *(Spanish)*.

**Thalente** *(Zulu)* Talent; God's gift.

**Thane** *(English)* Courtier.
*Variants:* Thaine, Thayne.

**Thanh** *(Vietnamese)* Serene; tranquil.

**Thayne** *See* Thane.

**Theo** *See* Theobald, Theodore.

**Themba** *(Zulu)* Hope; trust.

# T

**Theobald** *(Germanic)* Brave people.
   *Variants:* Theo, Thibaud, Tibald, Tibold, Tybalt.

**Theodore** *(Greek)* God's gift.
   *Variants:* Theodous; Teodus *(Czech)*; Ted, Teddy, Theo
   *(English)*; Theodor *(Germanic)*; Teodoro *(Italian, Spanish)*;
   Feodore, Fyodor *(Russian)*; Tudor *(Welsh)*.

**Theodoric** *See* Terry.

**Theodous** *See* Theodore.

**Théophane** *(French)* Presence; a French saint.

**Theron** *(Greek)* Hunter.
   *Variants:* Theran, Theren.

**Thibaud** *See* Theobald.

**Thierry** *See* Terence, Terry.

**Thomas** *(Aramaic)* A twin.
   *Variants:* Tomlin *(English)*; Tuomas *(Finnish)*; Tomas
   *(Germanic)*; Tamas *(Hungarian)*; Tomaso *(Italian)*; Tomaz
   *(Polish)*; Tavish *(Scottish)*.

**Thor** *(Norse)* The god of thunder in Norse mythology.
   *Variants:* Thorald, Thorbert, Thorgood, Thorin, Thorley,
   Thormund, Thorold.

**Thornton** *(English)* Thorn-bush town.

**Thorold** *See* Thor.

**Thurston** *(English)* Thor's stone.
   *Variants:* Thorstan, Thurstan.

**Tibald, Tibold** *See* Theobald.

**Tien** *(Chinese)* Heaven.

**Tiernan** *(Celtic)* Knightly.

**Tim, Timmy** *See* Timothy.

**Timon** *(Greek)* Reward; honour.

# T

**Timothy** *(Hebrew)* Honoured by God.
*Variants:* Timotei *(Bulgarian)*; Tim, Timmy *(English)*;
Timotheos *(Greek)*; Timoteo *(Italian, Spanish)*; Timoteus
*(Swedish)*.

**Tinan** *See* Tynan.

**Tioboid** *See* Tobias.

**Tirol** *See* Tyrol.

**Tison** *See* Tyson.

**Titus** *(Greek)* Honoured; a first-century Roman emperor.
*Variants:* Titos; Tito *(Italian, Spanish)*.

**Tobias** *(Hebrew)* God is good.
*Variants:* Tobie, Toby *(English)*; Tioboid *(Gaelic)*; Tobia
*(Italian)*; Tobiasz *(Polish)*.

**Tobikuma** *(Japanese)* Flying cloud.

**Todd** *(English)* Fox.
*Variant:* Tod.

**Tokori** *(Hopi)* Screech owl.

**Tomas, Tomaz** *See* Thomas.

**Tomi** *(Japanese)* Prosperous.

**Tomkin** *(English)* Little Tom.

**Tomlin** *See* Thomas.

**Tonio, Tony** *See* Anthony.

**Tor** *(Gaelic)* Rock.

**Toshiro** *(Japanese)* Smart boy.
*Variant:* Toshi.

**Tovi** *(Hebrew)* Good.

**Tracy** *(Latin)* Bold; courageous.
*Variant:* Tracey.

**Travers** *(French)* Crossing.
*Variant:* Travis.

# T

**Tremayne** *(Cornish)* Town built of stone.
  *Variants:* Tremain, Tremaine.

**Trefor** *See* Trevor.

**Trent** *(English)* A place name.

**Trevor** *(English)* Great village.
  *Variants:* Trever, Trevon; Trefor *(Welsh)*.

**Trey** *(Latin)* Three.

**Tristram** *(Celtic)* Din; tumult; *(Latin)* Sad.
  *Variants:* Tristran; Drostan, Tristan *(Celtic)*.

**Troy** *(French)* Soldier.
  *Variant:* Troye.

**Trueman** *See* Truman.

**Truitt** *(English)* Small; honest.
  *Variant:* Truett.

**Truman** *(English)* Loyal.
  *Variant:* Trueman.

**Trung** *(Vietnamese)* Faithful; loyal.

**Tshin** *(Gwich'in)* Rain.

**Tsubasa** *(Japanese)* Wing.

**Tucker** *(English)* Tailor.

**Tudor** *See* Theodore.

**Tulio** *(Latin)* Lively.
  *Variants:* Tullio, Tullius *(Italian)*; Tully *(Celtic)*.

**Tuomas** *See* Thomas.

**Turner** *(English, French)* Woodworker.

**Tuvaaq** *(InupiaQ)* Hunter.

**Ty, Tye** *See* Tyrone.

**Tybalt** *See* Theobald.

**Tynan** *(Irish)* Dark.
  *Variant:* Tinan.

**Tyrol** *(Germanic)* A place name in Austria.
*Variant:* Tirol.

**Tyrone** *(Irish)* Owen's land: a county in Ireland.
*Variants:* Ty, Tye *(English)*.

**Tyson** *(French)* Firebrand.
*Variants:* Tison, Tysen.

**Tzion** *See* Zion.

**Ualtar** *See* Walter.

**Uba** *(African)* Wealthy.

**Ubadah** *(Arabic)* Serves God.

**Uberto** *See* Hubert.

**Udeh** *(Hebrew)* Praise.

**Udo** *(Germanic)* Prosperous.

**Ugo** *See* Hugh.

**Uhu** *(Innu)* Owl.

**Uilliam** *See* William.

**Uistean** *(Irish)* Intelligent.

**Uiyula** *(InupiaQ)* Whirlwind.

**Ulan** *(African)* First-born twin.

**Uland** *(Germanic)* Noble country.

**Ulani** *(Polynesian)* Cheerful.

**Ulbrecht** *See* Albert.

# V

**Ulf** *(Germanic)* Wolf.

**Ulrich** *(Germanic)* Wolf ruler; prosperity and power.
  *Variants*: Ulric *(French)*; Ulrik *(Scandinavian)*.

**Ulysses** *(Greek)* Hater of injustice.

**Umialik** *(InupiaQ)* Captain; king.

**Umit** *(Turkish)* Hope.

**Unai** *(Basque)* Shepherd.

**Uner** *(Turkish)* Famous.

**Unni** *(Norse)* Modest.

**Unwin** *(English)* Unfriendly.

**Upendra** *(Hindu)* One of the names of the god Vishnu in Hindu mythology.

**Upshaw** *(English)* Upper part of the woods.

**Upton** *(English)* Upper part of town.

**Uriah** *(Hebrew)* The Lord is my light.
  *Variants:* Uri, Uria, Uriel.

**Urian** *(Greek)* From heaven.

**Uriel** *See* Uriah.

**Uzziah** *(Hebrew)* The Lord gives strength.

**Vachel** *(French)* Cowherd.

**Vaclav** *See* Wenceslas.

**Vadin** *(Hindi)* Speaker.

# V

**Vahe** *(Armenian)* Victor.

**Valdemar** *(Swedish)* Famous ruler.

**Valdis** *(Germanic)* Spirited in battle.

**Valentine** *(Latin)* Strong; valiant; two Christian martyrs.
*Variants:* Valentinus; Valentijn *(Dutch)*; Val *(English)*;
Valentin *(French, Scandinavian)*; Valentino *(Italian)*.

**Valerian** *(Latin)* Valiant one; a herb.
*Variants:* Valeray, Valerius; Valère, Valéry *(French)*.

**Van** *(Danish, Dutch)* From; of.

**Vance** *(English)* Marsh dweller.

**Vanya** *See* John.

**Varden** *(French)* Green hill.
*Variant:* Vardon.

**Varian** *(Latin)* Capricious; changeable.
*Variants:* Varien, Varion, Varrian.

**Varick** *See* Warwick.

**Varien, Varion** *See* Varian.

**Variya** *(Hindu)* Excellent one.

**Varrian** *See* Varian.

**Vartan** *(Armenian)* Rose giver.

**Varun** *(Hindu)* Lord of the waters.

**Vasilos, Vassily** *See* Basil.

**Vaughan** *(Celtic)* Little man.
*Variant:* Vaughn.

**Vayk** *(Hungarian)* Wealthy.

**Veasna** *(Cambodian)* Lucky.

**Verner** *See* Warner.

**Vernon** *(English)* Alder grove.
*Variants:* Vern, Verne; Verney *(French)*.

# V

**Victor** *(Latin)* Victorious conqueror; champion.
  *Variants:* Viktor *(Germanic, Hungarian)*; Buadhach
  *(Irish)*; Vitorio, Vittorio *(Italian)*; Victorio *(Spanish)*.

**Vidor** *(Hungarian)* Happy.

**Vidvan** *(Hindu)* Scholar.

**Viho** *(Cheyenne)* Chief.

**Vikram** *(Hindu)* Glorious king.

**Vilhelm, Viljo, Ville** *See* William.

**Vinay** *(Hindu)* Good behaviour.

**Vincent** *(Latin)* Conquering.
  *Variants:* Vincentius; Vincenz *(French)*; Vincentio
  *(Italian)*; Vincente *(Spanish)*.

**Virgil** *(Latin)* Flourishing.
  *Variants:* Virgio; Virgilio *(Italian, Spanish)*.

**Vitas** *(Latin)* Alive; animated.
  *Variant:* Vitalis.

**Vitéz** *(Hungarian)* Brave warrior.

**Vito** *(Latin)* Conqueror.

**Vitorio, Vittorio** *See* Victor.

**Vivian** *(Latin)* Vital; alive.

  *Variants:* Ninian, Vivien; Vivienne *(French)*.
  *See also* Ninian.

**Vladimir** *(Slavic)* Glorious prince.

**Vladislav** *See* Ladislav.

**Wade** *(Germanic)* Ford.

**Wagner** *(Germanic)* Wagon maker.
  *Variant:* Waggoner.

**Wain, Waine, Wainwright** *See* Wayne.

**Wakefield** *(English)* Wet field.

**Walden** *(English)* Wood valley.

**Waldo** *(Germanic)* Mighty ruler.

**Wallace** *(Scottish)* Welshman.
  *Variants:* Wallis, Welch, Welsh *(English)*; Wallache
  *(Germanic)*; Walsh *(Irish)*.

**Walter** *(Germanic)* Ruler.
  *Variants:* Walther; Gautier, Gauthier *(French)*; Ualtar *(Irish)*;
  Gualtiero *(Italian)*; Galterius *(Latin)*; Gualterio *(Spanish)*.

**Ward** *(English)* Guardian; watchman.
  *Variant:* Warde.

**Ware** *(Anglo-Saxon)* Wary.

**Warner** *(Germanic)* Protective warrior.
  *Variants:* Werner; Verner *(Scandinavian)*.

**Warren** *(French)* Game park; gamekeeper; *(Germanic)* Protector.

**Warwick** *(English)* Farm by the weir.
  *Variant:* Varick *(Germanic)*.

**Washington** *(English)* The estate of the wise one.

**Wate** *(Algonquin)* Northern lights.

**Watson** *(English)* Son of Walter.

**Waverly** *(English)* Tree-lined meadow.

# W

**Wayland** *(English)* Crossroads.
*Variant:* Waylen.

**Wayne** *(English)* Wagon maker.
*Variants:* Wain, Waine, Wainwright, Wayn.

**Webster** *(English)* Weaver.
*Variant:* Webb.

**Welby** *(English)* The farm by the spring.

**Welch** *See* Wallace.

**Weldon** *(English)* The hill with a spring.

**Wellington** *(English)* The town with the well; New Zealand's capital city.

**Wells** *(English)* The springs.

**Welsh** *See* Wallace.

**Wen** *(Chinese)* Cultured; refined.

**Wenceslas** *(Slavic)* Glory; a tenth-century saint.
*Variants:* Wenceslaus; Vaclav *(Czech)*.

**Wendell** *(Germanic)* Wanderer; seeker.
*Variants:* Wendall, Wendel.

**Wentworth** *(English)* Winter estate.

**Werner** *See* Warner.

**Wesley** *(English)* The west meadow.
*Variants:* Wesleigh, Wesly, Wessley, Westleigh, Westley, Wezley.

**Weston** *(English)* The town in the west.

**Wetherby** *(English)* Ram's meadow.

**Weylin** *(Scottish)* Son of a wolf.

**Wezley** *See* Wesley.

**Wheaton** *(English)* Wheat town.

**Wheeler** *(English)* A driver.

**Whit** *(English)* White.

**Whitby** *(English)* White town.

# W

**Whitely** *(English)* White field.

**Whitfield** *(English)* White field.

**Whitford** *(English)* White ford.

**Whitlaw** *(English)* White hill.

**Whitney** *(English)* White island.
   *Variants:* Whitny, Witney.

**Wickham** *(English)* Home in the meadow.
   *Variant:* Wykeham.

**Wieslav** *(Slavic)* Great glory.

**Wilbur** *(Germanic)* Brightly resolved.
   *Variants:* Wilber, Wilbert, Wilburt.

**Wiley** *See* William.

**Wilfred** *(English)* Much peace.

**Wilhelm, Wilkie** *See* William.

**Willard** *(Germanic)* Determined; strong-willed.

**William** *(Germanic)* Resolute protector.
   *Variants:* Wilhelm; Vilhelm *(Danish)*; Willem *(Dutch)*;
   Wilkie, Willie, Willis, Willy *(English)*; Viljo *(Finnish)*;
   Guillaume *(French)*; Quilliam, Wiley *(Gaelic)*; Liam, Uilliam
   *(Irish)*; Guglielmo *(Italian)*; Guilhermo, Guillermo *(Spanish)*;
   Ville *(Swedish)*; Gwilym *(Welsh)*.

**Wilmer** *(Germanic)* Resolute.
   *Variant:* Wilmot.

**Wilton** *(English)* Farm with a well.

**Wing** *(Chinese)* Glory.

**Winslow** *(English)* Friend's hill.

**Winston** *(English)* Friend's estate.
   *Variant:* Wystan.

**Winter** *(English)* The season.

**Wirt** *(Anglo-Saxon)* Worthy.

**Witney** *See* Whitney.

**Wolfe** *(English)* Like a wolf.
*Variant:* Wolf.

**Wolfgang** *(Germanic)* Advancing wolf.

**Woodley** *(English)* Meadow.
*Variant:* Woody.

**Woodrow** *(English)* Row of houses near the woods.
*Variant:* Woody.

**Woodward** *(English)* Forester.
*Variant:* Woody.

**Woody** *See* Woodley, Woodrow, Woodward.

**Wren** *(English)* A small bird; *(Welsh)* Chief.
*Variant:* Wrenn.

**Wright** *(English)* Craftsman; carpenter.

**Wyatt** *(English)* Little warrior.

**Wykeham** *See* Wickham.

**Wylie** *(English)* Beguiling; charming.
*Variant:* Wiley.

**Wyman** *(Anglo-Saxon)* Warrior.

**Wyndham** *(English)* Wandering path; windy village; a place name.

**Wystan** *See* Winston.

**Xan, Xander** *See* Alexander.

**Xanthus** *(Greek)* Golden-haired.
*Variant:* Xanthos.

**Xavier** *(Spanish)* Bright; new house.
  *Variant:* Javier, Zavier.
  *See also* Salvador.

**Xenophon** *(Greek)* Strange voice; a soldier and historian of ancient Greece.

**Xenos** *(Greek)* Foreigner; stranger.
  *Variant:* Zenos.

**Xerxes** *(Persian)* Prince; ruler.

**Ximen, Ximenes, Ximun** *See* Simon.

**Xylon** *(Greek)* Dweller in the forest.
  *Variant:* Zylon.

**Yaakov** *See* Jacob.

**Yadid** *(Hebrew)* Friend; beloved.

**Yael** *(Hebrew)* Strength of God; mountain goat.

**Yahya** *See* John.

**Yakov** *See* Jacob.

**Yakei** *(Tlingit)* "It is good."

**Yakim** *(Hebrew)* God will establish.
  *See also* Joachim.

**Yama** *(Japanese)* Mountain.

**Yana** *(Native American)* Bear.

# Y

**Yann, Yannick, Yannis** *See* John.

**Yaron** *(Hebrew)* He will sing.

**Yardley** *(English)* Enclosed meadow.

**Yasar** *See* Yasir.

**Yasahiro** *(Japanese)* Peaceful; calm; wise.

**Yasashiku** *(Japanese)* Gentle; polite.

**Yaseer** *See* Yasir.

**Yasin** *(Arabic)* Prophet.

**Yasir** *(Arabic)* Wealthy; easy.
   *Variants:* Yasar, Yaseer, Yassar, Yasser.

**Yasuo** *(Japanese)* Peaceful.

**Yates** *(English)* Keeper of the gates.
   *Variants:* Gates, Yeats.

**Yehosha** *See* Joshua.

**Yehudi** *See* Jude.

**Yemen** *(Japanese)* Guarder of the gate.

**Yeoman** *(English)* Attendant.

**Yervant** *(Armenian)* An Armenian king.

**Yestin** *See* Justin.

**Yevgenij** *See* Eugene.

**Yiannis** *See* John.

**Yin** *(Chinese)* Silver.

**Yiorgos** *See* George.

**Yitzhak** *See* Isaac.

**Yo** *(Cambodian)* Honest.

**Yobachi** *(African)* Pray to God.

**Yoel** *See* Joel.

**Yorick** *See* George.

**Yohann** *See* John.

# Y

**Yoland** *(Greek)* Violet.

**Yong** *(Chinese)* Courageous.

**York** *(English)* Yew tree.
  *Variant:* Yorke.

**Yosef** *See* Joseph.

**Yoshi** *(Japanese)* Better; best; good one.
  *Variant:* Yoshio.

**Yrjo** *See* George.

**Yu** *(Chinese)* Universe; jade.

**Yuan** *(Chinese)* Original.

**Yuki** *(Japanese)* From the snow.
  *Variant:* Yukio.

**Yul** *(Mongolian)* From the far horizon.

**Yule** *(Norse)* Christmastime.
  *Variants:* Yul, Yules.

**Yuma** *(Native American)* Son of the chief.

**Yun** *(Chinese)* Fair and just.

**Yura, Yuri** *See* George.

**Yusha** *See* Joshua.

**Yusuf** *See* Joseph.

**Yuudai** *(Japanese)* Great hero.

**Yuuta** *(Japanese)* Well-built hero.

**Yves** *(French)* Little archer.
  *Variants:* Ives, Ivo.

**Ywain** *See* Owen.

**Zabdi** *(Hebrew)* Gift.
  *Variant:* Zavdi.

**Zabulon** *See* Zebulon.

**Zachary** *(Hebrew)* God has remembered.
  *Variants:* Zaccaria, Zachariah, Zechariah; Zacharie *(French)*;
  Zacchaeus *(Greek)*; Zacharias *(Hungarian)*; Zacarius *(Latin)*;
  Sakari, Sakaria, Sakarios, Sakia, Zakarias *(Scandinavian)*;
  Zakarij *(Slavic)*.

**Zadok** *(Hebrew)* Righteous; just.
  *Variants:* Zadoc, Zaydoc.

**Zádor** *(Hungarian)* Violent.

**Zafir** *(Arabic)* Victorious.
  *Variants:* Zafar, Zafeer.

**Zaheer** *See* Zahir.

**Zahid** *(Arabic)* Self-denying.

**Zahir** *(Arabic)* Shining.
  *Variant:* Zaheer.

**Zahur** *(African)* A flower.

**Zaid** *(African)* Increase; grow.

**Zaide** *(Yiddish)* Elder.

**Zakai** *See* Zake.

**Zakarias, Zakarij** *See* Zachary.

**Zakariyya** *(Arabic)* Prophet.

# Z

**Zake** *(Arabic)* Innocent; pure.
   *Variants:* Zakai, Zaki, Zakia, Zakkai.

**Zalán** *(Hungarian)* Thrower; hitter.

**Zale** *(Greek)* The strength of the sea.

**Zalmai** *(Afghani)* Young one.

**Zalman** *See* Solomon.

**Zamiel** *See* Samuel.

**Zámor** *(Hungarian)* Ploughed land.

**Zander** *See* Alexander.

**Zane** *See* John.

**Zaniel** *(Latin)* Angel of Mondays.

**Zanipolo** *(Italian)* Little gift from God.

**Zanobi** *(Latin)* Scarcely alive.

**Zaránd** *(Hungarian)* Gold.

**Zareb** *(African)* Protector.

**Zared** *(Hebrew)* Ambush.

**Zarek** *(Greek)* May God protect the king.

**Zavdi** *See* Zabdi.

**Zaydoc** *See* Zadok.

**Zazu** *(Hebrew)* Movement.

**Zdenek** *(Czech)* From Sidon.

**Zeb** *See* Zebediah, Zebulon.

**Zebadiah, Zebedee** *See* Zebediah.

**Zebedeo** *(Aramaic)* Servant of God.

**Zebediah** *(Hebrew)* Gift of the Lord.
   *Variants:* Zeb, Zebadiah, Zebedee, Zedidiah.

**Zebulon** *(Hebrew)* Home; exalted and honoured.
   *Variants:* Zabulon, Zeb, Zebulun.

**Zechariah** *See* Zachary.

# Z

**Zedekiah** *(Hebrew)* Justice from God.
 *Variants:* Zed, Zedechiah.

**Zedidiah** *See* Zebediah.

**Zeeman** *(Dutch)* Sailor; seaman.

**Zefirino** *(Greek)* The wind of spring.

**Zeke** *See* Ezekiel.

**Zelgai** *(Afghani)* Heart.

**Zelig** *(Hebrew)* Blessed; holy.
 *Variant:* Selig *(Germanic)*.

**Zelimir** *(Slavic)* Wishes for peace.

**Zelman** *See* Solomon.

**Zemar** *(Afghani)* Lion.

**Zen** *(Japanese)* Religious.

**Zenas** *(Greek)* God's gift.

**Zeno, Zenon** *See* Zeus.

**Zenos** *See* Xenos, Zeus.

**Zenus** *See* Zeus.

**Zephaniah** *(Hebrew)* Treasured by God.
 *Variant:* Zephan.

**Zephyr** *(Greek)* Wind.

**Zero** *(Greek)* Seeds.

**Zeroun** *(Armenian)* Wise; respected.

**Zeth** *(Greek)* Investigator; researcher.

**Zeus** *(Greek)* The god of thunder and sky in Greek
 mythology.
 *Variants:* Zeno, Zenon, Zenos, Zenus.

**Zev** *(Hebrew)* Deer.
 *Variants:* Zevie, Zvi.

**Zia** *(Arabic)* Enlightened.

# Z

**Zigfrid** *See* Siegfried.

**Zion** *(Hebrew)* Excellent omen.
*Variants:* Sion, Tzion.

**Ziskind** *(Hebrew)* Sweet child.

**Ziven** *(Slavic)* Vigorous.

**Zobor** *(Slavic)* Gathering.

**Zoello** *(Greek)* Son of Zoe.

**Zoltán** *(Slavic)* Chieftain.

**Zorán** *(Slavic)* Dawn.

**Zorba** *(Greek)* Live each day.

**Zorro** *(Slavic)* Golden dawn.

**Zubin** *(Hebrew)* To exalt.

**Zuriel** *(Hebrew)* God is my way.

**Zvi** *See* Zev.

**Zwelethu** *(Zulu)* Our land/country.

**Zygfryd** *See* Siegfried.

**Zygmunt** *See* Sigmund.

**Zylon** *See* Xylon.